"This anthology opens up one of the most interesting and promising ideas in the study of narrative and story that we have had for a long time. Untold stories finally get their chance to be heard through the pages of this book and their importance becomes immediately apparent."
—*Yiannis Gabriel, University of Bath, UK*

"Organizations are full of untold stories. The authors bring them into the world of telling, and expose a need for critical management study of who they are untold. There is a relationship between unstoryable, the untold, and the storyable that is an important contribution to storytelling."
—*David Boje, New Mexico State University, US*

Untold Stories in Organizations

The field of organizational storytelling research is productive, vibrant, and diverse. Over three decades we have come to understand how organizations are not only full of stories but also how stories are actively making, sustaining, and changing organizations. This edited collection contributes to this body of work by paying specific attention to stories that are neglected, edited out, unintentionally omitted, or deliberately left silent.

Despite the fact that such stories are not voiced they have a role to play in organizational analysis. The chapters in this volume variously explore how certain realities become excluded or silenced. The stories that remain below the audible range in organizations offer researchers an access to study political practices which marginalise certain organizational realities whilst promoting others. This volume offers a further contribution by paying heed to silence and the processes of silencing. These silences influence the choice of issues on organizational agendas, the choice of audience(s) to which these discourses are addressed and the ways of addressing them.

In exploring these relatively understudied terrains, *Untold Stories in Organizations* comprises an important contribution to the organizational storytelling space, opening paths for new trajectories in storytelling research.

Michał Izak, PhD, is a senior lecturer in Management at University of Lincoln, UK. His research interests include emerging organizational discourses, Critical Management Studies, fiction as a reflection of organizational dynamics, and organizational storytelling. He publishes regularly in peer reviewed journals and is a member of the editorial board of Organization Studies as well as a guest editor of forthcoming issues of *Futures* journal and *Tamara Journal for Critical Organization Inquiry.*

Linda Hitchin is a principal lecturer at University of Lincoln, UK, and a sociologist of science and technology. Her research interests include ethnographic methods, sociology of translation, sociomaterial studies, and ontological politics of work.

David Anderson is a lecturer in management at University of Lincoln, UK. He has edited a special issue of *Tamara Journal* and is a reviewer for *Journal of Management Education.* His research interests include methodological anarchism, network studies, sociomateriality, and relationality.

Routledge Studies in Management, Organizations and Society

This series presents innovative work grounded in new realities, addressing issues crucial to an understanding of the contemporary world. This is the world of organizing societies, where boundaries between formal and informal, public and private, local and global organizations have been displaced or have vanished, along with other nineteenth century dichotomies and oppositions. Management, apart from becoming a specialized profession for a growing number of people, is an everyday activity for most members of modern societies.

Similarly, at the level of enquiry, culture and technology, and literature and economics, can no longer be conceived as isolated intellectual fields; conventional canons and established mainstreams are contested. **Management, Organizations and Society** addresses these contemporary dynamics of transformation in a manner that transcends disciplinary boundaries, with books that will appeal to researchers, student and practitioners alike.

Untold Stories in Organizations

Edited by Michal Izak, Linda Hitchin, and David Anderson

Routledge
Taylor & Francis Group

NEW YORK AND LONDON

First published 2015
by Routledge
711 Third Avenue, New York, NY 10017

and by Routledge
2 Park Square, Milton Park, Abingdon, Oxon OX14 4RN

First issued in paperback 2018

*Routledge is an imprint of the Taylor & Francis Group,
an informa business*

Library of Congress Cataloging-in-Publication Data

A catalog record for this book has been requested

ISBN 13: 978-1-138-34089-3 (pbk)
ISBN 13: 978-1-138-79001-8 (hbk)

Typeset in Sabon
by Apex CoVantage, LLC

Contents

PART II
Untold Stories on the Social and Political Agenda

PART III
Untold Story and Methodology

Figures

Tables

Acknowledgments

We would like to thank Professor Yiannis Gabriel for his support throughout this project. We are grateful to all the participants who contributed to *Untold Stories? A Storytelling Conference* organized at Lincoln in 2013, where the idea for this book originated. Lastly our thanks also go to the EGOS and SCOS communities which continue to be valuable sites for germinating new interests.

1 Introduction

Michal Izak, Linda Hitchin,
and David Anderson

ORGANIZATIONAL STORYTELLING

It is often argued that human lives are imbued with stories and storytelling. Common sense of research converge to suggest that stories do more than describe the sequence of events (Campbell, 1976). Story offers a space to vent emotions and collectively examine the word around us (Gabriel, 1995). Indeed, in our stories we find means to metaphorise reality. It is through stories that we can work to both secure or change such realities as story provides a means to challenge, change, or preserve deeply rooted meanings, inherent in our fictions and myths, across generations (Armstrong, 2005/2006).

Contemporary organization and management studies scholars have increasingly realized the importance of stories to organizational life. In organizations, stories are around us as our creations, companions, and oppressors (Boje, 1991, 1995; Gabriel, 2008; Rhodes & Brown, 2005; Sims, 2003). Thankfully, stories and storytellers come in all sorts of shapes and sizes and the work of story cannot be fixed or held down in particular places. Stories of success and failure are mirrored by organizational narratives of conquer, progress, or decline. Stories that attempt to overpower and control have counter stories that attempt to release and liberate. In such a melee of tales, storytelling shapes organizations (Boje, 2011).

Even where organizational stories appear to consist of a relatively limited range of themes (Martin, Feldman, Hatch, & Sitkin, 1983), they seem to have potential to fulfil a number of purposes. Research from different traditions has revealed how stories may serve as devices for mapping the territory of organizational sensemaking (Wilkins, 1984); disseminating knowledge (Campbell, 1972/1988); expressing deeply embedded organizational mythologies (Kostera, 2008); and glorifying past and/or future organizing ethos (Ybema, 2004). However, that is not an end to it, since somewhat shifting of research attention, stories have been revealed as technologies contributing to the formation of identity (Bamberg, 2010). Stories are at work in overtly managed spaces of organization enforcing control and performing resistance (Wilkins, 1983) and at work in psychic landscapes, including unmanaged spaces (Gabriel, 1995).

It is evident that stories provide means to make sense of human experiences (Sole & Wilson, 2003), shape individual lives (Sims, 2003), and access the worlds of others (Rennie, 1994). Crucially, by bringing external cogence and coherence to convictions, stories provide resources that shape appropriate responses to the stories and work of other people (Czarniawska-Joerges, 1995).

The criticality of the diverse approaches to story and storytelling is inherent in their intention to reveal the storyteller's strategies and hidden agendas, the mechanisms employed in creating stories or the unintended consequences which telling certain stories may entail. Hence, criticality resides in the ability to illustrate the politics of story whether that is from a position where story-politic contexts are considered subject to limits (Gabriel, 1995) or conceived as more open and 'messy' (Boje, 1991, 2006).

However, to date, research on storytelling typically focused on those stories the content of which is known from the start or *can* be revealed to the reader in the course of interpretation. The stories in question were somehow made explicit. Their authorship, even if multiple, was in principle discernible. We think that these (tacit) assumptions regarding storytelling should be problematised. Our goal is to provide an initial reflection on those experiences and emotions which for many reasons never entirely made it to the surface, which were not (fully) formulated and 'read' as stories, or which, despite appearing were ignored.

Our area of inquiry is a difficult one, yet not paradoxical—whether expressed, experienced, read or not, it is evident that there are untold interactions between individual and social worlds. The neglected, edited out, unintentionally omitted, or deliberately left silent stories provide blank spots—potential reference points on the map of organizational sensemaking that are no less indispensible to the map reader than those 'realities' which can be made explicit with current resources. Untold story research begins at the edges of current story research and attends to the emerging challenges in the field. Consequently, playing out the means to map 'blank spots' on the research agenda will inevitably challenge the limits of current analysis and possibly the politics of research conventions. The mature research offers a point of departure to reconceptualise story and story research through the very idea of 'untold'. In their own way untold stories may hold one key to making the complexity of the social world more comprehensible.

UNTOLD STORIES

To acknowledge the storytelling perspective means to denaturalise the ways in which the social world is typically construed by us and for us. As the focus is the social world, social context is inevitably a core concept and problem.

Consequently, denaturalising story poses certain challenges that are shared across social studies of action and meaning. Understanding human actions through stories and storytelling entails not only comprehending underlying intentions of story and teller by reference to a context as surrounding matter, but also examining context as relationships of social experience and thought worlds (as generative social interactions [Schütz, 1973; Kristeva, 1986; Berger & Luckmann, 1967]). Hence, it is through story interactions in context that we offer justifications and rationales for action and examine consequences. In (story) research, tracing story interactions, justifications, and rationales provide means to enhance contextual understanding (Garfinkel, 1984).

The degree to which any rationale can be sustained by popular reception depends on particular social expectations with which justifications are (or are not) aligned. Both social sensemaking frameworks (such as 'rationality') and meanings produced within them can be approached in terms of narratives (Reed, 1999; MacIntyre, 1981/1990, respectively). The repertoire of narratives or stories legitimised within and by such frameworks can be varied, but not infinite (Czarniawska, 2004) and therefore it may provide a key insight into the context of stories' production. The 'success-despite-obstacles' organizational story, for instance, will be sustained by its listeners provided that they share the notion of 'success' with the storyteller who, for example, may or may not qualify as such a government bailout covered by taxpayers' money. Similarly, a 'sacrifice story' may or may not be applauded depending on the current social weightings of particular values being saved and sacrificed (vide human offerings to gods in ancient Carthage or Warsaw uprising), and 'social progress story' may also be booed if the voices of those who were sacrificed in its name start to be heard.

However, we must also attend to the problem of criteria. Not only can criteria for 'acceptable' storytelling be themselves construed as stories, but also factors which shape criteria and carry their authority can also be rendered as narratives; as in the case of scientific paradigms (Czarniawska, 1995), or social agendas (Reed, 1999). Consequently, hidden under a story are precepts, tenets, and beliefs that precede decisions over how to arrange story-making ingredients and align them in a particular way. Which stories will appear and which will not depends on other stories, those which became expressed in the form of criteria for a particular form of storytelling. But these stories may become un-told, the criteria may change, the river-bed of thoughts may shift (Wittgenstein, 1969). Hence, not only very few stories get to be told, but also those that do, render a number of other untold. 'Telling' a story supplements the potentiality of an untold story to remain so. Whether such a 'supplement' merely adds a new ingredient to the untold or replaces it, seems not as much 'undecidable' (Derrida, 1976) as rather context-dependent, since stories may be variously constructed.

Typically, social scientists enjoy clarity and like to 'tell' their stories with confidence, indeed the very notion of academic argument tends to be struggle over the story. However, the same is not the case for managerial phenomenon where lack of clarity provides the space for managerial reproduction and action. It might seem that the only way in which a managerial phenomena such as motivation, teamwork, or strategy can be listened to attentively depends on ensuring that none of the multiple renditions of the phenomenon is in any sense 'final'. The space for reinterpretation and reformulations is not empty; on the contrary it is populated with multiple elements (interpretations, arguments, topics) which were discarded, forgotten, rejected, or which were never arrived at. These resources can be now mobilised into new forms or, more likely, reformulations of the existing ones. They may not be 'told', but they make 'telling' possible. The abundant ontology of the untold is not more problematic than human imagination itself, inasmuch as both enable creative sensemaking.

INTO THE UNTOLD

How can we talk about the 'untold'? We would like to suggest that possibilities are numerous. In fact, taking literary and cinematic fictions as reference points, when it comes to storytelling, we should expect that plots will unfold around organizational stories which are not told. Take for example, William Faulkner's *Yoknapatawpha* county saga (see for instance 1929, 1936, 1959). Faulkner employs the tactic of focusing the reader's attention on seemingly insignificant phenomena that appear as asides or spinoffs of the main story. The deliberate literary technique here, is to draw readerly attention to fringes or blank spots. If somewhere in the story crime is committed, we are more likely to learn about the texture of leafs in the distant part of the county rather than about any of the expected (normative) details of the crime scene. The crucial plot-driving details are typically enmeshed with immensely developed (rich) descriptions which not only seemingly, but often actually, have nothing to do with the plot kernel of the story. Hardly a surprising turn is we consider that Faulkner's work is often not plot-driven in the first place. The strategy of decentring the storyteller's (and story-reader's) attention away from where the action is may indeed be common. In John Barth's *The Sot-Weed Factor* (1960) we are faced with innumerable stories most of which appear as either dead ends or containing marginally important information or facts of *the plot*. The feeling is that the author remains ostentatiously uninterested in telling us anything about the main protagonist's story, in fact he appears to actively resist revealing what such a story might be. A different approach to not-telling-a-story can be found in the works of Mario Vargas Llosa (see *Conversation in a Cathedral*, 1978) or Julio Cortázar (see *Hopscotch*, 1966) who repeatedly undermine the reader's attempts to identify the storyline.

Although hiding a story away from the reader may appear to be a hallmark of our times, such textual tactics can be traced back to Cervantes

(1615/1950), Potocki (1815/2008), and to some extent Homer. Unsurprisingly, cinema recurrently employs similar storytelling tactics. In the culminating scene of Antonioni's *The Passenger* (1975), the camera ostentatiously turns away from the action to show us the empty space outside and leave us wondering what occurred. In *Blow-up* (Antonioni, 1966) by the same director we are once again reminded about the precariousness of a story—as implied in the final scene, we have to decide for ourselves whether the story (of a murder) was told to us or not. Francis Ford Coppola's *The Conversation* (1974) develops along the lines of a conspiracy-buster movie, only to take a drastic turn towards espousing a near metaphysical incapacity to grasp the actual story, which always eludes both the viewer and the protagonist. Perhaps less sophisticated non-telling unfolds in *The Divide* (Gens, 2011), which starts with the apparently apocalyptic scenario in which a city (or a country, or the whole planet) is under threat, but upon the conclusion of the first scene we find our protagonists in a cellar which (spoiler alert is in place) they practically never leave for the rest of the movie. They are vividly interested in what happens outside, and so are we, but this story is never revealed to us. Finally, in what may be one of the most explicit references to 'untold stories' in the history of cinema, Dalton Trumbo's antisystemic *Johnny Got His Gun* (1971) places the main protagonist in the position of losing any means to communicate with the external world and still having an intense inner life. It is not as much an inability to tell the story that is implied here, but rather the fatalistic conviction that some, even most beautiful stories may be ignored, and that there is nothing we can do about it.

Our interest in the untold is not motivated by epistemological scepticism, quite the opposite: we believe there is a great deal to explore in the 'realities' which remain hidden from us. Importantly, one can recently observe how organization scholars become inspired by such absent presences. The increasing multidisciplinarity in approaching organizational realities (Biehl-Missal, 2012) is to some extent underpinned by disenchantment across the social sciences with structuralist renditions (Lyotard, 1992). One path that work has taken is evident in emerging reconceptualisations of organization in terms of 'liquidity' (Bauman, 2000) or 'transparency' (Gabriel, 2005). These reconfigurations appear to overcome the postmodern stalemate and grasp recent social dynamics in a creative manner. Another path pursued by social theorists is to construe social interactions in non-representational terms (Cadman, 2009; Thrift, 2007), as witnessed by recent popularity in the field of management and organization studies of such non-categories as 'liminality' (Beech, 2011; Cunha & Cabral-Cardoso, 2006) and 'uncanniness' (Royle, 2003).

Significantly, such reconfigurations are proving valuable across organization studies and climates for organization theory are changing. In this connection, a special issue of *Organization Studies* committed to exploring the 'White Spaces of Organization' has particular relevance (O'Doherty, de Cock, Rehn, & Ashcraft, 2013). One of the contributors discussed the importance of structures, especially the invisible ones—the *white spaces* evoking Malevich's 1918 painting 'white on white', a Russian purist's asymmetrical square study in white. Working with simplicity this political study struggles for purity and in the process reveals necessary textures, shades, and discernible traces of the artist's hand and brush strokes at work in the 'pure'. Ironically, close attention to purity of whiteness revealed infinite variety rather than bounded pureness. Employing the trans-sensual notion of 'Sites/Sights', O'Doherty et al. investigate space and spatial experiences by unravelling concepts. In this case un-ness is analytically useful. Here, whiteness reveals otherwise invisible/unseen structures shown to be hidden agents of organizational domination and control (Conellan, 2013); uncomfortable and unfamiliar, or revealed as 'strangely familiar', spaces and objects inherent in the ones we take for granted (Beyes & Steyaert, 2013); and the spatial dispersion and mobility of geographically un-fixed organizations framed in terms of ephemeral ecologies and experiences of 'non-places' (Costas, 2013).

Clearly, the organizational importance of 'meaningful absences' does not end with emotions, spaces, and places. For better or worse, the conviction that organizations can be perceived as infinite entities or described in multiple terms has gathered force and it is this interest in un-ness and un-concepts that we seek to continue here through 'untold stories'.

WHY STUDY UNTOLD STORIES?

When the first specimens of platypus were sent to England in late 18th century the creature was generally believed to be a hoax—a mole with a duckbill attached to it (Moyal, 2002). Natural historians who first examined the platypus' body sought evidence of stitching on this fantastic creature. The search for stitches may have been natural: historians actively attempted to undo the platypus' existence and their disbelief was based on an un-awareness that the 'story' of their emerging discipline was more complicated than they thought. The fantastic unscientific platypus and the rational effort to un-find the creature is nicely illustrative of potential inertia in imaginative rational thought and inflexibility in cherished classifications and dualisms (O'Doherty et al., 2013).

Indeed, our goal is not to propose a 'science of the untold' with its rules and divisions, but to suggest that there is more in a story than meets the eye, ear, or any other sense organ. For, naturally, the 'untold' is not an auditory only (non) phenomenon.

Human interest in that which is absent is not new. The capacity to recreate an object in another space, which does not yet contain it, to re-present it, is the basic precondition not only for artistic conduct, but also for mathematics, music as well as (among other) writing and language. It is abstraction that enabled humans to create symbolic order in which most objects can be substituted by signs, and which in its turn makes it much easier to accumulate them and trade them. Abstracting from an immediate context, and therefore relating to something which is not immediately in front of us, is the feature distinguishing *Homo sapiens* from a great majority of animals. No wonder that discussing, describing, or theorizing about things which do not form the object of immediate intersubjective experience consumed an immense amount of time in human history, became an unspoken paradigm of social sciences and an increasingly important aspect of the natural ones. To relate to that which either is not there or is only for us (and perhaps a group of others, if we are fortunate) enabled humans to create not only science and art. This human capacity to story out from immediate contexts is the bedrock for any economic and institutional order which we create.

We commence our inquiry (Part I) with the reflection on the ecologies of the untold: the interconnected and varied strategies enabling to discuss organizational stories which have not been told. We open with David Sims' inquisitive exploration of storytelling, the narrative accomplishment of which may come, paradoxically perhaps, at the expense of presence. David Rae and Angela Lait in their separate chapters analyze the construction of 'untold' narratives and spaces which these occupy within organizational framework, thus creating a room for alternative paths of inquiry: Rae's 'momentary perspective' and Lait's role of explicit and untold stories in our cognitive processes. Bridging the themes of general exploration of the ecologies of the untold and bringing particular organizational untold stories to the fore Monika Kostera and Jerzy Kociatkiewicz propose a paradigmatic shift in marketing by reorienting customer relationship strategy towards attraction rather than seduction. Such step, according to the authors, could be enabled by opening communication channels towards the thought provoking and gender-liminal androgyne imagery—so far implicit and untold aspect of marketing. Part II of the volume focuses more explicitly on the potential social and political aspects of not-telling or actively untelling certain sets of stories, as well as not performing or un-performing realities which surround them. In this vein, Lucia Garcia-Lorenzo, Lucia Sell-Trujillo, and Paul Donnelly explore the implicit stories of 'necessity entrepreneurs', inviting us to reconsider the association of entrepreneurial figure with wealth and internal motivation, thus evoking more heterogeneous picture of entrepreneurship affecting political discourses. Maria Daskalaki, Alexandra Saliba, Stratis Vogiatzis and Thekla Malamou introduce performative and socially transformative aspects of enacting the stories which due to multiple social, political, and economic factors might have so far remained untold. Tom Boland and Ray Griffin delve into non-agentic silences surrounding the (non) actions associated with prolonged state of unemployment, and attempt to render the non-stories which surround it graspable as narratives by producing socially conscious imaginative narrative understanding of unemployment. Through the relevant textual vehicles offered by Beckett and Kafka the sensitive themes of meaninglessness, nothingness, and waiting are explored and translated into a societal narrative. What it means for storytellers to leave their stories untold or have them silenced is explained by Mónica Colón-Aguirre in her exploration of selectively shared stories among reference librarians and by Vaughan Roberts' rendition of the (again) selective manner of bringing certain stories out of the untold abyss of the Church of England's narrative pool. While most contributions in this section emphasise the non-appearance of a story or reflect on the lack of storytelling resources, Gillian Hopkinson, on a somewhat more reassuring note, discusses the alternative for untold stories to come into existence. Finally, in Part III, Linda Hitchin provides a methodological reflection on researching the untold and its relationships to the typically more explicit aspects of organizational life.

While we believe that the 11 contributions selected for this volume aptly grasp diverse aspects of untold stories in manifold organizational frameworks, we are also conscious that we can only hope to pose a question rather than provide the answer. Hence, the current work is designed as a preliminary study of the area rather than as a final rendition of this (yet untold) organizational story.

REFERENCES

Antonioni, M. (Director). (1966). *Blow-up* [Motion Picture]. UK/Italy/USA: Bridge Films; Carlo Ponti Production; Metro-Goldwyn-Mayer (MGM).
Antonioni, M. (Director). (1975). *The Passenger* [Motion Picture]. Italy/Spain/France: Compagnia Cinematografica Champion; CIPI Cinematografica S.A.; Les Films Concordia.
Armstrong, K. (2005/2006). *A Short History of Myth*. Edinburgh: Canongate.
Bamberg, M. (2010). Who am I? Narration and its contribution to self and identity. *Theory and Psychology*, 21(1): 1–22.
Barth, J. (1960). *Sot-Weed Factor*. New York: Doubleday.
Bauman, Z. (2000). *Liquid Modernity*. Cambridge: Polity.
Beech, N. (2011). Liminality and the practices of identity reconstruction. *Human Relations*, 64(2): 285–330.
Berger, P. L., & Luckmann, T. (1967). *The Social Construction of Reality: A Treatise in the Sociology of Knowledge*. New York: Doubleday.
Beyes, T., & Steyaert, C. (2013). Strangely familiar: The uncanny and unsiting organizational analysis. *Organization Studies*, 34(10): 1445–1465.
Biehl-Missal, B. (2012). Using artistic form for aesthetic organizational inquiry: Rimini Protokoll constructs Daimler's Annual General Meeting as a theatre play. *Culture and Organization*, 18(3): 211–229.
Boje, D. M. (1991). The storytelling organization: A study of story performance in an office-supply firm. *Administrative Science Quarterly*, 36(1): 106–126.
Boje, D. M. (1995). A postmodern analysis of Disney as "Tamara-Land". *Academy of Management Journal*, 38(4): 997–1035.
Boje, D. M. (2006). Breaking out narrative's prison: Improper story in storytelling organization. *Storytelling, Self, Society*, 2(2): 28–49.
Boje, D. M. (2011). *Storytelling and the Future of Organizations: An Antenarrative Handbook*. London: Routledge.

Cadman, L. (2009). Nonrepresentational theory/nonrepresentational geographies. In: R. Kitchin & N. Thrift (Eds.), *International Encyclopaedia of Human Geography* (Vol. 7, pp. 456–463). London: Elsevier.

Campbell, J. (1972/1988). *The Inner Reaches of Outer Space: Metaphor as Myth and as Religion*. London: Harper and Row.

Campbell, J. (1976). *Primitive Mythology*. Harmondsworth: Penguin.

Cervantes, M. (1615/1950). *Don Quixote*. London; Penguin.

Connellan, K. (2013). The psychic life of white: Power and space. *Organization Studies*, 34(10): 1529–1550.

Coppola, F. F. (Director). (1974) *The Conversation* [Motion Picture]. USA: Directors Company; The Coppola Company; Paramount Pictures.

Cortázar, J. (1966). *Hopscotch*. New York: Pantheon.

Costas, J. (2013). Problematizing mobility: A metaphor of stickiness, non-places and the kinetic elite. *Organization Studies*, 34(10): 1467–1486.

Cunha, M. P., & Cabral-Cardoso, C. (2006). Shades of gray: A liminal interpretation of organizational legality-illegality. *International Public Management Journal*, 9(3): 209–225.

Czarniawska, B. (2004). *Narratives in Social Science Research: Introducing Qualitative Methods*. London: Sage Publications.

Czarniawska-Joerges, B. (1995). Narration or science? Collapsing the division in organization studies. *Organization*, 2(1): 11–33.

Derrida, J. (1976). *Of Grammatology*. Baltimore: John Hopkins University Press.

Faulkner, W. (1929). *Sartoris*. New York: Harcourt, Brace and Company.

Faulkner, W. (1936). *Absalom, Absalom!* New York: Random House.

Faulkner, W. (1959). *The Mansion*. New York: Random House.

Gabriel, Y. (1995). The unmanaged organization: Stories, fantasies and subjectivity. *Organization Studies*, 16(3): 477–501.

Gabriel, Y. (2005). Glass cages and glass palaces: Images of organizations in image-conscious times. *Organization*, 12(1): 9–27.

Gabriel, Y. (2008). *Organizing Words: A Critical Thesaurus for Social and Organization Studies*. Oxford: Oxford University Press.

Garfinkel, H. (1984). *Studies in Ethnomethodology*. Malden, MA: Polity Press.

Gens, X. (Director). (2011). *The Divide* [Motion Picture]. Germany; USA; Canada: Instinctive Film; Preferred Content; BR Group.

Kostera, M. (2008). Introduction to the trilogy: Mythologies of organizational everyday life. In M. Kostera (Ed.), *Organizational Olympians: Heroes, Heroines and Villains of Organizational Myths*. London: Palgrave Macmillan.

Kristeva, J. (1986). Word, dialogue and novel. In T. Moi (Ed.), *The Kristeva Reader*. New York: Columbia University Press.

Llosa, M. V. (1974). *Conversation in the Cathedral*. New York: Harper & Row.

Lyotard, J.-F. (1992). *The Postmodern Explained to Children*. Sydney: Power Publications.

MacIntyre, A. (1981/1990). *After Virtue*. London: Duckworth.

Martin, J., Feldman, M. S., Hatch, M. J., & Sitkin, S. B. (1983). The uniqueness paradox in organizational stories. *Administrative Science Quarterly*, 28(3): 438–453.

Moyal, A. (2002). *Platypus: The Extraordinary Story of how a Curious Creature Baffled the World*. Sydney: Allen & Unwin.

O'Doherty, D., De Cock, C., Rehn, A. & Ashcraft K. L. (2013). New sites/sights: Exploring the white spaces of organization. *Organization Studies*, 34(10): 1427–1444.

Potocki, J. (1815/2008). *The Saragossa Manuscript*. Paris: Garnier-Flammarion.

Reed, M. (1999). Organizational theorizing: An historically contested terrain. In S. R. Clegg & C. Hardy (Eds.), *Studying Organization: Theory and Method*. London: Sage.

Rennie, D. L. (1994). Storytelling in psychotherapy: The client's subjective experience. *Psychotherapy: Theory, Research, Practice, Training, 31*(2): 234–243.

Rhodes, C., & Brown, A. D. (2005). Narrative, organizations and research. *International Journal of Management Reviews, 7*(3): 167–188.

Royle, N. (2003). *The Uncanny.* Manchester: Manchester University Press.

Schütz, A. (1973). *Collected Papers: The Problem of Social Reality.* The Hague: Martinus Nijhoff.

Sims, D. (2003). Between the millstones: A narrative account of the vulnerability of middle managers' storying. *Human Relations, 56*(10): 1195–1211.

Sole, D., & Wilson, D. G. (2003). Storytelling in organizations: The power and traps of using stories to share knowledge in organizations. (LILA Briefing Paper: Harvard University)

Thrift, N. (2007). *Non-representational Theory: Space, Politics, Affect.* Routledge: London.

Trumbo, D. (Director) (1971) *Johnny Got His Gun* [Motion Picture]. USA: World Entertainment.

Wilkins, A. L. (1983). Organizational stories as symbols which control the organization. In L. R. Pondy, P. J. Frost, G. Morgan, & T. C. Dandridge (Eds.), *Monographs in Organizational Behavior and Industrial Relations: Vol. 1. Organizational Symbolism* (pp. 81–92). Greenwich, CT: JAI.

Wilkins, A. L. (1984). The creation of company cultures: The role of stories and human resource systems. *Human Resource Management, 23*(1): 41–60.

Wittgenstein, L. (1969). *On Certainty.* New York: Harper & Row.

Ybema, S. (2004). Managerial postalgia: Projecting a golden future. *Journal of Management Psychology, 19*(8): 825–840.

Part I

The Silence, Subconscious, Meaning, and Narrative

The Ecologies of Untold

2 Storying as the Meaning, and the Evasion, of Life
Reflections on When Stories Might Be Better Left Untold

David Sims

THE STORY OF THIS CHAPTER

Introduction

This chapter tells the story of how I set off on a grand quest, discovered that my Holy Grail had holes in it, realised that I should have anticipated this, and set off on an even grander quest. I shall also acknowledge, later, that you, the reader, are probably not paying attention to what I say.

TAKING A LIFE FOR A WALK

At the 17th Organizational Storytelling Seminar, in Bath, I had been invited to give a paper which was supposed to be in some way helpful for researchers. Under the title "Taking a Life for a Walk", I told a story which was partly retrospective and partly prospective in which I looked at the development of my research on life, narratives, and everything. In the abstract I laid out my life project:

> Paul Klee described art as 'taking a line for a walk'. I have been fascinated for a long time by the way in which people take a life for a walk. My academic interest has been more in storying than stories. How do I develop the next chapters of the novel which is my life? How do I manage the interaction between my own pre-casting of the story and the events which impinge on it, but which are outside my control? I have also been interested in the relationship between the research which all people carry out in order to develop meaning and understanding in their worlds (in the tradition of Kelly, 1955) and research by those of us who are professional researchers. People are engaged in investigating how they can develop their stories both by expanding their imagination about where they could go next (is that one of the motivations for reading novels?) and by trying to research the costs, likelihood, and returns of different kinds of development. This is part of what we do when we take our lives for walks. I want to write about this without restricting

myself to an academic audience, and my discussion will be about how
I am going about this and how it relates to my experience of research.
In the process I am, of course, also wanting to tell you about how I am
taking my life for a walk.

(Sims, 2011)

In my paper I said that I now had the freedom to put together ideas that
I had been working on for a long time about some of the ways in which it is
enlightening to think of life as a story and the person as storyteller. I told the
audience of my excitement at the idea of trying to address a non-academic
audience with ideas that were emerging from applying a narrative framework to the world. I made the claim that we were better off for being able
to think of life as narrative, because it gives us more choice about how we
see the world and ourselves.

I talked about many of the themes which have emerged in my academic
study of narratives in organizations. For example, I discussed life narrative
as a form of research, where we test out our developing views by telling
ourselves and others stories about them, and applying the critical faculties
that we have spent a lifetime developing to those stories (Sims, 2008d). I
talked about understanding the mid-life crisis as a time when we get bored
with our own story, and are prepared to resort to desperate measures to
liven it up. I reflected on losing the plot of our story, and the possibility that this was a precondition for learning. I discussed the way self-
characterization can change to give a professional a narrative way to handle
changing levels of seniority in their own career (Sims, 2008b). I proposed
the notion of love as the willingness to engage in narrative intertwinement
(Sims, 2005b). I talked about the mystery of the love that people lavish on
their organizations (Sims, 2004). I shared my fascination with how angry
we can get when we cannot fit another person's actions into our narratives
(Sims, 2005a). I made the suggestion that the meaning of life is the extent
to which we can write ourselves into the stories of others (Edwards, 2000).
I said that we act like novelists, developing the next chapter of the story
that is our lives (Sims, 2005b). I described the humiliation of the middle
manager, caught in having to tell different stories upwards and downwards
(Sims, 2003). I gave a narrative view of organizational merger, from the
perspective of trying to bring together two different mythological traditions (Sims, 2008a).

The debate afterwards was helpful and useful to me. Some people
wanted to know whether my objective was to write a best seller and make
a lot of money, or to get ideas out to a wider public. I claimed that I was
aiming to get ideas out there. In that case, they said, why not at least start
this process with a blog, which may turn into a book later, but for the
time being will give you a more open and two-way communication with
an audience than a book can. Good idea, I thought, and went off to (a)
discuss with some blogging colleagues how the experience had been for

them and (b) sign up with Wordpress.com so that my blogging site was all ready to go.

So all is well, and I am set fair to put together my career reflections on what a wonderful thing all this storytelling is, and how it gives us insights that are not otherwise available.

Then I woke up.

Over time, with my continuing interest in stories and narrative, wise colleagues have asked me what is obscured by a storytelling approach. If a way of seeing is a way of not seeing, there must be something that is obscured by it. My evangelistic fervour for stories has not always been open to these counter voices, and I suspect I might have avoided hearing this point until, post retirement, with no academics to baby-sit any more, I too wondered what this approach might be obscuring from me. One of the joys of leaving the full time work place is that I no longer have to spend time constructing stories of the past or the future to satisfy the managerialist urges of vice-chancellors. I can visit the present more regularly.

Stories may be about filling the present with the past and the future. Could they be what we leave behind when we approach the present moment? Are they a part of the chatter with which we avoid meditation and meeting ourselves? Do they have an effect on the tense in which we lead our lives? This takes me to the second main input to this paper.

TIME PAST AND TIME PRESENT

Two or three years earlier I had been given another chance to indulge myself in a conference keynote paper by the organizers of the biennial Discourse conferences, and I gave myself the title, "Time Present, Time Past, and the Echoes of the Mind: Contemplating the Tense of Discourse" (Sims, 2008c). In it, I asked how we come by the state of near total inattention to the present moment that enables us to sit through plenary talks when we might prefer to be elsewhere? I ask that question as one who once walked out of the same plenary twice, and is quite proud of it. Why do people sit through a plenary session in a conference? When our inattention wavers for a minute we pick up enough to be able to build up a common history with others present—at least enough of a common history to have stories to try out at the intervals.

Some of the same issues were raised by Lanchester in a review of Google Glass:

> To dispense with one of the subtler consequences first, what does this mean for the users of Glass, in their interactions with other people? We already have an unprecedented range of tools for not-being wherever we are and for not-doing whatever it is we're supposed to be doing. But at least when we take a phone out to check our messages, people

can see that we're doing it. What if we could do that without anybody knowing? . . . The user of Glass has the option to be permanently not-there.

(Lanchester, 2013: 22)

I suggest that the same can apply to readers of a book. While you are reading this chapter, how are you getting on with preparing the stories you are going to tell others about what you have read? Would it be fair to suggest that, if you are not thinking about the stories you are going to tell others about this chapter, you are probably not paying much attention to it? You may want a range of stories, because you are likely to want to talk about it to different audiences. Sentences for these stories will have been passing through your mind already as a rehearsal of your story. My attention as writer, also, is partly lost to thinking about the stories that you, currently, are rehearsing. None of which leaves much time for the present moment. Does this matter? Do I have any reason to ask that your minds as well as your bodies should be with me in the present? Does our habit of inattention have consequences? Or is it an inevitable state? If language produces a necessary distortion in terms recognising reality might it not also carry a demand for inattention (Hitchin, personal communication, February 26, 2014).

Let me give you an example. When I was Associate Dean at Cass, I would be present at Executive Committee meetings of varying degrees of fascination. As with many meetings, much of the content would be sorted out beforehand, with the meeting acting as punctuation in the decision process. Numerous reports would be given, in which we would talk about our latest measures of each other's performance. On the basis of conversations before and after the meeting, I think I was typical in spending my time paying attention to the kinds of stories that were being told, which ones were going down well with the audience today, which ones were beginning to wear thin, which stories associated you with causes or colleagues that you did or did not want to be associated with, and therefore rehearsing how to tell the story for my department, when my turn next came around, in a way that would be most advantageous to us. This means that my attention would have been on what was being said in the present only in so far as it was an important contributor to this kind of thinking. I was listening more for keywords to inform my storytelling than for the content or inwardness of what my colleagues were saying. This is line with the argument of Pierre Bayard's wonderful book, *How to Talk about Books You Haven't Read*, which sounds like it should be the qualifying book for social scientists. In it he gives one of his chapters a subtitle which says:

in which we conclude, along with Oscar Wilde, that the appropriate time span for reading a book is ten minutes, after which you risk forgetting that the encounter is primarily a pretext for writing your autobiography.

(Bayard, 2008: 166)

We may not believe that Oscar Wilde really believed that all talk was so self-absorbed. "Perhaps Wilde the playwright is speaking, not Wilde the poet of Reading Gaol" (Hitchin, personal communication, February 26, 2014). However, don't we all frequently find ourselves in conversations, and particularly meetings, which can only really be understood by assuming that most of us only listen to others' talk in order to pick up one or two snippets (Sims, Huxham, & Beech, 2009) or keywords, on which we can hang our next comment.

Much of our storying may be a matter of writing our autobiography, or alternatively in my example of Cass Executive Committees, of rewriting organizational stories in ways that we think will lead other people into going along with what we want. We do this often for the best of reasons. We want to offer stories which give people hope, which help to create the better world described in those stories. We may be telling stories that help others to develop their own stories in very positive ways. But are we losing anything by our inattention, our absence from the present moment, when we are creating these storied worlds, and when we are inhabiting them as we are bound to do while rehearsing stories?

At times our flow of stories seems just like chatter, like an occasionally irritating background track that accompanies us wherever we go. At times we become aware of it and would wish to control or silence it, when we are aware of "the inner chaos going on in our heads, like some wild cocktail party of which we find ourselves the embarrassed host" (Laird, 2006: 4).

Our sense is sometimes that these stories drown out outer discourse; the continuous chatter from the internal cocktail party means that we are distracted from anything else that we might otherwise notice. Philosophers and spiritual teachers in many different traditions have pointed out that this internal discourse tends to be about the past or the future, and is part of what keeps us from being present in the moment. This matters. Many teachers have suggested that the lack of time spent in the present is spiritually impoverishing. As Ralph Waldo Emerson (2014) said, "To finish the moment, to find the journey's end in every step of the road, to live the greatest number of good hours, is wisdom". H. L. Mencken (2014) had a typically trenchant view of the present: "We are here and it is now. Further than that, all human knowledge is moonshine". The Chinese proverb which says: "The best time to plant a tree was 20 years ago. The second best time is now", points out the possible evasiveness of focusing our attention on the past.

Then we move on to spiritual teachers, and we start with the Buddha, saying: "Do not dwell in the past, do not dream of the future, concentrate the mind on the present moment". This is quite a central theme of the Buddha's teaching, French and Burgess (2009) p. 198, and he explained his purpose in saying this: "The Secret of health for both mind and body is not to mourn for the past, not to worry about the future, nor to anticipate troubles, but to live the present moment wisely and earnestly". We find the same theme among some Christian teachers, for example when Jean-Pierre de Caussade (1981 cited in Lallemont, et. al., 2006: 69) spoke of "The Sacrament of the present moment", which he elaborated by saying: ". . . in those early days, when people were more direct and unsophisticated. All they knew was that each moment brought its appointed task, faithfully to be accomplished". The same theme comes from the poet R. S. Thomas in a line from his poem, "Adam Tempted": "Too fidgety the mind's compass" (Thomas, 2004: 141).

Apologies to all those whose theological positions have not been catered for, but this is probably enough to make the point. Many traditions offer us ways of thinking about living more in the present moment and being less taken up with telling continual storytelling about our future or our past.

Why might this matter? One of the means by which investment is made workable is the deferral of gratification, the postponement of living, the focus on the future. We are accustomed to stories that encourage us to tolerate poor conditions in order to enjoy a bright promised future, this being both one of the more long winded definitions of investment and also the basis by which horrendous dictatorships retained control during the 20th century. We may feel that our Faustian pact is not so extreme as it is for those who work for Goldman Sachs, or in a labour camp, but the continual sacrificing of the present to stories of the future is something that we may at least wish to question. Are we colluding in our own loss of mindfulness?

So far I have discussed the idea that R. S. Thomas expresses as "Too fidgety the mind's compass", and we have had a look at the way we distract ourselves from the present moment by the stream of stories. We have all been students, so we are well versed in how to act out the non-verbal cues of attention, the noddies, the intelligent looks which reassure the speaker that we are still present and with them, as we remind ourselves of the shopping we need to do on the way home and as we prepare the stories to tell to our friends afterwards.

My theme so far has been that storytelling can be a flight both from the present and from presence. We are, in Christie and Orton's (1988) phrase, *homo narrans narratur*, that is, both the subject and object of storytelling. So one of the activities going on within us during plenary addresses, while reading chapters, and any other time when we are not fully engaged is the building, rebuilding, repair, outline planning applications, etc. for our own stories. How does this affect where we see ourselves in terms of tense and in terms of presence in the moment?

It seems to me that the tense of narrative is always ambiguous. In the past I have written about 'prospective' narratives, the ones where people cast themselves into the future and tell stories about the future of their careers. But this does not properly honour the way that narrative discourse works for us. Narratives enable us to travel through tenses. For example, if you watch a costume drama, you are watching a reconstruction of fictionalised events from a period that might be past or that might never have existed, depending on the level of confidence you have in the author and the adaptor. And yet you experience them in the present. Your emotions are present with Elizabeth Bennet as she fluctuates or develops in her emotions for Mr Darcy. You know how the story turns out, and yet you are still quite capable of hoping that it will turn out right again. This is true for romantic or tragic plots. It is equally possible to hope for a better outcome from King Lear's dementia, while knowing full well that the actors in front of you are not going to change Shakespeare's plot sufficiently to give you one. But you pay for the theatre ticket in order to be transported into a timeless present. Theatre is often said to involve a suspension of disbelief; does story involve a suspension of tense? Is story never fully past, present, or future?

When people tell stories they enter a narrative mode which sounds different. Their voices change, they very often move into the present tense. Test this notion for yourself. Next time you are part of a conversation where people are interspersing general chat with stories, notice whether there is a detectable difference to the voice, and whether the tense changes. My observation is that there are some distinct non-verbal cues that we emit when we are moving into story mode. When people tell stories about the future or the past there is a detectable change which can be thought of as, "I am about to perform a story". The tense is usually present, even if we know that the story is set in the past or the future. The tenses can break down in a story. However, when we are rehearsing and telling stories we are distracted from the present moment to the past settings of our stories and the future in which we hope to tell them. As T.S. Eliot said in Burnt Norton, "time past and time present are both perhaps present in time future" (Eliot, 1969: 171), at least when we are in a narrative mode.

If your mind has been fully engaged in the material of this chapter while reading it, you do not have the problem that I am trying to address! If, however, you have found yourself wandering from the text to think about past or future situations, to recall stories that people have told you about those situations, and to rehearse the stories that you might yourself tell, does this matter? Have you missed anything? Do we have the choice? Is our move into our past and future stories a conscious escape from being in the present? Within the current narrative turn of the social sciences, have we been too ready to accept stories and storying as a natural and universal part of working life, when they have more cost and potential toxicity than we have given them credit for?

A VIEW FROM PROBLEM CONSTRUCTION

So what? I now want to attempt to earth what I have been saying. I have always been interested in problem construction, the art by which we take the raw material in front of us and craft for ourselves problems for ourselves and others to work with.

Figure 2.1 shows the choices of story to tell that we might be faced with when constructing a problem. When problematic events occur, it is only after they have been set in the context of the story that they are defined as a problem. The figure captures some of the options available in the type of story that is constructed. It offers three dimensions on which different choices can be made about the story being constructed. We can define problems as being to do with me, us, them or someone: this, that or something: now, then or sometime. For example, I am driving past a car showroom and I see a car that I really fancy. But I do not have enough money for it. So I decide on a story in which the problem is that successive governments have failed to ensure that academic pay is as high as it should be (them, that, sometime), and that is the problem. This is a comforting way of telling the story because it has no action implications or, to put it another way, it is completely useless. However, for the purposes of a relaxed conversation in the pub it is excellent, as is all the whingeing to be heard about the things you cannot do because of 'company policy'. I could alternatively have told a story in which I cannot afford the car because we spent too much on our

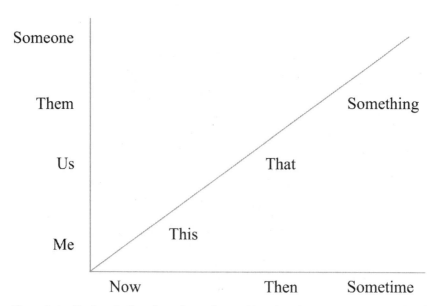

Figure 2.1   Options in Creating a Story from a Situation (Sims, Fineman, & Gabriel, 1993, p. 67).

holiday last year (us, that, then). This is less comfortable, because it has implications for the future in that it might affect our holiday planning for this year. Or I could tell a story about how I am not working hard enough, and am therefore doing silly things like looking at cars on forecourts rather than paying attention to what actually interests me much more (me, this, now). This has far more chance than either of the other stories of suggesting a problem on which I can actually take action. It also takes me into the present, but offers much less opportunity for carefully constructed self-presentations than storytelling, whether you are telling them for your own consumption or for others. Future-oriented or past-oriented stories through which we understand our situations can be a way of avoiding acting, as well as avoiding mindfulness and being.

BRINGING IT TOGETHER: WHY STORIES MAY BE BETTER UNTOLD

Viewing life as storytelling is a passion for me in that I have found many situations to be freshly illuminated when thought of in this way. The point of this chapter is to suggest that it has two associated pathologies that we should be aware of, two ways in which storytelling is a way of not seeing as much as a way of seeing.

Firstly, because we rehearse stories, improve and develop them, give them narrative legs, they risk making too much sense of the events that we tell stories about. Some events and situations should, perhaps, remain beyond storytelling, which gives too much of an aura of sense and understanding. I used to make a lot of use of a quote from Funkenstein (1993) and his claim that one of the crimes of the Nazis in the holocaust was robbing the victims of narrative; that is why so few holocaust survivors can make narrative sense of the event. I now see that differently. Making narrative sense of the holocaust is just as offensive as making any other kind of sense of the holocaust. Any sensible story must be a travesty.

Secondly, storytelling may drown out our mindfulness of the present moment. Stories may lead us to miss what is going on, and may be a form of escapism. As with the example from problem construction, storytelling may be an excellent leisure activity, but should not be confused with action, which takes place in the present. Stories can be about filling the present with the past and the future, and we may leave them behind when we approach the present moment; they are part of the chatter with which we avoid both flow (Csikszentmihalyi & Robinson, 1990) and meditation.

One of the reasons why the idea of hearing a story, watching a film or reading a novel is so attractive is that they offer us an exciting alternative to the present. This is true of other forms of storytelling too. It feels like the present—as suggested by the frequent use of the present tense in telling stories even when they clearly belong to the past. But the story is a relief from the present, an opportunity to be absent, rather like Google Glass. There is nothing necessarily wrong with wishing to escape the present. You may feel that anyone who has arrived at the end of this chapter had every reason to escape the present. But, if we collude with the narrative turn in the social sciences we should realize that this is a way of not seeing as well as a way of seeing, and we must choose whether we are ready to make the bargain of unbridled stories in exchange for being less present in the moment.

REFERENCES

Bayard, P. (2008). *How to Talk About Books You Haven't Read* (J. Mehlman, Trans.). London: Granta.

Christie, J. R. R., & Orton, F. (1988). Writing a text on the life. *Art History*, *11*(4): 543–563.

Csikszentmihalyi, M., & Robinson, R. (1990). *The Art of Seeing: An Interpretation of the Aesthetic*. Malibu, CA: Getty.

de Caussade, J-P (1981). *The Sacrament of the Present Moment* (K. Muggeridge, Trans.). San Francisco, CA: Harper Row.

Edwards, L. (2000). *A Narrative Journey to Understanding Self*. (Master's Thesis). Brunel University, London.

Eliot, T. S. (1969). *The Complete Poems and Plays of TS Eliot*. London: Faber.

Emerson, R. W. (2014). *Essay 14*. Retrieved from http://classiclit.about.com/library/bl-etexts/rwemerson/bl-rwemer-essays-14.htm.

French, F and Burgess, C. (2009) Into that silent sea: trailblazers of the space era, 1961–1965. University of Nebraska Press (Bison Books): Nebraska.

Funkenstein, A. (1993). The incomprehensible catastrophe: Memory and narrative. In R. Josselson & A. Lieblich (Eds.), *The Narrative Study of Lives* (Vol. 1, pp. 21–29). Newbury Park: Sage.

Kelly, G. (1955). *The Psychology of Personal Constructs: A Theory of Personality* (Vol. 1). New York, NY: Norton.

Laird, M. (2006). *Into the Silent Land: The Practice of Contemplation*. London: Darton, Longman & Todd.

Lallemant, L., Caussade, J. P., Colombière C. La., & Lafouge, J.-P. (2006). *For God's Greater Glory: Gems of Jesuit Spirituality*. Bloomington, IN: World Wisdom.

Lanchester, J. (2013) Short cuts. *London Review of Books*, *35*(10): 22.

Mencken, H. L. (2014). Retrieved from http://www.brainyquote.com/quotes/quotes/h/hlmencke124666.html.

Sims, D. (2003). Between the millstones: A narrative account of the vulnerability of middle managers' storying. *Human Relations*, *56*(10): 1195–1211.

Sims, D. (2004). The velveteen rabbit and passionate feelings for organizations. In Y. Gabriel (Ed.), *Myths, Stories and Organizations: Pre-modern Narratives for Our Times* (pp. 209–222). Oxford: Oxford University Press.

Sims, D. (2005a). You bastard: A narrative exploration of the experience of indignation within organizations. *Organization Studies*, *26*(11): 1625–1640.

Sims, D. (2005b). Living a story and storying a life: A narrative understanding of the distributed self. In A. Pullen & S. Linstead (Eds.), *Organization and Identity* (pp. 86–104). London: Routledge.

Sims, D. (2008a) Merging the myths: A study of the effect of organizational myth in an organizational merger. In M. Kostera (Ed.), *Organizational Epics and Sagas: Tales of Organizations* (pp. 288–301). London: Palgrave Macmillan.

Sims, D. (2008b). Managerial identity formation in a public sector professional: An autobiographical account. *International Journal of Public Administration, 31*(9): 988–1002.

Sims, D. (2008c). *Time Present, Time Past, and the Echoes of the Mind: Contemplating the Tense of Discourse.* Keynote paper presented at 8th International Conference on Organizational Discourse, London.

Sims, D. (2008d). *Constructing Stories and Storying Constructs.* Plenary address presented at 9th Conference of the European Personal Construct Association, Queen Mary College, London.

Sims, D. (2011). *Taking a Life for a Walk.* Paper presented at 17th Storytelling Seminar, University of Bath.

Sims, D., Huxham, C., & Beech, N. (2009). On telling stories but hearing snippets: Sense-taking from presentations of practice. *Organization, 16*(3): 371–388.

Sims, D., Fineman, S., & Gabriel, Y. (1993). *Organizing and organizations* (1st ed.). London: Sage.

Thomas, R.S. (2004). *Collected Later Poems.* Tarset: Bloodaxe.

3 Dr Harry Goes to Grantham

A Momentary Perspective on Narrative Construction, Omission, and Interpretation

David Rae

INTRODUCTION

This chapter explores the concept of the 'untold story' from a momentary perspective; that is, it aims to show how a single moment can become the turning point in constructing a narrative, and how the telling or untelling of this element of a story can have moral, political, and social dimensions and consequences.

It first explores the role of the moment in organizational storytelling, and introduces how interpreting the significance of the moment can draw on a diverse set of influences from a range of literatures, including philosophy, narrative, organizational, psychology, and even neuroscience.

It then deploys a short story to demonstrate the use of such moments and to explore the symbolic importance of the moment in narrative construction. This introduces a discussion of the contentious questions of whether such a story should, or should not be told, and of whether, once told it can be 'untold'. Storytelling (and writing) can be risky and morally hazardous; yet not telling stories can be freighted with similar consequences. The paper concludes by highlighting these dilemmas, and discussing whether such stories should, or indeed can, be untold as well as the implications of their telling; since what is omitted, or untold, may be significant.

THE MOMENT IN NARRATIVE

Considering the wider significance of the moment within the making of meaning and stories, the moment occurs in many aspects of everyday life, yet its definition is elusive, such as "a turning point in a series of events" (Shorter Oxford English Dictionary, 2007). Associated words include 'momentary', 'momentous', 'momentum', and others now obsolete. In this paper, the moment is taken as a point in time when we experience conscious mental awareness of what is going on, either within the mind, or around us, and are aware and able to remember our thinking and responses. Its meaning is related to the human experience and generation of meaning in a conscious attention span of subjective duration, rather than a fixed time interval, such as the 'blink' identified by Gladwell (2005). Our experience of lived existence is a sequence of moments, such as Damasio's (2000) understanding of consciousness as "the movie in the brain".

Moments are transitory, some bring retrospective realization that change has occurred through an event carrying significant meaning or enduring consequences, but most are incidental and pass without significance (Bergson, 1907/1911). Incidents and events are extrinsic phenomena which may trigger realizations with individual significance or meaning. A 'critical incident' (Cope, 2005) or 'entrepreneurial event' (Shapero, 1982) is distinct from the cognitive meaning or emotional response it creates in the subjective moment. Concepts connected with understanding of the moment include extrinsic time, context and serendipity, internal dimensions of memory, emotion, creativity, and learning. As Bergson (1907/1911) observed, the moment does not exist separately from its past, but rather there is a co-existent connection between the present, the past, and the future. Whilst the vast majority of Bergsonian '*durée*', or endured time, is lived in moments which are neither significant at the time, nor memorable in retrospect, a tiny number of incidents are exceptions to this flow of existence, being experienced either at the time or subsequently as 'momentous'; it is these which concern us.

The moment is significant in literature; the phrase 'moments of truth' is widely used and has been attributed (possibly erroneously) to the novelist Ernest Hemingway to describe the point at which the matador confronts and kills the bull in a bullfight. But Hemingway certainly incorporated the notion of the moment within the narrative structures of his novels: "In life people are not conscious of these special moments that novelists build their whole structures on" quoted from Hemingway's notes from *The Sun Also Rises* in Svoboda (1983: 12). Hemingway was influenced by James Joyce's use of 'epiphanies' in *Portrait of the Artist* and *Dubliners* as "'showing forth' of character through seemingly trivial action or detail" (Walton Litz, 1966: 23).

In a literary sense, the 'epiphany' (from the Greek, *epiphaneia* or sudden realization of the larger essence or meaning) is one where a deeper meaning in relation to the personal becomes apparent. There is a distinction between the concept of epiphany used as a structural term in literature to denote authorial meaning, and moment as a term in people's lived experiences when the realization of significant wider meaning occurs. The two concepts are connected and overlapping but distinct; epiphany is primarily literary, whilst moment is experiential. It is necessary to have experienced the moment to be able to reconstruct it as a narrative epiphany.

Time is an important concept in connecting narrative and the moment. Polkinghorne (1988) considered the role of temporality in narrative through readings of Ricoeur, Husserl, Heidegger, and Bergson in phenomenological philosophy. His interpretation explored the distinctions between an objective construction of time as moments interspersed along a geometric line, and understanding human experience through narrative over time, building on Husserl's prior conceptualisation of consciousness of time as: "a primal impression of a streaming present surrounded by an awareness of immediate 'retention' of the past and immediate 'protension' of the future" (Husserl, 1928/1964, in Polkinghorne 1988: 128).

Retention is the active recollection of memories and 'protension' the active expectation of imagined results. This moves beyond understanding the moment as simply now, being situated in consciousness between past experience and future anticipation. Referring to organizational narratives, Czarniawska (2004) refers to kairotic (from the Greek god Kairos, of 'right' or 'proper' time), or narrative, time, punctuated by events, which may run backward, forward, or even stand still, in their historical or social context. Brockmeier (2000) explores the concept of autobiographical time, introducing six different models of autobiographical narrative time construction. The concept of narrative time is of especial importance as a way of creating plots, stories, and meanings rather than simply chronicling events in an historical sense.

We can take narratives as central means of making sense of human experience within a schema or sequence of other moments. Narratives often use Kairotic time as an organizing device, with episodes being organized into a plausible plotline, rather than within strict chronological time. As well as being formed of retrospectively remembered events, they can also be prospective, building future conjecture based on past experiences, such as in the presentation of a business strategy for an organization. Also, previously experienced moments are inevitably remembered selectively, often in relation to their actual or narrative context and their subsequent significance. Pillemer (1998) identified six functional categories of personal event memories: memorable messages, symbolic messages, originating events, anchoring events, turning points, and analogous events. These provide useful categories which can help to connect memory, narrative, and the development of self.

Polkinghorne also referred to Bergson's and James' challenge to the notion of time as a series of instantaneous or momentary 'nows', but rather the 'duration' (*durée*) forming part of the progression of the past into the future: "The self is duration, a flowing, creative and productive process. Time is not located in an instantaneous moment. Time is a forceful movement that retains its past as it produces a new future" (Polkinghorne 1988: 128). Polkinghorne connected these philosophical understandings of the moment in time between the largely North American 'pragmatic' school, in particular William James, with European movements. He aimed to explain the difference between the representation of time as a mathematical construct, and the human experience of time as 'extended awareness'. Heidegger (1927/1980) referred to the moment of vision as 'ecstasis' which could not be clarified in terms of the 'now', only the future. Amongst extensive writing on the philosophical and sociological importance of time, often centring on the tension between an objective Newtonian 'scientific' time and the subjective time of human experience, Flaherty and Fine (2001) reinterpreted G. H. Mead's (1932) *Philosophy of the Present* lectures centring on the experience in the present, in which human action takes place not through conscious interpretation but through actualisation of the trajectory already established by the biographical self: "the self is more accurately understood as a momentary stance toward past and future events" (Flaherty & Fine, 2001: 157).

Boje (2012) develops the practice of 'quantum storytelling', away from a Bergsonian 'duration' approach towards a temporality which is "in-time, as well as in-space, and in-quantum-materiality" (Boje, 2012: 12); for example, he cites:

> Datable moments and events, not in calendar sense or chronology, but that stand out as living stories that are life-changing. . . . Each duration is like the yellow bucket incident I had on my Harley Electroglide while driving 90 mph on the 405 freeway in Las Angles, between the lanes. The duration of that moment when the bucket jumped out of the back of a pickup truck, and I kept swerving to avoid it, and finally, just throttled all the way up, to meet it head-on, and in that duration, time slowed way down, and I grabbed it by its handle, just before it got under the frame and rear wheels, and everyone in cars and trucks around me, let out a cheer. An event measured in nanoseconds, slowed to what was much longer.
>
> (Boje, 2012: 15)

For individuals in an everyday context of conducting their working and private lives, their practices, self, and social identities are constantly being affected and reshaped by such moments. Individuals may perceive events as a series of existential moments, most being of little lasting significance but some, either at the time or subsequently, will be recognised as having wider or lasting meaning. The moment is by definition transitory, certain moments bringing a realization that change has occurred through an event or interaction in which significant meaning is realized or which has enduring consequences. Existentially, being and lived reality are experienced in the moment, and it is in the moment and the perceptions of connections between them that we generate meaning and may decide to act, as creative ideas and realizations occur through mental association between the lived reality and memory. Existential writers such as Sartre stressed the role of authentic experience, self-actualisation, and living in the 'here and now' (Sartre, 1939). Lefebvre (1947) proposed that we seize and act on 'moments' of revelation, emotional clarity, and self-presence as the basis for becoming more self-fulfilled. The moment may have philosophical dimensions, sometimes historically significant, for example at times of crisis which prompt a re-evaluation of established praxis.

Such moments can occur within and among organizations, such as those during and following the financial crisis of 2008. They can be emancipatory, forming new reality in a revelatory moment which makes sense of individual or shared experience by accommodating and adapting prior knowledge. They may generate critiques of existing praxis, such as neoliberal capitalism, and result in the creation of new categories of meaning and values, possibly forming a working or lay theory. Such creative, constructionist associations enable the creation of new meanings and movement from periods of crisis, and may cause profound re-adjustments which affect us personally, organizationally, economically, and societally. But the meanings we adduce from making sense of such moments may not be logically coherent and consistent, and we may attribute disproportionate significance to them, as was the case post-2008. Balanced retrospection and critical reflection are needed, and are made possible by organizational storytelling, before the moment passes into the *durée* of history.

Qualitative research methodology has recently addressed the concept of narrative moments. Carlsen and Dutton (2011) gathered accounts from researchers of creative, generative moments in their work, and summarised these thematically as: "Seeing with new eyes; Feeling despair and movement; Daring to engage; Interrelating; and Playing with artefacts", illustrating their operation in idea-changes and self-change (Carlsen & Dutton, 2011: 216). This position informed the selection of moments as research material, as deployed in the making of the story told below, in which the researcher moved and dodged between these themes.

Finally, in exploring connections between Wittgenstein's philosophy and writing about managing and the production of a 'third kind of knowledge' from a social constructionist perspective, Shotter (2005) used the notion of moment-by-moment production of dialogically structured knowledge centring on grounded practices to describe the formative function of language. This again expands the role of narrative in (re)constructing reality:

> The very vagueness, ambiguity, and incompleteness that makes 'scientific' analysis seem hopeless, in fact allows for the moment-by-moment versatility, flexibility, and negotiability that we need in our talk, if we are to make clear the this or that to which at each moment we are referring.
>
> (Shotter, 2005: 159)

Philosophy, notably from the phenomenological, pragmatic, and existentialist movements, provided early and illuminating insights into the problem of time in relation to past, future, and present moments. Many of these insights remain valid observations on the human condition. However, cognitive science increasingly offers understanding of neural networks, processing, and how brain function operates in momentary operations which complement, and to some extent supersede, philosophical conclusions (Beeman & Kounios, 2009). Feeling and emotion are increasingly understood as highly significant in both cognition and momentary responses (e.g., Damasio, 2000, 2012; Lewis, 2004). Neuroscience has enabled understanding of the major role of the subconscious mind in everyday behaviours, including creativity and decision making. The subconscious is 'in control' of human behaviours to a far greater extent than we might otherwise (or wish to) think. We can suggest that the subconscious governs most momentary behaviours, whilst the conscious mind selects 'special' moments from memory in retrospect, through kairotic sensemaking, rather than being aware at the time of their significance.

A conceptualisation for a momentary perspective is outlined below. A momentary perspective is a way of gathering, conceptualising, sharing, and understanding the human experiences of 'what is going on?' in the moment. A single moment can be interpreted through multiple 'lenses' of knowing, such as those previously described as philosophical, narrative, and cognitive. This section develops a framework for a momentary perspective which can be applied in entrepreneurial creativity and learning, and possibly more generally. This is based on a model of the awareness of 'being in the moment' shown in Figure 3.1.

In this experience of 'being' in the moment, we are constantly perceiving, generating meaning, consciously and unconsciously, whilst acting in response, through speech and behaviour, in interconnected ways. This framework illustrates in a very simplified way these three essential and interdependent processes, which occur both consciously, with selective attention being paid to a small proportion of the sensory data being perceived in the mental foreground; and unconsciously, with awareness of a much wider range of experiential data taking place as background. This conceptualises the complex interactions which occur constantly in the experience of the moment.

The moment itself is taken to be an internal realization separate from any external incident which may trigger it. In the moment, perceptual processes operate both consciously and unconsciously (otherwise described as 'subconsciously'), with unconscious processing being more rapid (Banks & Isham, 2009). The perceptions generate a response, which may be of verbal or physical action which is elicited at the time, and hence likely to be recalled by the person as their response in the moment. An intuitive response is one arising from tacit knowledge not requiring conscious thought, or conditioned by experience or training, whilst an instinctive response results from core animal behaviour or personality. A response often expresses emotion: imagine the response to being hit or being kissed. A conscious response, the result of 'thinking about' how to respond, will be slower, occurring beyond or subsequent to the moment. At any time following the moment, there may

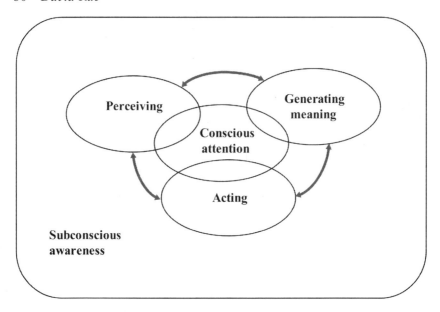

Figure 3.1   Momentary Perspective of 'Being' in the Moment (Rae, 2013). Copyright © 2013 IP Publishing Ltd. Reproduced by Permission.

be a conscious reflection on the meaning (new knowledge) produced from the moment.

In summary, the moment is constructed in both subjective consciousness of experience, which can be expressed in autobiographical narratives, as well as existing scientifically as an objectively observed neurological phenomenon, just as time may be taken to be either and both the flow of the *durée* and of chronological Newtonian time. Neither deny the other, since both are required to understand the momentary experience. David Lodge, in his novel *Thinks* (2001), expressed this gap between the creation of conscious understanding expressed through mindful narrative, and the neural operations of the brain. How we think, feel, and behave in the moment, and reconstruct these memories in narratives are at the centre of this matter. The reference to Lodge and the campus novel genre provides a plausible link to our (as yet un)told story.

DR HARRY GOES TO GRANTHAM

The University-centred narrative has developed a literary tradition in the UK. The 'campus novel' became established as a sub-genre, starting with CP Snow's *The Masters* (1951), reaching popularity with Kingsley Amis' resonant cultural critique in *Lucky Jim* (1954), and Malcolm Bradbury's

(1975) *The History Man*. It reached its apogee with David Lodge's sequence of novels from *Changing Places* (1975) to *Thinks* (2001). Whilst these novels defined a genre which has since waned (Bigsby, 2012), the 'real' narratives of university life have become more complex and contested. Yet for some reason, probably career survival, academics have been reluctant to use these stories as organizational narratives to enhance our understanding of 'what *really* goes on'. For there is little doubt that these 'untold stories' could reveal a rich and diverse sociological life-world of competing ideologies and contested narratives of politics, power, and control, in a 'reality' which many scholars share.

In what follows a short account has been fabricated. This fictional and experimental, in some ways risky, attempt to elicit 'an untold story' is derived from fragments of organizational narrative gathered from a distributed community of academic folk, in which the role of the 'critical moment' is central to its making. The location for this composition is the invented University of Grantham.

In the modern university, the recruitment advertising for senior management roles features a seductive discourse including (from recent recruitment advertising) "strong, passionate and empathetic academic leadership", "ambitious, highly motivated", "forward-looking, proactive and enthusiastic", and—well, you know the type. There is a form of courtship, or possibly stalking, played by the 'executive search' consultants who extract a lucrative rental from matching the holders of such attributes with the organizations who offer them arenas to perform their prowess. You may know how this works, with the call from the consultant asking 'would you be able to advise a suitable candidate?' But what happens after the anointed superstar leader is courted, seduced, and ends up in a marriage of convenience with diverse bedmates? Here is a salutary tale.

Imagine then a newish university in a traditional English midlands town, somewhere such as Grantham if you will, which did not have a university but where (like the university at Gloucester in David Lodge's *Thinks*) you might conceivably find one. This ambitious university has a Business School—transported from somewhere less glamorous, such as Peterborough, let us say. Grantham Business School has the vaunting rhetoric, the atrium-spanned building and the thrusting professoriate of an up-and-coming institution. Yet its identity, its base culture is a contested one, between the teaching and student-oriented roots of its polytechnic origins, shared by older staff who embody its biography, and its corporate aspirations to be a 'Top 40' institution. In short we find a large, aspiring, public-facing organization seeking growth and change in a highly competitive and volatile environment. Here many moments are constructed as memorable events and as individual epiphanies of self-realization.

Grantham required a Head of Business School, and so it was that the university turned to an executive recruitment firm, with their expensive West End office, and in due course, following a 'beauty parade', a candidate deemed to possess the necessary 'charismatic leadership', 'track record', and 'ability to drive change and achieve results' was appointed. Deus ex machina! However, the candidate is not the subject of this story. Rather, we follow the composite moments which followed the appointment of the leader and the dramas that unfolded which might otherwise remain untold. Let us visit the first meeting between this acknowledged inspirational figure, whom we shall call Dr Harry, and his (the Business School being an arena where the masculine tends to predominate) Executive Team.

Our new man is the centre of attention, and the rest of the group are laughing. The new man is streetwise, and picks—or attracts—his lieutenants, finding people who 'know how the place works' and 'can get things done'. Obviously, he is an agent of change. Almost every utterance, every aside he makes produces amusement from most of the men—for they are mainly men today—relieved that at least he has a sense of humour. Dr Harry appears to offer something deeply appealing to the group, the moment of seeing anew. The emotional dimension is of managerial bonhomie, a feel-good, 'up and at 'em' approach to picking fights with the University and coming off on top. It may be that the vacuum of leader has indeed been filled. Let us see.

Behind the scenes, this select little group are the product of change. For the most part the group comprises operational managers rather than senior academics—a familiar line up in new universities. By and large, the senior team consider their focus to be an upcoming national research audit—the Research Excellence Framework or REF. So, Dr Harry and his team initiate a 'review' of the school. This review will 'drive change', 'take no prisoners', and 'leave no stone unturned'. Sound familiar? The review goes on, and on, being referred to in every meeting as a kind of magic alchemy, yet never quite being materialised into tangible form.

From the shop floor things are also progressing and at first, the teaching staff are heartened by the new man and his obvious human character: demonstrated by his ability to entertain as a raconteur and his organization of a staff party. He's certainly changing the culture, seizing the reins of power . . . and yet, there are inevitably other stories here, other 'moments of truth', symbolic interactions which probe deep into the cultural web of this Business School.

Let us trace a different yet concurrent moment. Our fictional School has intentionally developed an international profile in teaching and learning, again a common theme in UK Business Schools. To complement this profile and growth, as with its competitors, it has rapidly become reliant on international staff, who take up junior faculty positions and depend on insecure work visas for their tenure. We drop into another composite meeting, on a hot summer afternoon, when Dr Harry has been tasked by the Human Resource Department to resolve a visa problem'. He is accompanied in his office by one of the 'old hands', a Principal Lecturer close to retirement who presides with apparently benign dictatorship over timetabling and staff work allocation. These organizationally powerful men are meeting with two international female lecturers, one Near-Eastern and one African. Both women are in the 'Catch-22' position of being near the end of their work visas, yet, as junior faculty, are too poorly paid to qualify for an application for permanent residency. Dr Harry, has a difficult problem to tackle. Having come to the UK to take their PhDs, the women's families are settled here and Dr Harry knows this. Yet, the women now face the prospect of loss of employment, income, and even deportation as a result. Dr Harry is in a difficult spot, stuck between immigration rules and conflicting managerial responsibilities. Here, then, is the moment when they put their case to Dr Harry who, in his symbolic role as Head of School and their ultimate line manager, is positioned both as immigration nemesis and protector of staff.

Later, in the women's retelling of the interlude only one moment travels. 'So why should we help *people like you* to stay in the UK?' asks Dr Harry; recollected by both women as a moment to chill the air and freeze the heart. Two memories are recounted—sitting side by side. Both come from the same plot line. Two stories now unfold when we are told that after desultory discussion the meeting ends without conclusion. One woman, tells of going quickly to the Ladies lavatory to burst into tears. The other stoically collects her bag and coat from her office and starts her long journey 'home' to her daughter. Sitting on the train the shock passes and she reflects. She draws parallels with what she knows so well from her own work: people like you are different, 'other' and not-us; here is politics at work. In such retellings, the multiple forces producing the actual moment are diffused and this politic is the story that is shared.

Dark work, from which hidden tales emerge. When the story of change within the School was retold only the surface story—the gloss—could travel and yet Dr Harry experienced, took part in and produced many *other* moments, which are not easily surfaced, yet which shape the sensemaking of the actors. Dr Harry, making up his story as he stumbled along, found that gradually his position was eroded as the gap between his narrative and the community's shared belief in it widened.

Inevitably, as stories ran through the corridors of Grantham, rumours started to circulate about his future, and speculation about who might step in to replace him. As stories abounded, Harry's own behaviours become unpredictable. Periods of absence and erratic attendance at meetings did not help, along with incidents which robbed such meetings of any symbolic value they might otherwise have had. In such moments, the informal goodwill and 'permission to manage' through which managers are able to operate was fast ebbing away.

Yet, one facet of the organizational ecology of university departments and similar communities is that they develop rhythmic patterns of practices, behaviours, and ways of coping which give them an inherent resilience and ability to survive even crass mismanagement, just as a forest can regenerate

surprisingly quickly after a fire. This can manifest itself as a form of organizational autopoiesis, in which a toxin or threat to the ecosystem is gradually eliminated by it (Hall, 2003). So whilst Dr Harry became increasingly
isolated, except for a group of like-minded chums, others took on necessary
responsibilities and quietly attended to human and relational processes in
the interests of the well-being of colleagues, students, and the practices of
educational management. In this way, the business of the school largely
continued without his active intervention and crises were, in most cases,
averted, coped with, or defused before becoming too serious. Undoubtedly,
Dr Harry had a remarkable series of moments, but he is neither our central
character, nor is the anti-hero. His story would be very different, were he
the victim of executive decision making and scapegoating, but here he is the
prompter and maker of untold stories.

Such dark and disturbing stories are rarely surfaced, and yet they reso-
nate strongly both within the University sector and across organizational
life. Academics may require fictive devices to retell such stories as we cau-
tiously pick our way through our responsibilities to all actors. On occasions
the moral imperative outweighs some of the professional ones and 'compe-
tency stories' need to be told, yet the less competent need to be protected.
This fiction is may be shocking, but simply reflects the unthinking incompe-
tence which can routinely arise.

So how do such stories end? There are different plot-lines available. One
hears, and occasionally witnesses, a kind of Stalinist purging in some institutions, where senior managers who have fallen from favour are summoned
summarily, to be informed they are to leave (or retire early) 'by mutual
consent', benefiting from that salve of HR conscientious ambiguity, 'the
compromise agreement'. Others are given loaded if well-meant advice that
it is time to 'seek fresh challenges'. When, inevitably, Harry announced his
intention to 'step down', staff feigned and dissembled 'gobsmacked' emotions of surprise and astonishment. Yet the underlying teleology of the narrative appears inevitable

Narratives such as this are acted out at different levels, none of the actors
ever being aware of all that is taking place, nor of the complex interactions
between the threads of the story. Also, there are parts of these stories which
remain untold; some which should not be told; and others, which have been
told, must be reclaimed or 'untold', if this is indeed possible. Such has been
the case with this narrative, parts of which have been redacted as being 'too
hot to tell'.

DISCUSSION

Several issues and questions are raised by this narrative and need to be
addressed. The primary one is that of risk and moral choice: should the
story be left untold, or is harm caused by its telling?

Let us assume that if the events in this narrative 'really happened' in some organization, then they have been reconstructed in the manner of Watson's ethnographic 'fiction science' (2000), as distinct from being invented, within a mimetic framework of drama imitating life (Bruner, 1990; Czarniawska, 2004). If so, it is possible, if unlikely, that the narrator actually witnessed all of the events which are reconstructed. Rather, let us assume that accounts of the events were relayed by people who were actually present. In that case, the stories of those moments would have already have been shared at least once, and so they cannot be 'untold'; they are 'out there' in the storied life of the organization. Hence the telling of this story is actually a re-telling of extant fragments in a constructed narrative in which the trajectory of the events reach their conclusion.

Is such a story better left untold? This may depend on whose interests are served by its suppression. This narrative hinges in part on the symbolic moment, and its aftermath, when the utterance: 'So why should we help *people like you* to stay in the UK?' is made. This speech act may have seemed trivial, possibly humorous and inconsequential at the time to the speaker. Yet in terms of its effect on the two women, this was anything but the case. Also, in relation to the politics of organizational discourse, it is suffused with latent, possibly unintended meanings of power, sexism, racism, and a denial of help and support for people in a position of powerlessness. Yet had either of them chosen, or felt able, to use the story to make a formal complaint about the incident, the position could have been quite different and it could have become a contested moment, one in which there are conflicting narratives over what took place, what was said, and the *context* to these events. The fact that neither woman did so meant that the 'untold story' helped perpetuate the moral consequences of this type of managerial behaviour. Telling the story, however, may help to make such behaviour morally accountable, even if this might be embarrassing for the perpetrator; who may, of course, have denied the utterance.

Gabriel (2000: 241) warned of the dangers of occluding "deeper issues of justice, politics, and human suffering". So the moral consequences of telling the story are at least no worse, and arguably better than, leaving it untold. Untold stories are often those of the powerless, those who fear they would not be listened to, or that the consequences of telling the story would be adverse for them. In this way, long-suppressed secrets, such as sexual abuses by the priesthood and celebrities emerge from their victims many years after the events. The 'cover-up' or suppression of the telling may be as, or even more, serious a crime as the deed itself.

The moment is symbolic, partly because as actors performing in organizational dramas, we often cannot dissemble in the moment. The actions and speech acts people perform are authentic enactions of their personalities and social identities. Even if the actors themselves do not realize this, those with whom they interact will recognise these 'moments of truth' and the meanings they convey. There are moral issues, as Watson and Harris (1999) concluded from their work on managerial emergence, managers set moral standards and their behaviours embody moral values. They also noted that the narrator as researcher must also make moral judgements which carry responsibility. Creating and shaping a constructed narrative is a selective process. Inclusions, exclusions, and the ordering of events reflect editorial choices and the underlying intentions behind the story. Narration is not a neutral act but also one in which power is used, or can be misused. This story could be seen as a fictive device used to attack Dr Harry, in which the narrator might deploy the tools of language, emotion, irony, and humour in describing the moments selected to create an unsympathetic portrayal of the character. However, such characterisation—but to what end?—is an integral part of the writer's work, whether in the genre of novel, history or organizational biography.

Story-making in this way may also be considered a therapeutic process of sensemaking at an organizational level (Weick, 1995). Incidents and interventions of the kind narrated in the story can be emotionally loaded, traumatic, and damaging for the individuals and work communities who are involved. People often deal with this on a mundane, daily basis through sharing accounts as organizational gossip. This can operate as a process of social coping, a phenomenon which is often evident during periods of organizational trauma. Such stories are told and shared, becoming part of the collective history of the organization. But can they enable the community to reflect, learn, and move on from the psychological, emotional, and moral damage of the events, actors and, interactions concerned?

There must also be a risk that readers will recognise (or think they do) 'real' people, events, and organizations behind those in the narrative. This is not a new problem, Watson encountered it in his thinly-disguised organization *In Search of Management* (1994). The possible danger or moral hazard can be recounted with two arguments. Firstly, such events are both specific and also fairly typical of the interactions which occur in managerial behaviour in many organizations, so it is legitimate to use them as naturally occurring organizational research resources. Secondly, if the stories and characters are already known, then no further harm should be caused by their sharing in a written narrative. Rather, the intention is that by placing them in a mimetic context removed from the original, the problematic issues and questions they pose can be considered, as intended, in a more detached and generalised way.

The story also aims to demonstrate the ways in which such moments can be symbolic turning points in narratives, in the way Hemingway observed. The deterioration in Dr Harry's managerial authority, and relationships with colleagues, was shown in the story to result from behaviours occurring in such moments. Of course, the story is constructed as just that—a narrative trajectory from a set of selected events. Alternative constructions of contested moments could be made and be equally valid. Were the character of Dr Harry to offer his, it would doubtless be quite different. Also, the moments when a listener or reader recognises that an 'untold story' is hidden in the shadow of the told and springs out may become significant points in its interpretation, as in the dénouement of Dr Harry's departure.

CONCLUSION

To observe that moments occur is a commonplace; they constitute the flow and 'twitter' of everyday life. This chapter proposes that 'critical', 'special', or even 'contested' moments are invested with both symbolic meanings within organizational narratives, and can act as 'turning points' within those narratives, whether or not they seemed to be significant to the people involved at the time. Such moments can be invested with meaning in a range of ways. This chapter has closed on the moral dimensions of managerial behaviour in the moment, as well as the implications of selecting and using 'real' material. There are of course, other dimensions as well, such as dimensions of power and gender.

The construction of time, and the differing ways this can be conceptualised, can alter the meaning and the way in which the moment is used and understood. The story could have consisted of the 'critical moment' in isolation, or juxtaposed with other information, rather than being placed within a linear narrative which provided contextual understanding as well as a teleological plotline. Yet it would be entirely valid to make such alternative choices.

The researcher-as-narrator has responsibility for the choices made in selecting, omitting, placing, and connecting moments in stories, in which the decision to 'tell', or 'untell', may be a risky one in terms of morality or personal consequences; 'whistleblowers' rarely prosper in organizations. Yet the story should be able to function as a 'safe' way of making managerial behaviour and practices, for example, morally accountable, and denying the implied power and suppression of 'untold stories' about such incidents.

So as researchers, how do we go forward, in using and interpreting the moment within our work? Carlsen and Dutton (2011: 216), in considering 'generative' (or creative) moments within qualitative research, offered six themes which can provide optimistic and constructive (in both senses) ways forward: "researchers come alive when turning to not knowing" (Carlson & Dutton, 2011: 232). This may provide hope in the risky and contested territories of our research, in working with the moments we perceive, invest with meaning and act to use in constructing our 'untold stories'.

REFERENCES

Amis, K. (1954). *Lucky Jim*. London: Victor Gollancz.
Banks, W., & Isham, E. (2009). We infer rather than perceive the moment we decided to act. *Psychological Science*, 20(1): 17–21.

Beeman, M., & Kounios, J. (2009). The *aha!* moment: The cognitive neuroscience of insight. *Current Directions in Psychological Science*, 18(4): 210–216.

Bergson, H. (1911). *Creative Evolution* (A. Mitchell, Trans.). New York: Henry Holt and Company. (Original work published 1907).

Bigsby, C. (2012, June 21). Farce majeure. *Times Higher Education Supplement*, 21–27.

Boje, D. M. (2012). *Quantum Storytelling*. Retrieved from http://business.nmsu. edu/~dboje/448/The%20Quantum%20Physics%20of%20Storytelling%20 in%20book%20format%20Jan%202011%20Boje.pdf.

Bradbury, M. (1975). *The History Man*. London: Secker & Warburg.

Brockmeier, J. (2000). Autobiographical time. *Narrative Inquiry*, 10(1): 51–73.

Bruner, J. S. (1990). *Acts of Meaning*. Cambridge, MA: Harvard University Press.

Carlsen, A., & Dutton, J. (Eds.). (2011). *Research Alive: Exploring Generative Moments in Doing Qualitative Research*. Copenhagen: Copenhagen Business School Press.

Cope, J. (2005). Toward a dynamic learning perspective of entrepreneurship. *Entrepreneurship: Theory & Practice*, 29(4): 373–397.

Czarniawska, B. (2004). *Narratives in Social Science Research*. London: Sage.

Damasio, A. (2000). *The Feeling of What Happens: Body, Emotion and the Making of Consciousness*. London: Heinemann.

Damasio, A. (2012). *Self Comes to Mind: Constructing the Conscious Brain*. London: Vintage.

Flaherty, M., & Fine, G. (2001). Present, past, and future: Conjugating George Herbert Mead's perspective on time. *Time & Society*, 10(2–3): 147–161.

Gabriel, Y. (2000). *Storytelling in Organizations: Facts, Fictions, and Fantasies*. Oxford: Oxford University Press.

Gladwell, M. (2005). *Blink: The Power of Thinking without Thinking*. London: Penguin Books.

Hall, W. (2003). *Organizational Autopoiesis and Knowledge Management*. Retrieved from http://www.researchgate.net/publication/216663463_Organisati onal_autopoiesis_and_knowledge_management/file/a3617c03edf885d76cbde 00d7cd5821c.pdf.

Heidegger, M. (1980). *Being and Time* (J. Macquarrie and E. Robinson, Trans.). Oxford: Blackwell. (Original work published 1927).

Husserl, E. (1964). *The Phenomenology of Internal Time-consciousness* (J. Barnett Brough, Trans.). Bloomington: Indiana University Press. (Original work published 1928).

Lewis, M. (2004). The emergence of mind in the emotional brain. In A. Demetriou and A. Raftopoulos (Eds.), *Cognitive Developmental Change: Theories, Models and Measurement* (pp. 217–240). New York: Cambridge University Press.

Lodge, D. (1975). *Changing Places*. London: Penguin Books.

Lodge, D. (2001). *Thinks*. London: Penguin Books.

Mead, G. H. (1932). *The Philosophy of the Present*. Chicago, IL: University of Chicago Press.

Pillemer, D. (1998). *Momentous Events, Vivid Memories*. Cambridge, MA: Harvard University Press.

Polkinghorne, D. (1988). *Narrative Knowing and the Human Sciences*. New York: SUNY Press.

Rae, D. (2013). The contribution of momentary perspectives to entrepreneurial learning and creativity. *Industry & Higher Education*, 27(6): 407–420.

Sartre, J-P. (1939). *Sketch for a Theory of the Emotions*. London: Routledge.

Shapero, A. (1982). Social dimensions of entrepreneurship. In C. Kent, D. Sexton, and K. Vesper (Eds.), *The Encyclopaedia of Entrepreneurship* (pp. 72–90). Englewood Cliffs, NY: Prentice Hall.

Shorter Oxford English Dictionary. (2007). Oxford: Oxford University Press.

Shotter, J. (2005). Inside the moment of managing: Wittgenstein and the everyday dynamics of our expressive-responsive activities. *Organization Studies, 26*(1): 143–164.

Snow, C. P. (1951). *The Masters*. London: Penguin Books.

Svoboda, F. (1983). *Hemingway & The Sun Also Rises: The Crafting of a Style*. Lawrence: University Press of Kansas.

Walton Litz, A. (1966). *James Joyce*. New York: Twayne Publishers.

Watson, T. J. (1994). *In Search of Management: Culture Chaos and Control in Managerial Work*. London: Routledge.

Watson, T. J. (2000). Making sense of managerial work and organisational research processes with Caroline and Terry. *Organization, 7*(3): 489–510.

Watson, T. J., & Harris, P. (1999). *The Emergent Manager*. London: Sage.

Weick, K. (1995). *Sensemaking in Organizations*. London: Sage.

4 Hidden Truths

Using Literature to Explore the Untold Stories of the Corporate Subconscious[1]

Angela Lait

OVERVIEW

This chapter begins by examining the presentation of a working professional in Ian McEwan's (2005) novel *Saturday*. The novel's fictional protagonist, NHS neuro-surgeon Henry Perowne, is unsettled by disturbing macro-political events (a post 9/11 anti-war demonstration) and a personal physical attack. These events have a sub-textual parallel in micro-political organizational change in the public sector, in which the structural transformation required for increased flexibility undermines Henry's occupational identity by turning him from 'surgeon' to 'administrator', causing stress that impedes his power of expression. One of the ways Henry copes with these disruptive forces is by continuing to narrate himself as a rational clinician. However, it is evident that the coherence and stability of this image is maintained only by leaving certain things about his character 'untold'. In this way, the story he tells about himself (i.e., how he presents and narrates his identity to others) relies on editing and the suppression of competing or contradictory character traits that would otherwise disturb the narrative act.

The analysis next focuses on the impact of organizational change on identity-formation in the 'real life' public sector workplace, at the point of its transformation towards the responsiveness needed for higher output at no extra cost. The quick and cheap approach that makes 'more for less' possible rests on the qualities of immediacy, flexibility, and mobility but this directly opposes the time-consuming and expensive production needed to ensure high-quality professional standards. This move from proper service to higher output is a transformation that undermines the public servant's occupational values causing dissonance. Inevitably, the organization faces a similar qualitative/quantitative conflict. Though the organization attempts to promote its new flexible identity through its corporate communication, analysis of its verbal and visual language can detect how, like the human character, it also employs a similar kind of editorial manipulation and suppression to manage contradiction and appear coherent. In other words, texts narrating the organization's identity struggle to contain this dichotomy, which suggests that it too, like the human agent, maintains the appearance of coherence on the surface only by suppressing, or leaving 'untold', some things the organization would rather not acknowledge. Thus, the conflicted organization can therefore be seen as producing "imaginary or formal 'solutions' to irresolvable social contradictions" (Jameson, 1981/2002: 64) while the organization's manipulated 'expressions' support Bauman's view that "the prime technique of power is now escape, slippage, elision, and avoidance" (2000: 11).

INTRODUCTION

This chapter explores factors affecting identity-making in the corporate body, human body, and textual body by claiming that a similar narrative dynamic operates in all three. It aims to show how the 'making' and 'expression' of identity are fundamental parts of a single creative act in which the process of narrating and presenting the self is the means by which an entity secures its stability and coherence.

Most importantly, that stability and coherence, which is entirely necessary for a corporation or human to function effectively in the world, is achieved because the 'story' that each tells about itself is a product of an editorial process. A literary author constructs a narrative by careful selection, ordering, and presentation of elements that result in a coherent and understandable 'whole'. This necessarily means that the author leaves out a great deal—background research, other possible plot directions, certain potential characters, and actions that form parts of the author's understanding. These elements, if included, would over-complicate the telling or make it unfit for purpose (e.g., by being too long, too digressive, or too technical). This chapter claims that the process of constructing a self-identity (human or corporate) is also an authorial process that necessarily requires the creator to leave some material 'untold'.

The 'untold' exists, therefore, as an ever present counterpoint to the 'told'. The following analysis aims to show how this operates in practice. It discovers that the 'untold' can occur as a set of ideas that form a subtext in a novel, as the failure of an individual to acknowledge characteristic behaviour that would undermine self-belief, or as elements that disclose the flawed underpinning of corporate ideology.

In other words, the way that an admitted 'story' achieves a semblance of formal unity and coherence is precisely by suppressing any potentially disturbing undercurrents. It is for this reason that a literary psychoanalytic approach is useful in probing what is kept hidden, either consciously or unconsciously, in order that the entity can function in a manner that appears sensible to others.

HENRY PEROWNE, THE VULNERABLE PROFESSIONAL

This chapter begins by examining a story produced by one of the UK's leading creative writers, Ian McEwan. His novel *Saturday* (2005), which deals with a day in the life of neurosurgeon, Henry Perowne, as he contemplates the circumstances of his existence, is a pertinent text for a number of connected reasons.

Chiefly, it is a narrative dealing explicitly with the importance of story for making sense of who we are and of the world in which we live. Typically for McEwan, *Saturday* is set in a context of changing and disturbing circumstances that impact the human agent. So, like other McEwan novels it deals with the contingent nature of existence. Yet the novel is presented in a well-wrought and coherent form, functioning, as story-telling exercises mostly do, to place order on experience. In other words, the disruptive content of the novel is 'contained' by its form (both in the sense of co-existing and being held in check). The containment aesthetic replicates the "conjoining of the ephemeral and the fleeting with the eternal and the immutable" that, according to Baudelaire are the opposing sides of a characteristic time-based tension in the creative work of art (Harvey, 1991: 10). This aesthetic is repeated by the novel's line-within-a-circle structure. The narrative is told in linear form, i.e., from beginning to end, spanning a 24-hour period. However, that timespan clearly establishes a relationship between itself and a natural order of cyclical time and being in which linear events (or lifetimes between birth and death) occur within a larger ordering where seconds make minutes that make hours, days, months, seasons, years, decades, centuries, and so on. This form functions to situate, or contain, the fragmentary and impermanent within a sense of the enduring and permanent (or at least works to [re]establish some connection between them) and as we shall see later, it is an aesthetic that is more problematic for corporate literature to manage.

McEwan is, effectively, like the modern corporation, interested in contingency, and in *Saturday* the disruptive impact of change on stability and security occurs on several levels. In this novel, as in his previous works, McEwan uses the unexpected event as a pivotal point in the plot. The main protagonist is an NHS neurosurgeon called Henry Perowne. Henry wakes one Saturday morning at 03.40 feeling disturbed. From this point on, we follow him through a single day, a 24-hour period ending at 03.40 on the Sunday morning. His early thoughts are about the changing pressures of his workplace, which have made him of late feel "baffled and fearful" (McEwan, 2005: 4) and in need of recovery. During the 24 hours he also witnesses a burning plane flying across the night sky, an event that he interprets against the backdrop of the New York Twin Towers' attack. He wanders through London on the day that the streets are thronging with demonstrators against the UK's involvement in the Gulf war. As the day progresses he follows the story of the burning plane through the various news media updates. He claims that he is not interested in 'stories', thinking that the imagination plays no transformative role in the world, unlike the science of medicine. In fact, he reflects on how his artistic and imaginative children, Theo and Daisy, musician and poet, respectively, are so different from him, though this is ironic given that, at the same time, Perowne's own imagination is dramatically casting him in the role of rescuer for the plane's occupants.

When driving through a narrow London street his car grazes another. There emerges from the second vehicle a man, Baxter, and two thugs who seem to be employed as Baxter's personal protectors. The heavies are intimidating and Baxter himself is clearly volatile. Perowne counters this physical threat by calling on his professional status and knowledge to question Baxter about his state of mind, suggesting that Baxter is suffering from a genetic neurological disorder, which could benefit from surgery.

Perowne then visits his elderly mother in a nursing home and plays a strenuous game of squash with a colleague, which is evidently a displacement activity for the competitive frustrations and general lack of control at work. He also shops and cooks for a family meal, an activity giving him considerable pleasure. By the evening the plane news story is resolved: the plane was not another terrorist attack but a cargo plane. The climax of the novel is when Perowne's defences (physical and psychological) are thoroughly breached. Baxter's threatened attack in the street turns into an actual attack on Perowne's house and family, when he enters the surgeon's home and holds a knife to Daisy's throat, at which point Daisy reads Arnold's poem *On Dover Beach* to Baxter. This has a dramatic, calming effect on the intruder allowing Perowne and his son, Theo, to overpower Baxter.

McEwan is, effectively, like the modern corporation, interested in contingency, and in *Saturday* the disruptive impact of change on stability and security occurs on three separate levels. It is evident, firstly, in the threat at a national (or even international) macro-political level (as anti-war demonstrations in London follow the 9/11 challenge to U.S. supremacy). It is also seen at an unsettling occupational micro-political level (where the call for public service accountability and responsiveness alters Perowne's NHS working conditions, requiring his alignment with emerging organizational values that will change him from all-medic to part-administrator). In addition, disruption appears at a worrying personal level (when Baxter's contact with Perowne sees the surgeon retreat to the padlocked and bolted safety of his home to defend a role as father and protector); or at a disturbed internal level (where neurological damage to Baxter's brain, as a result of illness, directly causes his volatile personality). In addition, the novel explores both what makes us who we are, and draws attention to the hermeneutic process and mechanisms of story-telling through which we each endeavour to secure and express an identity. These mechanisms include action, speech, and silences but the process is constantly challenged by the contradictory elements (or sub-texts) that we suppress in an effort to maintain our 'selves' as the personality we do wish to recognize. For example, recognizing oneself as a 'strong' person can require suppressing recall of incidences in which one was weak. So, as philosopher Kim Atkins says (2004: 350 quoting Ricouer) where we are caught up with multiple people and events, "the question arises concerning the 'actual stories the subject can take up and hold as constitutive of his personal identity'". In this way a narrative provides strategies for "coherence and continuity" by which one can carve out an actual story that one assumes responsibility for from all the potential fields of action (Atkins, 2004: 350). Finally, this novel establishes a connection between literary art and the life world as McEwan spent more than a year following a neurosurgeon to write *Saturday* and, though it is imaginative literature, its representation rests upon a thoroughly researched and recorded reflection of contemporary hospital work culture, thus illuminating the context of modern professional work and its effects on employees.

As McEwan's believes "we have probably not yet bettered a device than the novel for looking at what it is like to be other people" (Bragg, 2005) his novel follows in the introspective tradition for which the form was established and draws attention to 'story' as the cognitive instrument by which we (and Henry Perowne) comprehend ourselves, get to know others, and understand the world in which we live. We are first alerted to the importance of story for self-understanding when Henry sees a burning plane in the sky and immediately interprets this circumstance in the light of the 9/11 attacks on the twin towers of New York's World Trade Centre. He then spends the day obsessed by a developing news item about the plane in which he imagines a starring role for himself as a hero medic. Despite Henry's emotional investment in this imaginative construction, he (ironically) denies that 'story' has any relevance to his life. In fact, Henry is presented as a rational scientist in contrast to his two children, Daisy and Theo, who typify the emotionally literate and artistic temperaments of poet and musician, respectively. So when we are told that Henry thinks "this notion of Daisy's, that people can't 'live' without stories, is simply not true. He is living proof" (McEwan, 2005: 68), we are made aware that an element of illusion operates in order that Henry can recognize himself as he wishes. However, he is not a man who can admit that 'illusion' plays any role (let alone a significant one) in his existence, for part of his ability to achieve, maintain, and secure his self-identity as an entirely rational, emotionally detached clinician rests in maintaining the belief that stories don't matter. In other words, he denies the role that the imagination plays in interpreting the world because he must do so in order to recognize himself as himself.

In this characterization we see that Henry's self-coherence is dependent on suppressing any opposing traits of the emotionally driven, passive character that he associates with his literature- and poetry-loving daughter, Daisy. Thus the reader is alerted that Henry's preferred image of his 'self' is, in part, an illusion sustained by an achieved belief in a coherence that would be disturbed or, at least, weakened by any open acknowledgment of possessing opposing characteristics that challenge that identity. It is only when Daisy demonstrates that poetry can also actively alter Baxter's intentions, its mellifluous rhythms magically calming his violent demeanour, that her father's post-Enlightenment worldview, placing the active and rational in opposition to the emotional and passive, is exposed as cognitively faulty. In recognizing that surgery is not the only means to alter the brain functions of his attacker (and therefore that science is not the only force for transformation in the world) Henry is forced to face and acknowledge the power of imaginative creativity as an agent for change. In doing so he implicitly acknowledges the 'untold story' of his self, that part of him which, though still not fully conscious of the fact, engages with storytelling as part of his daily life and uses the narrative form for its cognitive processes as a means of achieving understanding. In this we can see that for consistent identity, one's orientation is consciously and unconsciously defended against threats to integrity that opposing positions or any challenging evidence represents. However, "because a coherent identity is an achievement it can also fail" (Atkins, 2004: 347). That potential failure is brought into focus by evidence in the novel of a further attack on Henry's self-image, one coming from another external political circumstance—the re-organization of the public service.

Following the altercation with Baxter in the street, and as a result of the post-9/11 threat to global security which transmits itself into the individual's consciousness, Perowne handles his growing vulnerability by the very practical means of ensuring his home is secure. His bid for self-protection includes:

> three stout Banham locks, two black iron bolts as old as the house, two tempered steel security chains, a spyhole with a brass cover, the box of electronics that works the entryphone system, the red panic button, the alarm pad with its softly gleaming digits. Such defences, such mundane embattlement.

> (McEwan, 2005: 36)

However, the physiological and psychological are directly inter-related in the novel by the description that the psychological stress of "not only his broken night, but the whole week and the weeks before bearing down on him" is manifest also in a physiological feebleness of his joints and muscles that limit his physical movement (McEwan, 2005: 36). This metaphoric link dissolves the categorical distinction between mind and body as both are equally vulnerable and threatened by days that are now "baffled and fearful" (McEwan, 2005: 4). We are thus made aware of how environmental change or actual events can have both physiological and psychological consequences. This becomes significant when the narrative describes how the changing working conditions in the public sector function effectively as an assault Perowne's psychic health and energy levels.

Henry is a professional in the NHS and, as discussed, much of his self-image rests on his occupational identity as a rational, scientifically minded, emotionally detached clinician. He uses certain psychological mechanisms to defend a status that is also outwardly signified by his personal possessions, his home—several storeys of grandeur in a prime London square[2]—and his car. His silver Mercedes S500 operates as an anthropomorphised 'other' version of his self that "breathes an animal warmth" (McEwan, 2005: 75). The car reflects his worth in economic terms and having now "accepted himself as the owner, the master of his vehicle . . . it's become part of him" (McEwan, 2005: 75–76). Its "padded privacy" (McEwan, 2005: 121) functions as concrete representation of his self, an outer casing of status and power, like his profession, that affords him a measure of protection and control. When Baxter's car hits Henry's Mercedes, as they attempt to pass each other in a narrow London street, it is a foretaste of the physical attack that seems imminent when Baxter and his men get out of the car to confront Henry. When Henry defends himself by calling on his professional identity to diagnose Baxter's illness, we become aware of how he uses his occupational status for self-confidence and protection.

Henry's occupation as a neurosurgeon is noted in the first line of the novel but this opening statement also describes him as naked, coupling the image of professionalism with vulnerability. Formally, this professional status is protected by qualifications, knowledge, and skills, attributes that indicate his level of authority. Personal identity through employment status is part of the codification, integral to Western daily life, by which we negotiate our relationships with, and expectations of, others. Indeed, Henry's occupational status is shown as the social currency that both defines him and guides his speech and action. Thus when diagnosing Baxter's neural disease Henry recognizes the "shameless blackmail" in which he "senses the power passing to him" (McEwan, 2005: 95) when the doctor/patient relationship re-establishes dominance in Henry's favour. Understanding the power Henry is afforded by his profession makes clear what any threat to that identity will mean for his self-security. So it is worth noting that Henry's workplace makes demands on him that are steadily diminishing the confidence borne from his professional status. In seeking an explanation for his malaise, Henry diagnoses his own mental state as being the "consequence of extreme tiredness [having] finished the week in a state of unusual depletion" (McEwan, 2005: 5). He locates his weariness in "this modern professional life. He works hard, everyone around him works hard and this week he's been pushed harder . . . balancing and doubling" (McEwan, 2005: 7) in order to work simultaneously in three operating theatres. The descriptor 'modern' indicates emerging circumstance, one not yet fully accomplished. Thus there is a telling semiotic lag when he uses the as-yet unmodified language of old-style, 'iron cage' stability commenting on "the discipline and responsibility of a medical career" (McEwan, 2005: 28). Trying to maintain traditionally recognised professional values in an increasingly lean and over-stretched system indicates a performative conflict and as there is "over much of it, a veil of fatigue" (McEwan, 2005: 28), ultimately causes the worker to tire and fail.

Here, 'modern professional life' (contrasting with orderly, stable, less pressurised traditional professional life) indicates instead the new economy's (oxymoronic) permanent state of flux that can be interpreted in two ways: the perpetually edgy position of readiness that is the basis for the responsive action required to supply a demanding and constantly changing market or as a transitional state without resolution known as the neurotic state of chaos or dissonance in which competing demands result in a total inability to act. While Sennett identifies the "confidence to dwell in disorder, [to] flourish in the midst of dislocation" as a characteristic of those successful in the new capitalist culture (Sennett, 1999: 62), the psychotherapeutic model, requiring resolution of contradiction and chaos for psychological welfare, suggests the certainty required for good mental health recommends against pursuing the kinds of rapid changeability now required for workplace success. While some are willing and able to immerse themselves in the seas of change, those mourning the old certain times are charged with previous generation nostalgia or seen as resistant to the adaptation necessary for survival. Existing among the fluctuations of new-economy conditions requires one to operate within its changeable currents for as long as that can be comfortably managed. When exhaustion ensues or if one stops, confused and directionless in eddying waters, one is sucked under—a method of natural selection in a system of occupational Darwinism by which those labelled indecisive or weak are identified as corporate losers and removed.

However, it is notable that hard work itself does not cause Henry trouble. In fact, the practical nature of Henry's occupation affords him fulfilment and he enjoys applying his skill to good effect, finding exhilaration in challenging work. It is the requirement for adaptability that pressures Perowne. Flexibility brings an increasing bureaucratic demand of peripheral tasks that are making him deskbound—less surgeon and more administrator. It is:

> the paperwork on Friday afternoon that brought him down, the backlog of referrals, and responses to referrals, abstracts for two conferences, letters to colleagues and editors, an unfinished peer review, contributions to management initiatives, and Government changes to the structure of the Trust, and yet more revisions to teaching practices. There's to be a new look—there's always to be a new look—at the hospital's emergency plan.
>
> (McEwan, 2005: 11)

The constant call for a new look is the 'fresh page' terminology that attempts to validate the changing policies associated with corporate restructuring undertaken in the too-frequent aim of cost-cutting. However, economist Richard Layard (2005) links change to the rising tide of misery and believes "we should . . . question policies of continuous change since they involve repeated losses" when any loss causes unhappiness greater than an equivalent gain would increase happiness (Layard, 2005: 141–142). The repetition "there's always to be a new look" hints at the weariness of a repeated process that, if not creating loss, certainly yields no gain. A similar lack of progress and more direct loss of freedom are implied by the paperwork. With the relentless accumulation of the administrative load, work in the new economy, aided by information technology, replicates the psychic problems of industrial conveyor-belt automation, i.e., work needing attention that arrives at a rate over which the worker has no control.

The name change from Health 'Authority' to 'Trust' is semantically interesting. Authority was once a guarantee that confidence could be placed in trained and experienced professional doctors. The alteration in descriptor occurs at a time when, according to Onora O'Neill (2002), "Mistrust and suspicion have spread across all areas of life and supposedly with good reason. . . , Patients . . . in particular no longer trust hospitals or hospital consultants". That the word 'trust' has replaced 'authority' is therefore deeply ironic (O'Neill, 2002: 8–9). Instead of trust there is accountability, which, particularly in the public sector "aims at ever more perfect administrative control of institutional and professional life" (O'Neill, 2002: 46), bearing out the Weberian prediction that bureaucratic administration would triumph over specialist, professional knowledge. The constant scrutiny of professionals is pernicious.

> Professionals have to work to ever more exacting—if changing—standards of good practice and due process, to meet relentless demands to record and report, and they are subject to regular ranking and restructuring . . . many public sector professionals find that the new demands damage their real work.
>
> (O'Neill, 2002: 49)

Specifically, "doctors speak of the inroads that required record-keeping makes into the time that they can spend finding out what is wrong with their patients and listening to their patients" (O'Neill, 2002: 50). It is clear that Henry is less able to define himself as surgeon while vast amounts of his time are spent as administrator. His work conditions are eating away equally at his autonomy, authority, and identity.

Like other aspects of his work, the administrative anxiety spills into his private life when following the car scrape, "with rising irritation . . . he already sees ahead into the weeks, the months of paperwork, insurance claims and counterclaims, phone calls, delays at the garage" (McEwan, 2005: 82), so just when his characteristic clinical detachment could be of use, it fails him, and the emotional surfaces with his "rising unease about the encounter" (McEwan, 2005: 102). This is perhaps because paperwork, requiring time he would rather devote to other activity but needing none of the professional skill and knowledge through which he experiences pride and achievement, seems fundamentally purposeless and unproductive. Unlike Henry's clinical work, ending pain and restoring function, these tasks do not 'make a difference'. We know how Henry feels about useless toil for when seeing a litter collector jabbing away at individual items of detritus he says, "what could be more futile than this underpaid urban-scale housework when behind him . . . cartons and paper cups are spreading thickly under the feet of demonstrators" (McEwan, 2005: 74). His ever-growing mountain of paperwork is similar in having little practical and no personal benefit, and the speed and volume of arriving email leaves recipients feeling overwhelmed. While dealing with administration Henry is unable to experience the more fulfilling part of his job, the harmonies and satisfactions he finds when operating on patients, an activity in which knowledge, skill, and experience are applied to good practical effect such as when his intervention means "three years' misery, of sharp, stabbing pain, ended" (McEwan, 2005: 7). The growing volume of e-communication defines Henry not as surgeon but as administrator as more and more of his time is spent in the office.

Thus:

> Perowne dictated monotonously, and well after his secretary went home he typed in his over heated box of an office. . . . At eight in the evening he concluded the last in a series of e-mails and stood up from his desk where he had been hunched since four.
>
> (McEwan, 2005: 12)

Described here Henry is imprisoned, has assumed a fetal protection position and appears to lack control and achievement or the power to do anything about it, a situation recognised as the classic condition of stress and depression (Layard, 2005: 68, quoting Marmot).[3] This passive position contradicts the view Henry holds of himself and the effects of this are absorbed internally producing the classic symptoms of trauma—the lack of verbal facility, or in the words of the text, "an unfamiliar lack of fluency" described as follows:

> Now he was stumbling. And though the professional jargon did not desert him—it's second nature—his prose accumulated awkwardly. Individual words brought to mind unwieldy objects—bicycles, deckchairs, hangers—strewn across his path. He composed a sentence in

his head, then lost it on the page, or typed himself into a grammatical cul-de-sac and had to sweat his way out. Whether this debility was the cause or consequence of fatigue he didn't pause to consider.

(McEwan, 2005: 12)

When he does '"pause to consider" he observes that:

In the past year he's become aware of new committees and sub-committees spawning, and lines of command that stretch up and out of the hospital, beyond the medical hierarchies, up through the distant reaches of the Civil Service to the Home Secretary's office.

(McEwan, 2005: 12)

This multi-layered, hierarchical structure is far from the level structures that today's business organizations claim as the distinguishing features of a devolved system of responsibility that puts everyone in charge of their own workload. In fact, it confirms itself as part of the accountability trend identified by O'Neill who says:

For those of us in the public sector the new accountability takes the form of detailed control. An unending stream of new legislation and regulation, memoranda and instructions, guidance and advice floods into public sector institutions . . . [arousing] a mixture of despair and disbelief.

(O'Neill, 2002: 46)

So, where trust has been replaced by accountability, as O'Neill claims (2002), it results in the punishing hours and wearying amounts of checking and measuring now placed on public sector professionals. While it seems entirely reasonable to allow prospective patients to access information regarding a surgeon's reliability based on the consistent performance of skill and knowledge over time, it is not acceptable for institutions to require the collection of such data by the same surgeons in a burdensome manner that makes their necessary demonstration of such diligence ever harder. This unreasonable requirement marks a performative contradiction that undermines the very standards it seeks to measure. Moreover, it gives the medic an ethical dilemma in addition to the logistical one and denies that some valuable things to do with quality of care—the nurse's hand-holding, the doctor's kind words, the teacher's support of a pupil—just cannot be easily measured even though they contribute to good performance and controlling costs. According to O'Neill

the new accountability is experienced not just as *changing* but . . . as *distorting the proper aims of professional practice* and indeed as damaging professional pride and integrity . . . professional and public servants understandably end up responding to requirements and targets and not only to those whom they are supposed to serve. . . .

(O'Neill, 2002: 50, emphasis original)

This distortion evidently impacts Perowne's identity in two ways: it surfaces the emotion he would rather keep suppressed, and it disturbs the integrity of his persona. In total, *Saturday* paints a portrait of a professional feeling physically and psychologically vulnerable by a number of destabilizing circumstances. He inhabits a world now made nervous by the radical challenge to power relations caused by the 9/11 bombings. In addition, he suffers a physical assault in the street, which eventuates in the breach of his home security when the 'outside' terror comes 'inside' his house. He is dependent on stories even when denying they have any relevance for him, for he exists in the empirical world only through the story McEwan tells about him, and in the fictive world uses story constantly as the means to shape and understand experience. Thus it is important when another external circumstance, his changing employment environment, affects his identity and his powers of expression, each of which depend on the stability or equilibrium of internal psychological processes.

So, the analysis of the subtext illustrates a clash between self and institution in which professional insecurity indicates Perowne's bid for identity survival when time pressure and the demands of a flexible, responsive, new-economy business model threaten to overwhelm him. Certainly, the literary idea of a subtext operating below what is made visible is a useful notion for understanding both the construction and presentation of identity, particularly so where it can be seen that the adopted identity of the main protagonist also involves a degree of withholding. By being aware of this dynamic we know that containment of specific elements is an integral part of producing a certain impression. This form of editing indicates that the untold may have as much to say about an entity as any story about itself it chooses to declare. Moreover, the surface presentation of identity can be examined critically and analytically to discover the existence of points of stress, silence and fracture that indicate precisely what is being kept hidden. The question is does this, or the way that story operates to secure a preferred identity, have any relevance for the professional in the empirical world?

THE IDENTITY STRUGGLE OF THE 'HUMAN' CORPORATION AND ITS EMPLOYEES

The key point to notice from Perowne's fictional account of his work experience is that when he is under pressure of administrative overload, work of a type that heralds an identity conflict, the impact is exhibited in the failure of language—a conceptual breakdown in his sensemaking structures. What follows is a discussion about organizational identity, which exhibits how the telling or presentation of a coherent corporate 'story' about identity also relies on suppressing certain factors and how a failure of sensible communication similarly occurs where those underlying stressors are too disturbing. In other words, the mechanics of any form of identity story-telling—individual, organizational, fictional—are very much the same, a process of editing in which the 'untold' constantly challenges the coherence and intelligible surface of what is 'told'. Turning now to the corporate body we can examine the ramifications of these circumstances.

A psychoanalytic analysis of the corporate body is made in consideration of the various moves made by business to present itself as having not only a human face but also a human soul. The first PR campaign was launched in 1908 by the U.S. telephone giant AT&T, which "imbued the company with human values in an effort to overcome people's suspicions of it as a soulless and inhuman entity" (Bakan, 2004: 17). A following move "in the middle of the nineteenth century" saw the corporation become "a legally designated 'person' designed to valorize self-interest and invalidate moral concern" (Bakan, 2004: 28) about its activities. Since then business has adopted what Thomas Frank calls "people-friendly styles" to explain itself in more appealing and responsible terms to a wider public (Frank, 2000: 39) while internal and external marketing has focussed on corporate branding designed to define the organization's 'personality' through the attributes of products, services, and behaviour with which its stakeholders can identify. In addition, the corporation has attempted to promote its own humanity specifically to employees through the development of nurturing personnel policies derived from Maslow's and Herzberg's human needs models. The corporation's transformation from impersonal object to personal subject is completed by the full and willing acknowledgment it makes of its contingent existence amid the altering circumstances and pressures of the external world. With business now cognisant of, and attentive to, the adaptations it must make to 'survive' it is hardly fanciful to extend the 'humanising' metaphor further so that the utterances and presentations made by the organization, its communication practices, function in a similar way to anything that is said or done by any individual in an effort to negotiate the circumstances of her existence.

Organizations strive for effectiveness and efficiency as a means of surviving in the world of business. The public sector became used to the language that supports this drive after 1997 when it was given the task to shed its old identity as a lumbering, inefficient, and over-stuffed bureaucracy and to adopt the principles of lean efficiency that characterize the New Economy. There is no doubt that such a move was warranted in order to make good use of taxpayer's money and that this effort was spearheaded, as are many change management programmes, by communications designed to align employees with the attitudes and behaviour required by the new model.

Using the Department of the Environment Food and Rural Affairs (DEFRA) as an example, a simple word count of its Annual Reports over the 3-year period after it was formed shows how 'new economy' thinking began to dominate the department as language urging responsiveness, immediacy, and flexibility colonised its corporate utterances and, by doing so, determined its culture and placed new identity demands on its workforce (Lait, 2012: 18–20).[4] The human effect of this was brutal. The 10-fold increase in the use of the word 'change' and the tripling of the word count, 2,720 to 8,930, is testimony to the discursive thrust the new direction is given while, in an uncanny reversal of those figures, what this adaptability means in practice for employees is volatility—a reduction from "8,000 people in the core department when DEFRA was formed in 2001, to around 3,200 in 2008" (DEFRA, n.d.-a: 86). A "leaner more effective Department" (DEFRA, n.d.-b, 8) actually means less costly (DEFRA, 2003: 96) and a further statement that efficiencies will be achieved by "moving resources (money and people) quickly and easily", (DEFRA, website) makes clear that humans, like photocopiers, are thought of only in instrumental terms. Unsurprisingly, workers treated like replaceable machines, overloaded by work of their now-redundant colleagues experience low self-esteem, uncertainty, and psychological stress.

By controlling the language through which its image is both constructed and reflected the department's communications activities are designed to effect a makeover, to rebrand not only the company but the workforce also, to instil in employees the innovative, flexible, and agile attitudes and behaviours that promote the business efficiency of a "responsive service provider" (DEFRA, 2003: 103). And yet, contradicting the chameleon behaviour and constant reinvention proposed by its new flexible model, DEFRA still trails a Fordist goal-oriented claim to be "planning for the long term as well as the present" (DEFRA, 2003: 6–7). In this we begin to see a tension existing at the bedrock of the organization. The values, attitudes, and behaviour—the identity—of the institution organized for flexible responsiveness are very different from the fixity and stability it requires to inspire confidence in the electorate and to govern with authority, or from the loyalty and care it requires from its employees to deliver proper service outcomes.

The transformation proceeded with the department's corporate communications—design, typography, and logos—all designed to establish the new DEFRA ethos, character, and image, which is publicly defended by brand managers and professional communicators. While externally directed effort is gauged by brand recognition and sales (or in the case of government, policy) success, employee 'buy in' is judged by the absence of dissent and low staff turnover. The pressure to conform is immense. Musson and Duberley's fieldwork entitled *Change, Change or be Exchanged* (2007), recognises the role of workplace discourse in "targeting and moulding the human subject" (Musson & Duberley, 2007: 148). The organization chooses the discourse within which identity can be forged no less authoritatively than the fictional writer constructs character, and personnel management practices operate to marginalise, expel, or silence any resistors or gainsayers who undercut, subvert, or miscommunicate the corporate messages and so detract from its preferred image.[5] The preference for those whose speech signals conformity proves that "organizational control is accomplished through the self-positioning of employees within managerially-inspired discourses about work and organization within which they may become more or less identified and committed" (Alvesson & Willmott, 2002: 620). Those who commit to the greatest extent will fully replicate the organizational language in their own communication. These workers are often singled out for promotion as they willingly demonstrate that they are truly 'company' people. Others are merely pragmatic. They are less willing to give their wholehearted commitment to the firm but still find benefit in "using representations that are officially sanctioned by the organization [as this] reduces the possibility for dissonance, provides a sense of existential security, and gives the individual a sense of protection from sanctions" (Alvesson & Spicer, 2012: 1208). There are certainly costs for workers unable to identify and commit to the new public service ethos. Those still holding to the (now inappropriate) notions of quality, trying to do a good job, rather than the cheap or fast job that is required by the agile employee, may consequently foul their own occupational and professional standards, fail promotion, and suffer psychological stress. Even worse, as with recent case of so-called uncompassionate NHS nurses, they may also find themselves scapegoated for the poor outcomes that have actually resulted from economically inspired managerial choices. At the very least they may find themselves suffering cognitive dissonance because they are trying to hold in their heads two conflicting stories about who they are.[6] Are they the thorough and caring public servant able to act with professional pride or are they the efficient, quick, and agile operator more concerned with quantity than quality? To be one means actively suppressing the other.

It matters because these divided selves lack the psychological continuity necessary for the human individual to conduct itself as what Kim Atkins terms a practical and ethical subject through time, that is a subject who must continually act in the world and whose reason for acting attests to the subject's essentially held values (Atkins, 2004: 341–366).[7] That psychological continuity, Atkins considers, is only found in a narrative model. She believes that "as a practical being whose existence is structured by action, the meaning and continuity of my life and identity—who I am—is structured through the textual resources of narrative" (Atkins, 2004: 350). Moreover, only a narrative model "is oriented to the need for meaning in the lives of embodied, practical beings existing within the constraints of a temporal world" because it is able to "articulate a form of continuity in identity consistent with the importance a person attaches to being the same experiential subject over time" (Atkins, 2004: 341–342).[8] Where change management and 'flexible responsiveness' forces repeated ruptures in continuity (just as disruptive events challenge Perowne in *Saturday*) and only a specific vocabulary of changeability is validated, the result is narrative difficulty.

This is evidenced by the fact that it is no longer possible to make a progressive narrative of one's life that was once afforded by the word 'career' since the traditional values associated with craftsmanship, those of continuity and permanence, doing something well for its own sake, practising to perfect an ability or skill over time, have been replaced by fragmentation, impermanence, a requirement to jump from job to job, and move on quickly and uncritically from failure. This prejudicial shift in the relationship of time to activity means that valuable character traits like trust and commitment, which can only be demonstrated through continuities of time and through enduring relationships, are no longer part of experience (Sennett, 1999: 22–23 and 48). Where one narrates identity through experience, the language that is available, or more critically, that is socially sanctioned for that narration also has a direct bearing on who one is able to be particularly when "words and language are [used as] powerful and seductive rhetorical implements" (Amernic & Craig, 2006: 4). Employees given a new language in which the terms of success are those of flexibility and fast turnover are faced with dissonance if their natural inclinations and personal values are those of old-style stability, continuity, and slowness but they are required to adopt the 'new economy' values to secure their employment.

However, if identity and narration problems arise in the demand for employees to adapt from the structural stabilities, fixity, and continuities of one managerial system to the flexibility, mobility, and responsiveness of another, the transformational call has no less significant repercussions for organizational identity and the way the resulting conflict is reflected in its communications output.

DEFRA's adoption of "people-friendly styles" (Frank, 2000: 39), which serve the market model's customer-focus, can be seen in the photographs of the Minister in the annual Departmental Reports.

In the 2002 photo (Figure 4.1) she has a forward-facing gaze conveying directness, stability, and gravitas against a backdrop of historic architecture, taken from a low-angled camera so the viewer must look up to her. A very clear shift away from this authoritative image is evident in another portrait 2 years later in which she appears against a softened studio backdrop, with her body angled to the camera, her hair cut, coloured, and shaped, and crucially, from a higher angled camera so that her eyes are tilted upwards (in the pose of vulnerability made famous by the late Princess of Wales) and in the viewer's eyes she is diminished. This shape-shifting occurs also on the cover where the centrally placed, capitalized acronym DEFRA and the single image on the 2002 publication breaks down into three areas on the 2003 report with a lower case logo now situated on the right-hand lower corner, and is fragmented still further in the 2004 version, where the cover

Figure 4.1 The Changing Defra Departmental Report Covers (DEFRA, 2002, 2003, 2004) and Accompanying Ministerial Photos for the Years 2002 to 2004 Illustrate the Transformation from Monolithic Authoritarianism to Flexible Approachability.

now sports nine images, each representing an aspect of the department's responsibilities, with upper and lower bands carrying the title and logo, respectively. This inclusive diversity is the publications' equivalent of the eclecticism and multidimensionality that David Harvey notes is central to postmodern structural aesthetics (Harvey, 1991: 66–98) and it mirrors the structural fragmentation that supports the agility of modern business. However, the replacement of the capitalized acronym with the lower-case one, the change of the authoritarian Times font to the more relaxed Arial and the repositioning of the logo on the lower right-hand corner on the cover is not the literal and symbolic decentring it at first appears. In left-to-right reading cultures the prime position for assimilation (as advertising charges inform us) is where the reader places a finger to turn the page. So the friendly style may appear less dominant yet has replaced its obvious impressive power with a far cannier but equally affecting one that escapes detection.

A key linguistic technique declaring coherence against all other presentational evidence is the use of the corporate 'we', a magical pronoun that co-opts and excludes at will. Sentences using 'we' or 'DEFRA' presume an unproven unity and intimacy that is fouled by the comment that "the DEFRA family will be examined for potential rationalization" (DEFRA, 2003: 105), an emotionally detached statement whose passive construction carefully avoids pinpointing the responsible agent(s). The key relationship is rather better proved by the statement claiming that the organization is geared to "efficient service to our customers" (DEFRA, 2002: 17–18), which indicates that the 'widely-shared' company values extend between corporations and the market and not between corporations and employees.

The general growth of stress management output by HR departments, across industry, testifies to the increasing psychological difficulties experienced in today's workplace. This is particularly evident in the public sector where the tensions between the old and new economic models appears at its most keen. The following is an interesting structural example produced by DEFRA's HR department of how corporate-speak attempts to handle the wider irresolvable tensions between business needs and those of its employees in the new economy workplace. The sentences have been separated and are numbered for identification purposes.

1. A stimulating and supportive working environment can have a positive effect on mental health, but adverse situations can have a negative effect (see Section 5).
2. Dealing with stress is not just about individual coping mechanisms but also about looking at the causes and developing corporate approaches to the problem.
3. DEFRA is subject to financial and other resource constraints, as are other similar organizations.
4. However, good management practices and concern for staff go a considerable way to reducing excessive pressures on individuals.

5. The aim of this booklet is to provide guidance for managers and staff to assist them in recognising and dealing with stressful situations.
6. It is in the interests of DEFRA and all its staff that harmful levels of stress should be minimized.

(DEFRA, n.d.-a: 2)

The six sentences are thematically linked through the idea of stress. However, there is no strong logical argument or narrative line dependent on the current sequence. Sentences 1, 2, 5, and 6 are separate, semantically discrete statements, but although each is internally grammatical, they bear no critical relationship to each other and can be placed in any order. Unlike these entirely separate statements, the conjunction 'however' refers the 'management practices' in Sentence 4 to the 'resource constraints' in Sentence 3. In this way the central two sentences are interdependent and their meaning lies in their logical sequencing, while the other four sentences can be paired in any way to provide the outer casing either side of the inner sentiment.

Sentences 3 and 4 are the critical, literal, and metaphorical heart of the matter, and it is worth looking at their content and logical pairing. The first part of Sentence 3, "DEFRA is subject to financial and other resource constraints", indicates cost-dependency, while the second part of the sentence, that DEFRA's constraints make it "like other similar organisations", locates responsibility outside itself and, significantly, obscures the distinction between the public sector organization and public shareholder companies. The next statement (at the beginning of Sentence 4), that "good management practices and concern for staff go a considerable way to reducing excessive pressures on individuals", is a rhetorical expression which acknowledges the benefit of personal interaction and support but, given that 'resource constraints' are going to heavily influence 'management practices,' the extent of 'concern for staff' looks set to diminish. The 'considerable way' leaves unspecified what else needs attention for the elimination of stress, including responsibility for locating the precise causes of the admitted "excessive pressures on individuals".

Ironically, these two sentences appear to be written in plain English but their very simplicity is the linguistic poverty of a presentational style that prohibits full understanding and conceals irresolvable paradox beneath a gloss of openness and clarity. Their placement at the centre of the paragraph is significantly metaphoric, as the linguistic elision is a symptom of contradictions emanating from the heart of the organization. The sentences appear straightforward, individual, and incontrovertible (and uncontroversial) statements of fact, but they are emblematic of the way structural fragmentation conceals ideological contradiction. In fact, the organization of the paragraph reflects and represents the organization itself: the site of contest for opposing ideological ideas; apparently coherent but actually structurally fragmented and internally driven; tensioned by the public sector's incorporation of corporate business ethics; using communication that ostensibly informs and comforts but truly perplexes understanding and so prohibits question; employing indirect grammar to shift responsibility away from itself; and calling on its management professionals to reconcile contradictory objectives of concern for staff welfare with cost-cutting priorities. Such contradiction seems very much like O'Neill's "incompatible or barely compatible requirements [that] invite compromises and evasions" (DEFRA, 2002: 54). The textual avoidance bears witness to the need to speak clearly about something that cannot be spoken. It results from a market-oriented focus which has to subordinate the needs of employees to corporate success but which it tries not to acknowledge openly. It is evidence of a continuing agenda of public sector cutbacks and accountability that sit uneasily together and prove Bauman's view that "the prime technique of power is now escape, slippage, elision and, avoidance" (Bauman, 2000: 11). These tensions surface in DEFRA's communications when the organization attempts to negotiate and reconcile the competing organizational priorities by using what Jameson calls "imaginary or formal 'solutions' to irresolvable social contradictions" (Jameson, 1981/2002: 64). However, the organization's expressive structures do not manage the co-existence of the ephemeral and the fleeting with the permanent and the immutable anywhere near as successfully as McEwan does in *Saturday*. In other words, there is a similarity in the way any expressive form manages to disguise inherent contradictions beneath the gloss of an apparently coherent surface but the artistry of McEwan's novel contains those contradictions in the sense of holding them in perfect tension, while the containment effort in organizational material is less perfectly executed and results in those contradictions appearing as logical flaws in the organizational order of things.

CONCLUSION

The structural dissolution and ideological contradictions in these examples of DEFRA's corporate output are well-hidden but analysis reveals three important contradictions. Firstly, that narrative fragmentation fights linearity and unity. Second, that lean efficiency striving for faster, higher, and cheaper output battles with the time-consuming and expensive matter of genuine staff welfare. Third, that the impersonality and disconnection needed for hard business decisions contests the humanity required of the truly responsible and caring workplace. The identities of both the public sector organization and its employees are seriously compromised in the move from monolithic stability to agile and flexible responsiveness, and while the corporate communication machine tightly controls and coordinates the messages and images it shows to the world as an impression of unity and being fit-for-purpose, those polished surfaces conceal much that needs to be suppressed in the achievement of that seemingly coherent presentation. In other words, just as a human being constructs a self-narrative that avoids knowledge harmful to its ego, as we have seen with the character of Perowne, so the corporate body operates a similar mechanism of self-protection by relegating some 'untold stories' about itself to what might be called the corporate unconscious so that its preferred identity can be maintained and presented through the various forms of (apparently) intelligible communication it has with the world.

On the other hand, the many employees who are self-committed to quality rather than quantity of output may not have the expressive capabilities to manage their identity trauma and may more explicitly show the resulting symptoms. If they are not like Perowne, and can willingly suppress less dominant parts of the self in order to be who they are or want to be, they are likely, instead, to exhibit the stress, depression, and introverted silence of the worker being forced to be someone they do not want to recognize as themselves, finding themselves called to act against personal or professional ethical codes already held as constitutive of their preferred identity and deprived of power over the language, actions, and attitudes that attest to their essentially held values.

So, where at first McEwan's contemporary novel and DEFRA's corporate output may seem strange bedfellows, it can be claimed that their use of story for the presentation of human or organizational identity shows particular similarities, especially with regard to how disruption and contradiction are 'managed' in order to maintain coherence. Bringing one discursive form (the novel) alongside another (the corporate story) also shows the ramifications for the real or fictional professional employee—the 'subjects' of the story forms—when new economy principles begin to alter working conditions in the public sector. Certainly, in both, suppressed meaning has a presence (even if only obliquely) proving that wherever there is a 'story' an 'untold story' lurks somewhere beneath the surface as an implicit challenge to any understood and apparent truth.

NOTES

1. This article is adapted from the author's book, *Telling Tales: Work, Narrative and Identity in a Market Age* (2012). (Manchester: Manchester University Press).
2. According to Peter Childs (2005: 151), Perowne's house is modelled on McEwan's own. Several clues in the text place the house in a square (McEwan, 2005: 196–197) near Warren Street, Maple Street, and Fitzroy Street (McEwan, 2005: 78), probably Fitzroy Square.
3. Social science research has found that low-status work produces higher levels of the stress hormone that curtails life expectancy, concluding that for labour to be fulfilling, "the most important issue is the extent to which you have control over what you do" (Layard, 2005).
4. At this time DEFRA's publications saw the introduction of a vocabulary beloved by private sector CEOs—customer, change, delivery, prospectus, vision, journey, reform, challenge, lean, effective, etc.

5. See Edwards (1979: 155), who claims that although individual acts of resistance have not brought capitalism to its knees, the proliferation of print, broadcast, and Internet channels endows the individual with a disruptive power unequalled in earlier times. Tighter controls and 'gagging clauses' may be the result of organizations recognising that.

6. Alvesson and Spicer (2012) say workers engage "in a process of *stupidity self-management*" to avoid reflexive questioning that would cause dissonance. Psychological well-being is achieved by "focusing on the more positive aspects of organizational life which are more clearly aligned with understandings and interpretations that are officially sanctioned and actively promoted" (p. 1207) so that "they can avoid fragmentation, contradiction and vulnerability" (p. 1210).

7. The concept of being as a "practical and ethical subject" through time is similar to Sennett's use of the French philosophic definition "mantien de soi"—maintenance of oneself over time, and "constance a soi"—fidelity to oneself (Sennett, 1999: 145).

8. See also Galen Strawson, *A Fallacy of Our Age: Not Every Life is a Narrative* (Times Literary Supplement, 2004: 13–15). Strawson asserts that 'Diachronic' types see their lives in narrative terms but not so 'Episodic' types who accept 'one has long-term continuity' (in terms of bodily existence through time) but whose psychology resists or is wary of employing the privileged position of the 'I' to determine meaning from the available facts of experience. This willingness to exist with uncertainty is, however, recognisable as an element of postmodern forms that narrate disruption, contingency, and discontinuity by drawing attention to their own limitations in making meaning from a chaotic reality.

REFERENCES

Alvesson, M., & Spicer, A. (2012). A stupidity-based theory of organizations. *Journal of Management Studies*, 49(7): 1194–1220.

Alvesson, M., & Willmott, H. (2002). Identity regulation as organizational control: Producing the appropriate individual. *Journal of Management Studies*, 39(5): 619–644.

Amernic, J. & Craig, R. (2006). *CEO-Speak: The Language of Corporate Leadership*. London: McGill Queen's University Press.

Atkins, K. (2004). Narrative identity, practical identity and ethical subjectivity. *Continental Philosophy Review*, 37(3): 341–366.

Bakan, J. (2004). *The Corporation: The Pathological Pursuit of Profit and Power*. London: Constable.

Bauman, Z. (2000). *Liquid Modernity*. Cambridge: Polity.

Bragg, M. (2005, February 20). *South Bank Show* [Television Broadcast]. Season 28, Number 638. London: ITV.

Childs, P. (Ed.). (2005). *The Fiction of Ian McEwan*. Basingstoke: Palgrave MacMillan.

Department for Environment, Food and Rural Affairs (DEFRA). (2002). *Departmental Report*. Retrieved from http://webarchive.nationalarchives.gov.uk/2003122022 1853/http://www.DEFRA.gov.uk/corporate/deprep/default.htm#2002.

Department for Environment, Food and Rural Affairs (DEFRA). (2003). *Departmental Report*. Retrieved from http://webarchive.nationalarchives.gov.uk/20 031220221853/http://www.DEFRA.gov.uk/corporate/deprep/2003/deprep2003. pdf.

62   *Angela Lait*

Department for Environment, Food and Rural Affairs (DEFRA). (2004). *Departmental Report*. Retrieved from http://webarchive.nationalarchives.gov.uk/2007 0101084356/http://www.DEFRA.gov.uk/corporate/deprep/2004/2004repo rt.pdf.
Department for Environment, Food and Rural Affairs (DEFRA). (n.d.-a). *Stress at Work: Policy and Guidance*. Retrieved from DEFRA intranet.
Department for Environment, Food and Rural Affairs (DEFRA). (n.d.-b). *Working for the Essentials of Life*. Retrieved from http://webarchive. nationalarchives. gov.uk/20050301192907/ http://www.DEFRA.gov.uk/corporate/prospectus/DEF RAwork.pdf.
Edwards, R. (1979). *Contested Terrain: The Transformation of the Workplace in the Twentieth Century*. New York: Basic Books.
Frank, T. (2000). *One Market Under God: Extreme Capitalism, Market Populism and the End of Economic Democracy*. London: Doubleday.
Harvey, D. (1991). *The Condition of Postmodernity: An Enquiry into the Origins of Cultural Change*. Oxford, UK: Blackwell.
Jameson, F. (2002). *The Political Unconscious: Narrative as a Socially Symbolic Act* (2nd ed.). London: Routledge. (Original work published 1981).
Lait, A. (2012). *Telling Tales: Work, Narrative and Identity in a Market Age*. Manchester: Manchester University Press.
Layard, R. (2005). *Happiness: Lessons from a New Science*. London: Penguin.
Marmot, M. (2004), *Status Syndrome*, London: Macmillan.
McEwan, I. (2005). *Saturday*. London: Jonathan Cape.
Musson, G., & Duberley, J. (2007). Change, change or be exchanged: The discourse of participation and the manufacture of identity. *Journal of Management Studies*, 44(1): 143–164.
Sennett, R. (1999). *The Corrosion of Character*. New York: W. W. Norton & Co.
Strawson, G. (2004, October 15) A fallacy of our age: Not every life is a narrative. *Times Literary Supplement*, pp. 13–15.

5 Marketing beyond Seduction
Androgyny and the Untold Tale of Socially Responsible Advertising

*Jerzy Kociatkiewicz and
Monika Kostera[1]*

INTRODUCTION

In the beginning there was Chaos, the emptiness that is everything and nothing at the same time, the blinding darkness out of which all was born. Then Gaia, the mother, came into being. She emerged splendidly, as immanence, the great becoming, creation and death all in one. Between them Eros sprang into life, the most beautiful of all beings: gods, humans, all things that ever existed. Eros, the irresistible power of attraction, infinitely desirable and desired yet always slightly distant and detached, complete within him/ herself, indefinite, and undefinable. Eros, the androgynous, the kinetic potential that makes gods and people approach each other, that brings them together, makes them reach out beyond their private worlds, the primordial force of attraction, beyond stereotypes, dichotomies, or shallow figures of beauty. Eros, the elemental force that remains, deep within the very heart of our humanity and perhaps our souls, the inexhaustible power to move towards one another. Eros, the force that brought together Chaos and Gaia and gave birth to all of creation.[2]

In our times mainstream stories of gender have been compartmentalised into two main categories: male and female. All that falls in between is categorised as transgendered or transsexual. All these types are supposed to endurable identities, possibly connected to solid genetic predispositions (Heilburn, 1973; Kłosińska, 2010). Such an essentialization may have beneficial political reasons and consequences, but we believe it is harmful to the human potential for real creativity and imagination (Butler, 1990; Haraway, 1991), as it erodes liminality, the stuff that radical stories are made of (Izak, forthcoming).

The strikingly beautiful model, Andrej Pejic, does not mind any of the existing categories but sees himself as an androgyne:

> He thinks of himself neither as gay nor straight. 'For me, love has no boundaries. I'm not an extremely sexual person, but I am romantic'. He doesn't object to the word transgender, but says it isn't accurate—he has

no desire to be a woman. Androgynous, he says, best sums it up. 'I'm pretty happy with how I am now'.

(Pejic, 2012, as quoted in: Guardian, 2012)

Our aim with this chapter is to propose, by the means of a textual analysis of Polish computer advertisements, a model of using the androgynous image in marketing which, we believe, may bring back the romance and happiness into socially responsible management (Syed & Kramar, 2009). We would like to tell the untold tale of the androgyne, as an archetype of liminal gender in the area of critical marketing management. The androgyne can help to shift the focus of marketing strategies from the managing of the consumer, but, instead to developing a relationship. This becomes possible due the fact that liminality is the main attribute of this archetype, and it powerfully brings forward and confronts us with the unmanageable.

Yiannis Gabriel and Tim Lang (2006) point out that despite the vast and gigantically costly apparatus of marketing science and research directed towards understanding and controlling consumer behaviour, the actual effectiveness of these attempts remains dubious at best. Managing the consumer proves to be close to impossible; the success of a product cannot be planned or even predicted. Even the most recent scientific developments such as neuromarketing, or brain-scanning technology did not actually increase the odds of consumer management (Opitz, 2011). Together with the old techniques and methods, they did, however, succeed in a profound erosion of social trust and ethos, leading to adiaphorization: the placing of certain events and human beings outside of the moral categories (Bauman & Donskis, 2013). This chapter is dedicated to the exploration of the unmanaged and unmanageable, but not by proposing even more intrusive methods of management, but the means of radical learning from narratives, through liminal sensemaking processes (Izak, forthcoming).

CRITICAL MARKETING AND THE USES OF ALTERNATIVE GENDER IMAGES

While the marketing discourse has, since the inception of the discipline sometime in the early 20th century, been largely focused on promoting the culturally dominant perspectives (Skålén, Fougère, & Fellesson, 2008; Tadajewski & Jones, 2008), there has nevertheless developed a rich undercurrent of critical, and often subversive, reading of the totalizing discourse of mainstream corporate marketing. Tracing its roots to Adorno and Horkheimer's (1947/1969) critique of the consumer society, the critical marketing perspective came of age in the last 20 years (e.g., Alvesson, 1994; Brownlie, Saren, Wensley, & Whittington, 1999; Saren et al. 2007) and encompasses work conceptualizing marketing not as a set of business tools but rather as a bundle of practices and ideology and assessing its societal impact. The facets of explored discourse include such disparate issues as normalization of exploitative work practices (Sharp, 2002) unsustainable identities (Parmentier & Fischer, 2011), commoditization of public goods (Brei & Böhm, 2011) of social and cultural activities (Applbaum, 2000), and reification of gender roles and relations (Mizielińska, 1997).

Advertisements, comprising the most discursive aspect of marketing, present a particularly useful research venue for insight into the dominant discourses of consumer society and there exists a considerable body of work detailing presentation (Gončarova, 2010) and propagation (Nelson, 2008) of gender roles in various forms of advertising. Most of such research, starting with Erving Goffman's (1979) seminal study, analyses the objectification and power imbalance made evident in the portrayal of women where femininity is limited to one image only, usually totalised within a time and a culture (Onyejekwe, 2008). This chapter builds on this tradition, but aims at incorporating insights from the performative understandings of gender developed in recent scholarship (Butler, 1990; Entwistle & Mears, 2013), and focuses on exploring how the richness of cultural patterns represented in advertisements cannot be reduced to or contained in a hegemonic discourse of gender.

Retelling the tale and bringing up to the surface what usually remains untold, we form a critical reexamination of mainstream advertising images in ways that foreground subverting dominant representations, and draw upon the richness of culturally significant archetypal images (Kociatkiewicz & Kostera, 2012a; Kostera, 2012), often invoked in advertising, but usually reduced in their representation to stereotypes conveying only the most superficial messages of the dominant discourse. Our aim is not to expose gender biases present in mainstream advertising discourse, as this has already been demonstrated convincingly and ubiquitously by previous research (e.g., Paek, Nelson, & Vilela, 2011). Instead, it is to recover latent meanings present but subdued in the studied material, focusing on ambiguous and ambivalent representations of gender practice and traces of androgyny that resist reification into any stable gender dichotomy. This approach enables us to propose a model for socially responsible marketing management, based on ideas of diversity and attraction, rather than hegemony and seduction.

The untold yet compelling narrative driving force we are looking for in the studied text is desire, understood as a positive and radical creative force, capable of production of original output (Deleuze & Guattari, 1972/2004). This is a narrative able to resist the currently dominant marketing tale of seduction, which is establishing a hegemonic relationship (Bauman, 2000).

STUDYING GENDERED IMAGES

The designers, administrators, and users of computing equipment have historically constituted a strongly male-dominated population (Breene, 1992).

The growing popularity of personal computers and increasing pervasiveness of information technologies in daily life, as well as ongoing changes in patterns of work, led to a rapid and significant influx of female computer users throughout the 1990s and 2000s (Ono & Zavodny, 2003). This change, accompanied by a symbolic shift away from the perception (and presentation) of computer hardware and software as male attributes marks out the studied discourse, that of computing-related advertisements published at the turn of the millennium as particularly valuable for studying complexities of gender representation.

In order to examine the ways in which the discourse of computers and information and communication technologies evokes gender imagery, we studied advertisements published in four popular Polish computer magazines: *Chip*, *Enter*, *www*, and *PC World: Komputer (PCWK)*, covering, in total, 100 issues published from 1998 to 2001. While we have analysed and discussed all images found in the studied magazines, this text focuses on the few we have chosen as the most interesting and relevant for the purpose of examining the complexity of gender representations.

In regards of methodology, our approach is narrative (Czarniawska, 2004; Gabriel, 2000). We focus on stories or

> narratives with simple but resonant plots and characters, involving narrative skills, entailing risk, and aiming to entertain, persuade and win over [the listeners].

(Gabriel, 2000: 22)

Instead of following the mainstream readings, we interpret them by means of liminal sensemaking (Izak, forthcoming), by drawing upon the toolkit of visual anthropology (Olechnicki, 2003) and image-focused cultural studies (Denzin, 1991). This approach, according to Norman Denzin (1992), allows finding and description of the unintentional elements of a text as well as reflection on their impact on the construction of culture by people who use the symbols for meaning making. The deeper layers of sensemaking symbols, or its cultural fabric of the text, used for cultural (and political) negotiations is usually concealed (Denzin, 1997) and these hidden layers can be revealed through the systematic reading of the text (Ingarden, 1960). We adopt a social constructivist approach (Berger & Luckmann, 1966), assuming that our studied reality is socially constructed and can be read as a cultural creation. Our reading is ethnographic, we study the cultural fabric in the text and, as Denzin (1997) calls for, we adopt a messy, multi-layered analysis, and aiming at a narrativization of the findings. Ultimately, our aim is to contribute to what Donna Haraway (1991: 149) describes as

> an ironic political myth faithful to feminism, socialism, and materialism. Perhaps more faithful as blasphemy is faithful, than as reverent

worship and identification. Blasphemy has always seemed to require taking things very seriously.

Thus, we do not look for ideological or political underpinnings, typical of Denzin's analyses; instead, we are interested in tracing the symbols and flows of desire (Deleuze & Guattari, 1972/2004). It is emphatically an over-interpretation, in the sense that our reading goes beyond the intent of the text and draws upon its wider cultural context. To that end, we juxtapose many of the analysed images with significant works of art touching upon similar themes, noting both the continuities and the shifts in cultural imagery as represented by the studied advertising discourse.

We do not, however, consider our approach a misreading (Eco, 1993), a violation of authorial contribution, but what Richard Rorty (1992) labels "inspired reading", or an effect of an "encounter which has rearranged . . . [the] priorities and purposes [of the reader]" (p. 107). The opposite of inspired reading is methodical reading, ordered and un-poetic. Rorty claims there is little difference between interpreting and using a text. He stresses the pragmatist pleasure of "blurring the distinction between finding an object and making it". (Rorty, 1992: 97).

> Reading texts is a matter of reading them in the light of other texts, people, obsessions, bits of information, or what have you, and then seeing what happens.
>
> (Rorty, 1992: 105)

This is exactly how we go about analysing the advertisements for the sake of this study, with the aim of uncovering and describing archetypes embedded in the cultural context of the advertisements, with our accompanying commentary taking the form of a narrative response to the presented images rather than a reasoned analysis. For this purpose, advertising images form a particularly useful source material, as they can be understood as thick representations of the cultural context (in the Geertz, 1973, sense) in which the processes of cultural signification are embedded.

In our study, we were looking for the symbols of desire on the level of underpinning cultural archetypes. We understand archetype in the Jung (1968) way, as images of human inspiration

> concealed in the collective unconscious domain of reality and shared by all humans. They are the substance that myths and symbols are constructed of and because of their universality they have the capacity of turning individuals into a group and can be seen as the underpinning of culture and society.
>
> (Kostera, 2008: 67)

Archetypes are like riverbeds, ready to embrace images, narratives, ideas, and characters. They are fundamental cultural figures—and they can be understood as central symbols and genres, inspiring humanity to tell stories and to interpret them anew, and thus a kind of particularly strong plots (Czarniawska & Rhodes, 2006). Alternatively, they can be seen as embedded in the collective unconscious, connecting humanity through time and space (Jung, 1968). They turn up in tales about management and organizations, both in the form of field stories collected in the field, and taking the shape of theoretical reflection (e.g., Bowles, 1991; Carr, 2002; Kostera, 2012). As we were focusing on archetypes related to gender, the archetypes of the most interest to us were, from the beginning of our study, Anima and Animus, the most popular gendered archetypes. In the course of our analysis, we found, however, a third archetype which turned out the most interesting—the Androgyne. The Anima is the female aspect of the soul, and the Animus, its male side (Jung, 1972). The archetype of the Anima contains images and roles held by women and Animus—elements associated with men. The contents of these archetypes vary with culture and time, and they may include stereotypes as well as alternative and counter-cultural images. They are the sum total, or the full potential of ideas inspiring people to play gendered roles. In order to be emancipating and empowering, the archetypes need to be made conscious in a person and then made mature through the experiencing of their diverse potential. Immature Anima and Animus are typically projected on men and women in the environment, bringing misogyny, violence, unrealistic expectations of one's partner, objectification, etc. Anima and Animus together result in a powerful union, which Jung calls the Syzygy (Jung, 1968). It brings enormous energy to the person and opens up a potential for communication, not necessarily limited to language and discourse but at the same time embodied and spiritual. The Androgyne is one of the manifestations of this archetype, with powerful examples such as the primordial Eros which we presented in the beginning of this text. It has been the theme of many famous myths and images, from Plato's spherical wholes (2001), Ovid's double-gendered Hermafroditus (2008), to Eliade's recurring tale of the Androgyne (1981), to the more recent popular celebration of unisex and gender indeterminacy in the glam culture of the 1970s (Kłosińska, 2010).

All three archetypes have been the topic of writing of organization researchers. For example, Hart and Brady (2005) believe organizations hold collective images of the Animus and Anima, shared by the participants of all genders. The Anima inspires and motivates, but due to its marginalization in contemporary corporations, its manifestation tends to become limited to an orientation towards career. The Animus, a potential for success and empowerment, is much more present but mostly in its immature version, as an obsession with winning and corporate power. Höpfl (2002) presents some of the consequences of the loss of and desire for Anima in organizations nowadays. Organizations make their Animus, or masculine archetype, the central focus of their (rational) activity, expressed in practices such as benchmarking which treat organizations as mere assortments of interchangeable parts devoid of any human presence or expression. Batko (2013), in a study of Polish public administration describes the abandonment of Anima in even stronger terms: as a loss of soul. Similar points about the domination of the male element, or Animus, and deeply felt lack of the female principle, or Anima, in contemporary organizations are also made by numerous other authors working in disparate methodological and theoretical traditions, such as Kanter (1977), Jacobsson (1993), Zanetti (2002), Kostera (2003), and Buckle-Henning (2007).

Androgyny is not a mainstream topic of management or marketing discourse but its fleeting presence is nevertheless important. Alice Sargent (1981) argues that androgyny in management is both constructive and needed. It makes it possible to combine and orientation for effectiveness with personal development and opens ways for maturation. In the context of marketing, androgyny has received relatively little attention, and the few articles that do pick up the theme describe androgyny as a fad (American Marketing Association, 1984), as a product feature increasing appeal to specific audiences (Jamieson, 2007), or, conversely, as a characteristic describing a particular musical subculture (Goulding, Saren, Maclaran, & Follett, 2004). The one book chapter we have found adopting a similar research stance on androgyny to our own (Vänskä, 2002) has been published in Finnish and not received wider distribution.

The potential of gender liminality to inspire creative and liberating ideas of management and organization has been taken up by few studies. Jerzy Kociatkiewicz (2004) presents the potential for imaginative synergetic interactions between Information Technology and social actors. Such technology allows the creation of places where different aspects overlap, The body, active within physical spaces, the soul, functioning in the virtual spaces, the mind located within technical spaces, experience, placed within the personal space, and logic, acting in the abstract spaces, come together to constitute the space of a possible alchemical marriage. It holds an enormous potential for transformation, producing a new quality, rich in new dimensions. A syzygic mode of management learning, based on the contraposition of different modes of experiencing, has been proposed (Kociatkiewicz & Kostera, 2012b) in the form of the co-narrative study. It enables students to engage with otherness through direct and powerful narrative immersion in modes of experience that are unusual or opposite to what their everyday experience brings them. Syzygic learning could also apply to gender archetypes and stereotypes, bringing together differences and learning from gendered Otherness. Similarly, Fotaki and Harding (2013) make a case for an empathetic and conceptual bisexuality in academia, defining bisexuality as a merger and powerful experiential joining of different gendered positions. This would bring a force for change and understanding.

SHADES OF ANIMA

Femininity in Polish and, more generally, in Western culture has traditionally been rigidly defined, mostly by male subjects such as church fathers
(Ostrowska, 1997) or authoritative voices of patriarchy hidden in educational texts such as schoolbooks (Buczkowski, 1997). Mainstream media
propagate this patriarchal voice, as when they define what is and what is
not feminine in management and business (Kostera, 2003). As noted before,
advertisements serve as an established arena for propagating these dominant ascriptions of femininity (Goffman, 1979; Mizielińska, 1997). All such
attempts at defining femininity present it as the Other, the object of male
gaze and desire, unmistakably placed as the subservient position in the hierarchy of genders, the passive element to male activity, the negative to male
positive energy. Thus, a computer monitor is advertised superimposed over
an image of a feminine eye (sporting fake eyelashes and blue eyeliner), looking not at the reader but rather unfocused into the distance: point of focus of
the reader's gaze rather than an autonomous origin of vision (*Enter* 1999/5:
29). Another monitor ad (*Enter* 2000/12: 141) repeats the linkage of gaze
and femininity by showing a full-page image of a steam iron, an implement
for traditionally female housework.

However, the archetype of the Anima allows for many more shades of
the feminine gender than patriarchal definitions would allow. There is the
active, assertive and even violent femininity of Phoolan Devi as described
by Graff (1997), or the passionate diversity of female gender aesthetics
actualizing itself in female authorship (Górnicka-Boratyńska, 1997; Kozak,
1997). Women want to define their own gender and the range of the definitions is very broad: from soft and traditionally feminine (but as a subject
and not an object) via androgynous (be it hetero- or homosexual), to plainly
human (Graff, 2001). This is a fairly recent acknowledgement of a diversity already present but hidden beneath the intransparence of the dominant
discourse. Davies (1990) presents an in-depth historical analysis of varied
visions of femininity and feminism, and concludes:

> We need to write and speak utopias, we need to rewrite the past and the
> present, we need to write and speak all of our selves, not just our minds
> but our bodies, to imagine who we might be if we were not constituted
> within the bonds of the male/female dualism.
>
> (p. 515)

Femininity appears in the analysed material most often in association
with monitors (made to be looked at), but also with Internet services (communication is a traditionally feminine sphere of influence), software, and
assorted peripherals. Women rarely appear on images presenting entire
computers or computer systems.

Of the many full-page monitor ads, one struck us as particularly alluring and somehow tantalising (*PCWK* 1998/11: 155, Figure 5.1): it shows an image of an attractive young woman bending over a monitor, almost (but possibly not quite) touching it. Bluish mist swirls in the background. The figure is dressed in stylish and tight-fitting black clothes, and her sporty silhouette reminds us of a ballet performer. Her gaze is turned towards the monitor case (she cannot see the screen image from where she is standing) and not at the reader. The entire scene is replicated on the monitor screen and then recursively again and again . . . ad infinitum. Two bolded slogans proclaim "There are things one cannot resist" and "For now, forever" (*PCWK* 1998/11: 155). The image is striking for its multiple ambiguities: the implied flirt (or love) between the woman and the monitor their possible bodily contact,[3] the infinity implied in the recursive image and evoked in the slogan.

The scene replicates, updates, and reverses the dynamics and composition of Velázquez' *Las Meninas*: a 1656 court painting showing both a court scene (featuring mostly female subjects) and the artist painting a court scene (Velázquez himself). In Velázquez' masterpiece, the viewer cannot see the artist's handiwork, and indeed there is some debate over whether the in-picture Velázquez is shown painting *Las Meninas* or a portrait of the royal couple who are implied (via a reflection visible in a mirror) to stand just outside the frame (Dayan, 1974). Both the advert and the painting are self-referential, each showing a contemporary mode of image reproduction together with the social actor enacting such reproduction (the painter and the monitor screen). Both foreground female subjects engaged primarily in interactions that do not immediately involve the viewer. In the case of the ad, the focal relation runs between the woman and the machinery. In the painting, the viewer shares the perspective and the voyeuristic power with the royal couple. In the advertisement, the viewer can still enjoy his (or possibly her) role as a voyeur, but is left with no hint of possible agency.

Another advertisement, promoting desktop computers (*PCWK* 1998/4: back cover), shows a vision of female agency much more active than a denial of interaction. It depicts an athletic young woman in black leather and black lipstick, facing the reader and shouting at or towards him or her. Her pose is dynamic and aggressive but indeterminate: she might be about to jump at the reader, or just dramatically flex her muscles. The image is clearly erotic, yet also challenging.

This picture, too, evokes comparison with a much older piece of art. In 1865, Manet exhibited *Olympia,* a painting depicting a nude prostitute gazing provokingly at the viewer. Its presentation of non-submissive female sexuality, as well as the choice of the subject, provoked widespread criticism and hostility as well as interest and fascination. *Olympia*, combining eroticism with a reversal of traditional power dynamics, or at least with a denial of implied social hierarchy, helped to create a visual language for showing female assertiveness (see: Berger, 2008). The advert uses signifiers already

Figure 5.1   (Source: PCWK 1998/11: 155).

available within the mainstream cultural repertoire (black leather, dark lip-stick, coiled up pose reminiscent of superhero comic book representations) and does not mount any challenge to conventional morality, but it presents a similar vision of powerful femininity as Manet's transgressive painting.

It is worthwhile to note that forceful female characters, such as the one described above, tend to be relegated firmly into the realm of virtuality or fantasy, while the yielding, hesitant, or at least gentle women inhabit more accessible spaces on the advertisements. Similar displacement of female strength can be seen in well-known characters of computerised fantasies, with Lara Croft of the *Tomb Raider* game series (cf. Schleiner, 2001) being probably the most obvious contemporaneous example.

One more notable point is the seemingly missing factor of age—all the women appearing on the ads are young (more so than men), and all are presented as attractive; in that sense, the gaze of the viewer is construed as stereotypically male. At the same time, some of the depicted women, includ-ing both described above, seem to question the patriarchal power of the observer to a lesser or greater extent.

TONES OF ANIMUS

The traditional feminine role is rigidly defined, but so is the traditional essentialist masculine role. Even if ascribed to dominance and power, it allows little or no personal variation, perhaps less even than the feminine (Arcimowicz, 1997). Masculinity appears as a single-variable scale:

> Most discussions of masculinity tend to treat it as if it is measurable. Some men have more of it, others less. Those men who appear to lack masculinity are, by definition, sick or genetically inadequate.
>
> (Brittan, 2001: 51)

The discourse of hegemonic maleness culminates in the ideology of masculinism, but does not, and cannot, encompass the entirety of men's gendered experiences. In order to foreground this multiplicity, we "cannot talk of masculinity, only masculinities" (Brittan, 2001: 51). Masculinism does not acknowledge these diverse masculinities, as its role is that of disciplining the real and eradicating existing variety. However, men are increasingly vocal about their wish and desire to define their gender on their own terms, with the diversity and spontaneity that it brings about (Whitehead & Barrett, 2001). The archetype of the Animus can inspire a diversity of readings and meanings. The impetus to redefine and accept the variance has come mainly from two directions: feminism and gay movements (Connell, 1995). The men who define their own masculinities construct their gender is a variety of ways: there are aggressive masculinities and soft ones, changing and immutable, gay and straight, and bisexual too.

In the analysed material, hardware equipment such as printers and monitors, as well as software products and Internet services are advertised slightly more often by images featuring male characters than female ones. In case of complete computer systems the disproportion is much higher. There are many images of apparently asexual men in white shirt and tie (e.g., software ad *PCWK* 1998/11: 93; e-business services *Enter* 1999/6: 19; monitors *PCWK* 1998/11: 171; computers *PCWK* 1998/4: 9), sometimes looking at the viewer with a strictly business like smile (printers, *PCWK* 1998/6: 131; software *PCWK* 1998/11: 131). Other depictions of masculinity are less common, but still not exceedingly rare. These can involve spatial exoticism as in the case of a group of colourful South American Indian men, wearing hats and smoking pipes in an ad for an Internet provider, or a temporal dislocation: a nostalgic fantasy in the form of a scowling gangster with a smoking bomb in his hand (advertising printers, *PCWK* 1998/6: 15), simultaneously an icon of tough masculinity and a mythical brute with a heart of gold.

Several other ads take up the muscle bound, heavyweight image of the male subject, including a smug car mechanic (*Enter* 20001/1: 29), a triumphant cowboy (*Enter* 2000/4: 35), and a moustached strongman about to swallow an earthworm (*Enter* 2000/12: 23). Masculine power is also clearly present in many of the advertisements featuring sportsmen. Thus, a black athlete, jumping over the crossbar is pictured in an ad of data storage solutions (*PCWK* 2000/5: 33 while monitors are promoted with images of male football players legs, each pair framed within its own screen (*PCWK* 1998/6: 29).

A few advertisements portray a traditional image of masculinity that is, however, softened in some significant way. Thus, a formal looking office worker in full suit, but with his feet bare, relaxes in a hammock while promoting desktop computer systems (*Enter* 2000/12:73). He is peaceful, smiling, holding his glasses in his hand, looking slightly to the right and up from the reader. The slogan says: "We ensure everything you need", so he probably just took an impromptu vacation and left the work to the computer. Another man, dressed like an office employee but looking tiredly beyond the picture but not meeting the reader's gaze advertises monitor filters (*Enter* 1999/12: 121). His eyes are an intense shade of blue, his visibly dyed hair is ruffled and there is something irresistible in his pose, in spite of the suggestion of exhaustion. "Listen to your eyes" says the text. The man leans over a keyboard but does not touch it.

More ambiguous is a portrait of a bald man with a hand brush tied atop his head, pursing his lips covered in blue lipstick (*PCWK* 1999/5: 13; Figure 5.2). He is wearing shades in thick plastic frames and looks focused on his performance. Though the character's face is clearly visible (apart from the eyes hidden behind the dark glasses), the image puts us in mind of René Magritte's 1964 surrealist painting *Son of Man* (and a similar and contemporaneous *Man in a Bowler Hat*). Magritte's subject, a formally dressed man in a bowler hat, stands with his face obscured by an apple apparently floating in the air before him. He appears serious and composed, unimpeded by the strangeness of his situation. The painting, which might be the artist's self-portrait, plays on the theme of hidden and apparent features, with its Biblical title hinting at possibilities of deeply symbolic interpretations. The advert, providing no explanation for the depicted character's appearance, additionally riddles the viewer with the expected connection between its subject and the hardware components displayed below. The accompanying slogan, "Get Serious. Get AOpen" (in English) only adds to the confusion when juxtaposed with the utter seriousness of the subject[4]. And the masculinity presented is just as contradictory: appearing as both an object of ridicule and as the literal face of the advertised products, the depicted character is not business-like but neither is he playful. Idiosyncratic in his tastes and meticulous about his grooming, his presence rests uneasily with the smaller print text proclaiming (this time in Polish) that "the new series of AOpen components shows how much weight we give to efficiency" (*PCWK* 1999/5: 13). Not a role model but and yet the spokesperson for business products, this male character epitomises contradictions of transgressing the traditional cultural codes and thus fits quite well alongside the surrealist canon, and alongside Salvador Dali's similarly exotic looking self-portrait photographs.

Interestingly, not many of the men appear to exercise their traditionally gendered power of control—indeed, one is shown tightly bound (and looking dejected) in front of his computer (*PCWK* 1998/12: 109), another one stands dwarfed by an enormous desktop computer (*PCWK* 1998/12: 9), and

Figure 5.2 (Source: PCWK 1999/5: 13).

yet another looks up at the reader in apparent exasperation (*Enter* 1999/12: 122). Perhaps hypermasculine technology overwhelms their ability of exerting control, as phallic symbols appear quite often in relation to computing equipment, usually in images devoid of human beings: computer screen filters are promoted by a picture of a gun and a banana (*Enter* 1999/7: 27), both pointing in the same direction. The caption instructs the viewer that "It's better to be certain". Elsewhere, a very phallic tie accompanied by sperm-shaped computer mouse promote an Internet service provider (*www* 2001/6: 27). But perhaps the lack of asserted control signifies the changing milieu, different now than the phallogocentric competition the manly protagonists expected? We surely cannot tell.

ENTER ANDROGYNE

The most remarkable imagery present in the analysed discourse are not, however, the portrayals of masculinity and femininity that broaden or transgress the boundaries of mainstream definitions of gender, but the relatively frequent depictions that we identify as the androgynes.

Since in examining representations of the androgyne we are looking for the untold archetype, our approach is perforce slightly different than in the analysis of depictions of masculinity and femininity. While we started our research by explicitly looking for the representations of masculine and feminine gendering, the category of the androgyne emerged in are reading through repeated encounters with figures whose gendering appears potentially significant and yet ambiguous. Androgynes are thus rarely explicitly presented as such (since, as we argue, this is a figure largely hidden from explicit public discourse), yet appear as a distinct set of representations failing to conform to the rigidly circumscribed roles we dubbed Animus and Anima. They include adult human characters of indeterminate gender, such as a clown advertising printers (*PCWK* 2000/5: 157). S/he has a sunny colourful face, looking confidently and a bit flirtatiously straight at the viewer. In another ad, a figure of ambiguous gender, dressed in a suit jacket and a t-shirt, talks on the phone while promoting Internet mail and hosting (*Enter* 2000/4: 13). A more intriguing advertisement shows a feminine face, puckered up and wearing bright red lipstick yet with cheeks covered in shaving foam and apparently engaged in shaving. In this ad (*Enter* 10/1999: 183; Figure 5.3), the face is displayed on a computer screen, though other versions of the same advert show the same face outside of the monitor frame. The figure, accompanied by the slogan "monitor screen with character", appears as the embodiment of the said product, described in smaller print as economical, safe, and user friendly. With strong signifiers pointing to both femininity and masculinity of the figure, it emphatically represents androgyny rather than uncertainty or genderlessness.

As already mentioned, the idea of androgyny has a long and interesting history. The name derives from Greek, a combination of the terms of male and female and it was often used to describe an ideal, perhaps supernatural state. Androgyny derives from the divine bi-genderedness and is a sign and condition of true perfection (Eliade, 1961). It is also seen as an ideal of sexuality, uniting male and female attractiveness and somehow producing a synergetic effect of all sexual energies (Singer, 1976). But it is not

Figure 5.3   (Source: *Enter* 1999/10: 183).

just an abstract ideal. Cultural anthropology describes many manifestations of androgyny. A liminal 'third' gender, has existed in many cultures, such as the Polynesian *fa'afafine* (Besnier, 1996), the North American berdache (Roscoe, 1996), Indian eunuchs—the hijras (Nanda, 1996), or biologically defined hermaphrodites in New Guinea (Herdt, 1996a). However, it has not been considered legitimate in the Western mainstream Judeo-Christian culture for the most part of recent history, even though there are numerous examples of more or less accepted androgyny in the course of that history (Heilburn, 1973; Herdt, 1996b; Kosińska, 2004), and the recent surge of interest in the issues of transgender identities (e.g., Beemyn & Rankin, 2011; Vries, 2012) shows the possibility of expanding gender categories beyond the male/female dichotomy. It is, thus, a more and more widely recognised reality, that:

> Certain individuals in certain times and places transcend the categories of male and female, masculine and feminine, as these have been understood in Western culture since at least the later nineteenth century. The bodies and ontology of such persons diverge from the sexual dimorphisms model found in science and society—in the way they conceive their being and/or their social conduct. Furthermore, in some traditions—cultures and/or historical formations—these persons are collectively classified by others in third or multiple cultural-historical categories.
>
> (Herdt, 1996b: 21)

The discourse of androgyny is surfacing in many areas of knowledge, such as philosophy and sociology of work (Vetterling-Braggin, 1982), epistemology (Pakszys, 2000), literary studies (Vedeer, 1987), sociology of technology (Haraway, 1997), and organization and management studies (authors referred to at the beginning of this paper). An example of androgyny often quoted in organizational context is Donna Haraway's (1991) cyborg. It is an alternative to dichotomic gender concepts, a hybrid of a human being with technology where the genders combine into androgyne. Haraway argues that technology makes androgyny common and open to use by all who wish to tap into the energetic potential it stands for, offering in the process a possibility of understanding otherness and an ability for peaceful communication. The cyborg metaphor opens perspectives for "transgressed boundaries, potent fusions, and dangerous possibilities which progressive people might explore as one part of needed political work" (Haraway, 1991: 154).

Yet the analysed ads also feature genderings that are not easily identifiable as either any point on the male/female spectrum nor any combination of male and female features. Such images can also draw from the readily available cultural repertoire as, for example, does a drawing of God and an angel (*PCWK* 1998/11: 93). God has a male outlook, he wears a beard—but he is not expressly a man, while the angel's gender is indefinite. Together, they advertise software. In a few pictures the equipment itself looks sexual and sensual but it is hard to say what gender it should be ascribed translated to human terms. One picture shows a UPS (Uninterrupted Power Supply) unit, resplendent with curved flowing lines and blinking lights, set against a red background (*PCWK* 1998/5: 33). It appears distinctly erotic, perhaps due to the arched lines, the colours and the sense of its gazing seductively back at the viewer. In another advertisements, two juxtaposed printers are on the brink of touching, seemingly leaning in for a caress (*Enter* 1999/4: 33).

ANDROGYNY AND TECHNOLOGY MARKETING

All in all, the advertisements did not dazzle us with their varied and inventive ways of challenging and subverting the traditional gender roles, nor in innovative gendering of relations with technology.[5] This is not particularly surprising, as mainstream advertisements usually reflect the dominant, rather than the subversive, values of the society. Nevertheless, there is ample space for rereading the messages and refiguring the socio-cultural associations embedded within. One trope worth pursuing is the linkage between traditional gender archetypes, nostalgic image of idealised past, and the attempts (or promises) to rebuild such past using cutting edge technology (cf. Ross, 1999)—thus numerous images with a retro look, with 1950s as the most favoured period. Similar ideas appeared in the 1995 brief, and very unsuccessful, campaign to promote Microsoft Bob—a computer personal assistant, or agent, stereotypically gendered as a very traditional male. The campaign involved images stylised as 1950s, and met with very little customer interest. Retro imagery can be also seen as an attempt to domesticate unknown (and threatening) technology: much as early electric appliances (radios, radiators, TV sets) were constructed along the lines of traditional furniture (Forty, 1986), technologised social actors are presented as traditional, or even old fashioned, gendered constructs. Yet the opposite trend is also clearly present: many ads present actors (both human and nonhuman) that are hip, edgy, and outrageous. Such actors are rarely anchored in everyday settings, yet carry immense symbolic power of the transformative promises of technology.

In the end, we are left with no easy answer to the question of gendering of IT—much as we expected, there is no clear gender(ing) of the ads, of their subjects, or of their addressees. Born with the assurance of preserving traditional values, tempting with glimpses of transgression, advertised computers flicker between conservatism and avant-garde. And of course, computer users are drawn into that very net of contradictory definitions, constructing the social space of computing in between unreal promises and empty assurances. The archetype of the androgyne remains untold, though not absent from the analysed ads, again bringing up the figure of the cyborg reimagined by Donna Haraway:

> The cyborg is a cybernetic organism, a fusion of the organic and the technical forged in particular, historical, cultural practices. Cyborgs are not about The Machine and The Human, as if such things and subjects universally existed. Instead, cyborgs are about specific historical machines and people in interaction that often turns out to be painfully counterintuitive for the analyst of technoscience.
>
> (Haraway, 1997: 51)

The complex, contradictory cyborg presented by Haraway is androgynous, unambiguously sexual, though its sexuality is both ambiguous and ambivalent. He/she/it carries the legacy of macho phallic origin, the dreams of feminine liberation, and the scars of the daily struggles. It can be seen as a good model for the attraction between organizations and human actors.

TOWARDS SOCIALLY RESPONSIBLE MANAGEMENT THROUGH THE TELLING OF UNTOLD GENDER STORIES

Giles Deleuze and Félix Guattari (1972/2004) conceive of desire as of a positive force working in the unconscious, not a lack, as it is usually understood, but something both creative and real. Because of its mechanical nature, they describe it as a machine, the desiring-machine, functioning in the context of other machines, and creating its own output—which is desire. They regard desire as part of all important cultural processes, including the economic and institutional ones. The effect of desiring production is realized and even materialised within many spheres of social life, among them—marketing management. We regard the flows of attraction that we described above as a product of the desiring machine. Famously, Deleuze and Guattari did not presuppose a dichotomic gendered order but rather saw a multitude and endless diversity of desiring-machine (Delezue & Guattari, 1980/1996). The machine are interconnected and the sexuality they represent is all encompassing, transgressive, and all-pervasive, according to Deleuze and Guattari (1972/2004) "we always make love with worlds" (p. 323). Desire is revolutionary, explosive, subversive. It is the energy that bursts existing orders and structures. Therefore we think it ideal for the development of socially responsible marketing management, beyond attempts at consumer management (cf. Gabriel & Lang, 2006). Such marketing management is non-hegemonic and rooted in the Deleuzian idea of desiring-machine as the producer of an all-pervasive archetypical attraction underpinning communication with consumers. It is not of a dichotomic nature but takes the shape of the Androgyne as the primal inspiration, and includes images of Anima and Animus. We believe that, as our reading of the advertisements shows, many shades of the gendered archetypes can with advantage be used to attract the reader/consumer. The greatest power of attraction was traced to androgynous images—and, as we explained, at first we did not find them there, but they emerged as a potent category in the course of our analysis. A marketing which does not have to follow the overpowering imperatives of economic growth and increasing shareholder value, used in broader and socially responsible contexts, can be dedicated to other goals than mainstream marketing, such as the original aim—communication with the consumers (Saren et al., 2007). For this purpose it may take advantage of one of the key attributes of archetypes which generates attraction but not seduction.

Archetypes are the opposite of stereotypes, because while the latter limit areas of interpretation, the former inspire original understandings, they stimulate to look for what is individual and unique (Kostera, 2012). They wake consciousness and engage powerful and complex feelings in the process of experiencing, connected with the necessity of making difficult decisions. They can be said to be exceptionally open texts (Eco, 1989). Stereotypes are closed texts, offering easy answers and unproblematic solutions to the reader's questions. They lull attention and disactivate conscience, because they allow people to communicate without an active use of judgement and consciousness, as if automatically. In that sense their role in social communication is to seduce, because they have the ability to persuade to fulfil a desire without the hint of any difficult consequences. Longman Dictionary (2012a) defines seduction in the following way:

se·duce [transitive]

> 1 to persuade someone to have sex with you, especially in a way that is attractive and not too direct
>
> . . .
>
> 2 [often passive] to make someone want to do something by making it seem very attractive or interesting to them
>
> . . .

SEDUCE SOMEBODY INTO DOING SOMETHING

The same source characterises 'seduction' as "something that strongly attracts people, but often has a bad effect on their lives" (Longman Dictionary, 2012b). Seducing, or using the power of desire without responsibility or empathy, excludes true communication with the Other, such as Levinas (1969/1999) advocated. Instead it is all about the establishing of a one-sided power position and taking advantage of it. Seduction has been postulated, not only in critical marketing literature but also in Zygmunt Bauman's sociological analysis (Bauman, 2000; Blackshaw, 2008) as the prime structuring principle of the economy of desire underpinning mainstream marketing, and largely based on stereotyped hegemonic gender premises.

Socially responsible marketing is, instead, based on responsibility for the Other and an interest taken in him or her. It is about attraction rather than cold rational information and it is a proposition of mutual commitment. The archetypical gender nuances can be used to attract a certain type of consumers, the advertisements can be personalised and directed to more specific groups without the streamlining of the gendered images according to hegemonic standards. Creative marketing management is based on an archetype of gender beyond the current—or any other—social order. Gender diverse images, including the androgyne, are symbols that constitute an empowering desire that helps us move beyond the male/female dualism (Davies, 1990). The message reaches the customer not with seducing but impossible images of quick fixes and happy endings, producing a culture of permanent disappointment, by with a more difficult promise of establishing a relationship. This can be beneficial for both sides in many areas, not least in technology marketing where customer loyalty is of high value (Gummesson, 2002). As Hatch and Schultz (2008) show using the example of LEGO, such a mutual relationship between a brand and its loyal customers may have highly beneficial long-term effects of the brand's sustainability and ability to follow the customers' real needs and desires. Desire is a powerful narrative machine and we have shown how is able to unfold radical stories if the untold liminal archetypical tale of the androgyne is allowed a voice in the discourse of marketing.

NOTES

1. Monika Kostera's part of the text is based on a research project supported by the European Union Marie Curie Fellowship Programme: FP7, 627429 ECO-PREN FP7 PEOPLE 2013 IEF.
2. Creation story based on Hesiod's *Theogony* (1999).
3. Humans are almost never depicted touching machinery on the ads we have analysed: touch is apparently strongly transgressive (cf. Kociatkiewicz, 2004).
4. More superficially, of course, this message implies that the man in the picture is not serious enough and should, by the acquiring of AOpen, get so. Our Ingardenian (Ingarden, 1960) readings seek to contrapose the visible with the concealed, to look for meanings not always intended by the author but nonetheless brought to life by the text, understandings provoked, perhaps non-consciously, drawing the reader into a symbolic realm of its own. A text does that, just as a picture might, when we understand looking as a creative relationship (Berger, 2009). We do not claim exhausting such possible symbolic confrontations and our readings here follow just one of many possible directions.
5. However, in comparison with more conventional advertisements in the Polish press (Kostera, 2003) the ads in computer magazines were much more diverse and considerably less based on gender stereotypes.

REFERENCES

Adorno, T. W., & Horkheimer, M. (1969). *Dialektik der Aufklärung* [Dialectic of Enlightenment]. Frankfurt: S. Fischer. (Original work published 1947).

Alvesson, M. (1994). Critical theory and consumer marketing. *Scandinavian Journal of Management*, 10(3): 291–313.

American Marketing Association. (1984). Androgyny is a fad, but women are adopting some male characteristics. *Marketing News*, 16(1): 1–5.

Applbaum, K. (2000). Marketing and commoditization. *Social Analysis*, 44(2): 106–128.

Arcimowicz, K. (1997). Współcześni mężczyźni: Przegląd problematyki badań [Modern men: review of research issues]. In J. Brach-Czaina (Ed.), *Od Kobiety do Mężczyzny i z Powrotem: Rozważania o płci i kulturze* [From Woman to Man and Back Again: Reflections on gender and culture] (pp. 145–168). Białystok: Trans Humana.

Batko, R. (2013). *Golem, Awatar, Midas, Złoty Cielec: Organizacja publiczna w płynnej nowoczesności* [Golem, Avatar, Midas, The Golden Calf: Public organization in liquid modernity]. Warszawa: Sedno.

Bauman, Z. (2000). *Liquid modernity*. Cambridge: Polity Press.

Bauman, Z., & Donskis, L. (2013). *Moral Blindness: The Loss of Sensitivity in Liquid Modernity*. Cambridge: Polity Press.

Beemyn, G., & Rankin, S. (2011). *The Lives of Transgender People*. New York: Columbia University Press.

Berger, J. (2008). *Ways of Seeing*. Harmondsworth: Penguin.

Berger, J. (2009). *About Looking*. London: Bloomsbury.

Berger, P. L., & Luckmann, T. (1966). *The Social Construction of Reality*. Garden City, NY: Anchor Books.

Besnier, N. (1996). Polynesian gender liminality through time and space. In G. Herdt (Ed.), *Third Sex, Third gender: Beyond Sexual Dimorphism in Culture and History* (pp. 285–328). New York: Zone Books.

Blackshaw, T. (2008). Bauman on consumerism: Living the market-mediated life. In M. H. Jacobssen & P. Poder (Eds.), *The Sociology of Zygmunt Bauman: Challenges and Critique* (pp. 115–136). Aldershot: Ashgate.

Bowles, M. (1991). The organization shadow. *Organization Studies*, 12(3): 387–404.

Breene, A. L. (1992). Women and computer science. *Initiatives*, 55(2): 39–44.

Brei, V., & Böhm, S. (2011). Corporate social responsibility as cultural meaning management: A critique of the marketing of 'ethical' bottled water. *Business Ethics: A European Review*, 20(3): 233–252.

Brittan, A. (2001). Masculinities and masculinism. In S. M. Whitehead & F. J. Barrett (Eds.), *The Masculinities Reader* (pp. 51–72). Malden, MA: Blackwell.

Brownlie, D., Saren, M., Wensley, R., & Whittington, R. (Eds.). (1999). *Rethinking Marketing: Towards Critical Marketing Accountings*. London: Sage.

Buckle-Henning, P. (2007). Dancing in the white spaces: Exploring gendered assumptions in successful project managers' discourse about their work. *International Journal of Project Management*, 25(6): 552–559.

Buczkowski, A. (1997). Dwa różne światy, czyli jak socjalizuje się dziewczynkę i chłopca [Two different worlds, or how girls and boys are socialized]. In J. Brach-Czaina, (Ed.), *Od Kobiety do Mężczyzny i z Powrotem: Rozważania o płci i kulturze* [From Woman to Man and Back Again: Reflections on Gender and Culture] (pp. 169–196). Białystok: Trans Humana.

Butler, J. (1990). *Gender Trouble: Feminism and the Subversion of Identity*. New York: Routledge.

Carr, A. (2002). Jung, archetypes and mirroring in organizational change management: Lessons from a longitudinal case study, *Journal of Organizational Change Management*, 15(5): 477–489.

Connell, R. W. (1995). *Masculinities*. Berkeley: University of California Press.

Czarniawska, B. (2004). *Narratives in Social Science Research*. Thousand Oaks, CA: Sage.

Czarniawska, B., & Rhodes, C. (2006). Strong plots: Popular culture in management practice and theory. In P. Gagliardi and B. Czarniawska (Eds.), *Management Education and Humanities* (pp. 195–218). Cheltenham: Edward Elgar.

Davies, B. (1990). The problem of desire. *Social Problems, 37*(4): 501–516.

Dayan, D. (1974). The tutor-code of classical cinema. *Film Quarterly, 28*(1): 22–31.

Deleuze, G., & Guattari, F. (1996). *A Thousand Plateaus: Capitalism and Schizophrenia* (B. Massumi, Trans.). London: Althone Press. (Original work published 1980).

Deleuze, G., & Guattari, F. (2004). *Anti-Oedipus: Capitalism and Schizophrenia* (R. Hurley, M. Seem, & H. Lane, Trans.). London: Continuum. (Original work published 1972).

Denzin, N. K. (1991). *Images of Postmodern Society: Social Theory and Contemporary Cinema*. London: Sage.

Denzin, N. K. (1992). *Symbolic Interactionism and Cultural Studies: The Politics of Interpretation*. Oxford: Blackwell.

Denzin, N. K. (1997). *Interpretive Ethnography: Ethnographic Practices for the 21st Century*. Thousand Oaks, CA: Sage.

Eco, U. (1989). *The Open Work*. Cambridge, MA: Harvard University Press.

Eco, U. (1993). *Misreadings*. Orlando, FL: Harcourt.

Eliade, M. (1961). *Images and Symbols: Studies in Religious Symbolism* (P. Mairet, Trans.). London: Harvill Press. (Original work published 1952).

Eliade, M. (1981). *Mephistopheles et l'Androgyne* [Mephistopheles and the Androgyne]. Paris: Gallimard.

Entwistle, J., & Mears, A. (2013). Gender on display: Performativity in fashion modelling. *Cultural Sociology, 7*(3): 320–335.

Forty, A. (1986). *Objects of Desire: Design and Society 1750–1980*. London: Thames and Hudson.

Fotaki, M., & Harding, N. (2013). Lacan and sexual difference in organization management theory: Towards a hysterical academy? *Organization, 20*(2): 153–172.

Gabriel, Y. (2000). *Storytelling in Organizations: Facts, Fictions, and Fantasies*. Oxford: Oxford University Press.

Gabriel, Y., & Lang, T. (Eds.). (2006). *The Unmanageable Consumer*. London: Sage.

Geertz, C. (1973). Thick description: Toward an interpretive theory of culture. In *The Interpretation of Cultures* (pp. 3–30). New York: Basic Books.

Goffman, E. (1979). *Gender Advertisements*. New York: Harper & Row.

Gončarova, T. (2010). Genderový hudobný stereotyp v televíznych reklamách [Musical gender stereotype in TV commercials]. In J. Vereš (Ed.), *Hudba—Integrácie—Interpretácie 12: Hudobná kultúra a vzdelávanie v mediálnej spoločnosti* [Music—Integration—Interpretation 12: Music Culture and Education Media Company] (pp. 153–165). Nitra: UKF.

Górnicka-Boratyńska, A. (1997). Odwrotna strona rzeczy, czyli dlaczego Izabela Filipiak jest pisarką feministyczną [The reverse side of things, which is why Izabela Filipiak is a feminist writer]. In J. Brach-Czaina (Ed.), *Od Kobiety do Mężczyzny i z Powrotem: Rozważania o płci i kulturze* [From Woman to Man and Back Again: Reflections on Gender and Culture] (pp. 330–352). Białystok: TransHumana.

Goulding, C., Saren, M., Maclaran, P., & Follett, J. (2004). Into the darkness: Androgyny and gender blurring within the gothic subculture. In L. Scott & C. Thompson (Eds.), *Gender and Consume Behaviour* (Vol. 7, n.p.). Madison, WI: Association for Consumer Research.

Graff, A. (1997). Phoolan Devi—kobiecość niezłomna [Phoolan Devi—steadfast femininity]. In J. Brach-Czaina, (Ed.), *Od Kobiety do Mężczyzny i z Powrotem: Rozważania o płci i kulturze* [From Woman to Man and Back Again: Reflections on Gender and Culture] (pp. 288–296). Białystok: TransHumana.

Graff, A. (2001). *Świat Bez Kobiet: Płeć w polskim życiu publicznym* [World without Women: Gender in Polish Public Life]. Warszawa: W.A.B.

Guardian, The. (2012, March 2). Meet the models breaking the mould. Retrieved from http://www.guardian.co.uk/fashion/2012/mar/02/models-breaking-mould.

Gummesson, E. (2002). Relationship marketing in the new economy. *Journal of Relationship Marketing, 1*(1): 37–57.

Haraway, D. (1991). A cyborg manifesto: Science, technology, and socialist-feminism in the late twentieth century. In D. Haraway (Ed.), *Cyborgs, Simians, and Women: The Reinvention of Nature* (pp. 149–181). New York: Routledge.

Haraway, D. (1997). *Modest_witness@second_millennium. FemaleMan©_meets_ OncoMouse™: Feminism and Technoscience*. New York: Routledge.

Hart, D.W., & Brady, F.N. (2005). Spirituality and archetype in organizational life. *Business Ethics Quarterly, 15*(3): 409–428.

Hatch, M. J., & Schultz, M. (2008). *Taking Brand Initiative: How to Align Strategy, Culture and Identity through Corporate Branding*. San Francisco, CA: Jossey-Bass.

Heilburn, C.G. (1973). *Toward a Recognition of Androgyny*. New York: Harper & Row.

Herdt, G. (1996a). Mistaken sex: Culture, biology and the third sex in New Guinea. In G. Herdt (Ed.), *Third Sex, Third Gender: Beyond Sexual Dimorphism in Culture and History* (pp. 419–446). New York: Zone Books.

Herdt, G. (1996b). Introduction: Third sexes and third genders. In G. Herdt (Ed.), *Third Sex, Third Gender: Beyond Sexual Dimorphism in Culture and History* (pp. 21–84). New York: Zone Books.

Hesiod (1999). *Theogony: And, Words and Days* (M.L. West, Trans.). Oxford: Oxford University Press. (Original work written ca. 700 B.C.).

Höpfl, H. (2002). Strategic quest and the search for the primal mother. *Human Resources Development International, 5*(1): 11–22.

Ingarden, R. (1960). *O Dziele Literackim: Badania z pogranicza antologii, teorii języka i filozofii* [On Literary Work: Research on the Borders of Anthology, Language Theory, and Philosophy]. Warszawa: PWN.

Izak, M. (forthcoming). Learning from a fool: Searching for the 'unmanaged' context for radical learning. *Management Learning*, DOI 10.1177/1350507613486426.

Jacobsson, H.K. (1993). Organization and the mother archetype: A Jungian analysis of adult development and self-identity within the organization. *Administration & Society, 25*(1): 60–84.

Jamieson, D. (2007). Marketing androgyny: The evolution of the Backstreet Boys. *Popular Music, 26*(2): 245–258.

Jung, C.G. (1968). *Man and His Symbols*. New York: Dell.

Jung, E. (1972). *Animus and Anima* (H. Nagel, Trans.) Zurich: Spring.

Kanter, R.M. (1977). *Men and Women of the Corporation*. New York: Basic Books.

Kłosińska, K. (2010) Feministyczna Krytyka Literacka [Feminist Literary Criticism]. Katowice: Wydawnictwo Uniwersytetu Śląskiego.

Kociatkiewicz, J. (2004). *The Social Construction of Space in a Computerized Environment*. (PhD dissertation). Polish Academy of Sciences, Warszawa, Poland.

Kociatkiewicz, J., & Kostera, M. (2012a). The good manager: An archetypical quest for morally sustainable leadership. *Organization Studies, 33*(7): 861–878.

Kociatkiewicz, J., & Kostera, M. (2012b). The speed of experience: The co-narrative method in experience economy education. *British Journal of Management, 23*(4): 474–488.

Kosińska, K. (2004). Androgyn, który spadł na ziemię [The Androgyne that has fallen to earth]. *Kwartalnik Filmowy, 25*(47–48): 107–108.

Kostera, M. (2003). Reflections of the other: Images of women in the Polish business press. *Human Resource Development International, 6*(3): 325–342.

Kostera, M. (2008). Archetypes. In S. Clegg and J.R. Bailey (Eds.), *International Encyclopedia of Organization Studies* (pp. 67–68). London: Sage.

Kostera, M. (2012). *Organizations and Archetypes.* Cheltenham: Edward Elgar.

Kozak, B. (1997). Frauenliteratur i obrzeża [Women's literature and its borderlands]. In J. Brach-Czaina (Ed.), *Od Kobiety do Mężczyzny i z Powrotem: Rozważania o płci i kulturze* [From Woman to Man and Back Again: Reflections on Gender and Culture] (pp. 309–322). Białystok: TransHumana.

Levinas, E. (1999). *Totality and Infinity: An Essay on Exteriority* (A. Lingis, Trans.). Pittsburgh: Duquesne University Press. (Original work published in 1969).

Longman Dictionary of Contemporary English. (2012a). *Seduce.* Retrieved from http://www.ldoceonline.com/dictionary/seduce.

Longman Dictionary of Contemporary English. (2012b). *Seduction.* Retrieved from http://www.ldoceonline.com/dictionary/seduction.

Mizielińska, J. (1997). Matki, żony, kochanki, czyli tak nas widz;: kobieta jako podmiot i przedmiot reklamy [Mother, wife, mistress, or so we see: a woman as subject and object of advertising]. In J. Brach-Czaina, (Ed.), *Od Kobiety do Mężczyzny i z Powrotem: Rozważania o płci i kulturze* [From Woman to Man and Back Again: Reflections on Gender and Culture] (pp. 224–246). Białystok: TransHumana.

Nanda, S. (1996). Hijras: An alternative sex and gender role in India. In G. Herdt (Ed.), *Third Sex, Third Gender: Beyond Sexual Dimorphism in Culture and History* (pp. 373–418). New York: Zone Books.

Nelson, A. (2008). The pink dragon is female: Halloween costumes and gender markers. In J.Z. Spade & C.G. Valentine (Eds.), *The Kaleidoscope of Gender: Prisms, Patterns, and Possibilities* (pp. 222–230). Thousand Oaks, CA: Sage.

Olechnicki, K. (2003). *Antropologia Obrazu* [Anthropology of the Image]. Warszawa: Oficyna Naukowa.

Ono, H. & Zavodny, M. (2003). Gender and the Internet. *Social Science Quarterly, 84*(1): 111–121.

Onyejekwe, C.J. (2008). Media issues of concern to women: Some observations on gender roles in advertising in South Africa. *Jenda: A Journal of Culture & African Women Studies, 12*(1): 17–28.

Opitz, S. (2011). *Marketing Self: Negotiating Moral Conflict in the Profession* (Unpublished PhD thesis). University of Essex, Colchester, UK.

Ostrowska, D. (1997). Wizerunek kobiety w pismach Ojców Kościoła [The image of women in the writings of the Church Fathers]. In J. Brach-Czaina, (Ed.), *Od Kobiety do Mężczyzny i z Powrotem: Rozważania o płci i kulturze* [From Woman to Man and Back Again: Reflections on Gender and Culture] (pp. 53–75). Białystok: TransHumana.

Ovid. (2008). *Metamorphoses.* New York: Oxford University Press.

Paek, H-J., Nelson, M.R., & Vilela, A.M. (2011). Examination of gender-role portrayals in television advertising across seven countries. *Sex Roles, 64*(3–4): 192–207.

Pakszys, E. (2000). *Między Naturą a Kulturą: Kategoria płci/rodzaju w poznaniu* [Between Nature and Culture: Gender/sex Category in Cognition]. Poznań: Humaniora.

Parmentier, M-A., & Fischer, E. (2011). You can't always get what you want: Unsustainable identity projects in the fashion system. *Consumption, Markets & Culture, 14*(1): 7–21.

Plato. (2001). *The Symposium.* Provincetown, MA: Pagan Press.

Rorty, R. (1992). The pragmatist's progress. In U. Eco (Ed.), *Interpretation and Overinterpretation* (pp. 89–108). Cambridge: Cambridge University Press.

Roscoe, W. (1996). How to become a berdache: Toward a unified analysis of gender diversity. In G. Herdt (Ed.), *Third Sex, Third Gender: Beyond Sexual Dimorphism in Culture and History* (pp. 329–372). New York: Zone Books.

86   Jerzy Kociatkiewicz & Monika Kostera

Ross, A. (1999). *The Celebration Chronicles: Life, Liberty, and the Pursuit of Property Values in Disney's New Town*. New York: Ballantine Chronicles.

Saren, M., Maclaran, P., Goulding, C., Elliott, R., Shankar, A., & Catterall M. (Eds.). (2007). *Critical Marketing: Defining the Field*. Oxford: Butterworth-Heinemann.

Sargent, A. G. (1981). Training men and women for androgynous behaviors in organizations. *Group & Organization Studies*, 6(3): 302–311.

Schleiner, A-M. (2001). Does Lara Croft wear fake polygons? Gender and gender-role subversion in computer adventure games. *Leonardo*, 34(3): 221–226.

Sharp, L. (2002). Are public relations campaigns commercial speech? *Sport Marketing Quarterly*, 11(3): 190–192.

Singer, J. (1976). *Androgyny: Toward a New Theory of Sexuality*. New York: Anchor Books.

Skålén, P., Fougère, M., & Fellesson, M. (2008). *Marketing Discourse: A Critical Perspective*. London: Routledge.

Syed, J., & Kramar, R. (2009). Socially responsible diversity management. *Journal of Management & Organization*, 15(5): 639–651.

Tadajewski, M., & Jones, D. G. B. (Eds.). (2008). *The History of Marketing Thought*. London: Sage.

Vänskä, A. (2002). Pojista tulee tyttöjä, tytöistä tulee poikia: Calvin Kleinin mainoskuvien androgynian ristiriitaisuus [Boys will be girls, girls will be boys: Calvin Klein's advertising images androgyny contradiction]. In P. von Bonsdorff & A. Seppä (Eds.), *Kauneuden Sukupuoli: Feministisen estetiikan* kysymyksiä [Beauty Gender: Feminist Aesthetics Issues] (pp. 159–180). Helsinki: Gaudeamus.

Vedeer, W. (1987). *Mary Shelley and Frankenstein: The Fate of Androgyny*. Chicago: The University of Chicago Press.

Vetterling-Braggin, M. (Ed.). (1982). *'Femininity', 'Masculinity', and 'Androgyny': A Modern Philosophical Discussion*. Totowa: Rowman & Allanhead.

Vries, K. M. (2012). Intersectional identities and conceptions of the self: The experience of transgender people. *Symbolic Interaction*, 35(1): 49–67.

Whitehead, S. M., & Barrett, F. J. (2001). The sociology of masculinity. In S. M. Whitehead & F J. Barrett (Eds.), *The Masculinities Reader* (pp. 1–26). Malden: Blackwell.

Zanetti, L. A. (2002). Leaving our father's house: Micrologies, archetypes, and barriers to conscious femininity in organizational settings. *Journal of Organizational Change Management*, 15(5): 523–537.

Part II

Untold Stories on the Social and Political Agenda

6 A Telling Silence

Beckett, Kafka, and the Experience of Being Unemployed

Tom Boland & Ray Griffin

Vladamir: What do they say?
Estragon: They talk about their lives.

Vladamir: To have lived is not enough for them.
Estragon: They have to talk about it.

Beckett (1998: 58), Waiting for Godot

INTRODUCTION

It is commonly noted that answering the question 'what do you do?' presents an unpleasant difficulty for people who are unemployed. This observation incorporates an understanding that unemployment is more than just a technical economic calamity, because it also presents social and self-identity problems. So it is against this backdrop of self-identity (Elias, 2000; Foucault, 1984; Giddens, 1991) mediated through social recognition (Honneth, 1993), that this chapter explores what it means to be unemployed.

This chapter reports on storytelling interviews in which we ask unemployed people about what they do, a methodological practice which is deeply ambivalent and implicated in the construction of being as doing. Thus we attempt to represent the stories of unemployed persons in their own vernacular, dwelling on themes around the psycho-somatic consequences of unemployment for the self. In this, we draw on existing work around the experience of being unemployed particularly Jahoda and Zeisel (2002), Burhman and Rheinhart (1990), Ezzy (2001), and Gabriel (2012) whose work inspired this chapter, before introducing the various narrative strategies deployed by unemployed people as they account for their experience. It is not difficult to reconfirm the deprivation theory of unemployment as being an unpleasant alienating state of anomie and nothingness.

However, such a straightforward conclusion is neither enough for fresh academic work, nor is it analytically honest to the ellipses and silences that we encountered when we attempted to elicit stories. As a result we attempt to offer an interpretation, or an interpolated analysis built around Beckett and Kafka's writings, particularly those which illuminate narrative failure.

In this way we hope to make two contributions. On safe ground we add to the body of literature on the experience of unemployment, demonstrating the alienation and anomie in terms of ellipsis and silence. On a more speculative footing, we try to re-imagine the experience of unemployment through the literary works of Beckett and Kafka. Eschewing a treatment of literature as entertainment or a reflection of values, we attempt to recover the theoretical and reflexive potentials of literature as an extended meditation on experience. Following Heidegger (2002), 'poesis' can be considered as the world 'worlding', in the sense that creative writing discloses emergent properties of social reality. In this sense, the general use of the terms *Beckettian* or *Kafkaesque* to typify certain situations reflects our collective struggle to tell the complex stories of modernity. Whilst this does entail 'privileging' canonical writers as storytellers, these two authors worked within social and literary traditions, and just like our interviewees, assured narratives belie early, falteringly-narrated obscure efforts. That their writings have since been widely recognised arguably demonstrates that they have, at least in part, expressed some form of collective experience.

ON METHODS AND MATERIALS

People use story to make sense of their lives and it is natural for them "to tell stories of those lives" (Connelly & Clandinin, 1990: 2), "to make sense of the world that surrounds them, and their place in it", (Forster et al., 1999). To get a "thick description" (Ryle, 1971; Geertz, 1973), and to gain access to the sensemaking activities of people as they offer an interpretation of their unemployment, a novel method of inquiry is required. Weick (1995) suggests that stories are a kind of retrospective sensemaking device which allow us to narrate the events in our lives. A method of the moment, storytelling is increasingly being used to "capture organizational life in a way that no compilation of facts ever could" (Czarniawska, 1999: 15). During the past 20 years, a body of work has emerged (Boje, 1991, 2008; Czarniawska-Joerges, 2004; Gabriel, 1991, 2000, 2004; Sims, 1999, 2003) that champions the use of story as a way to understand people's lives in organizational settings. Taken together this work constitutes a narrative turn in organization studies, but separately each contribution offers subtle and distinct conceptions of narrative and story. So whilst Czarniawska-Joerges (2004) does not make much of the distinction, Boje (2001: 5) argues that story and narrative interact in intriguing ways, "story is folksy" and narratives is the retrospective sense that comes after story, adding plot and coherence. Arguing for a firmer distinction, Gabriel (2000: 5) suggests that stories must be poetic; advocating that "factual or descriptive accounts of events that aspire at objectivity rather than emotional effect must not be treated as stories". Sims is much more focused on the curious interaction between story and narrative, particularly in how the effect of story is subjectively constructed by the research participants, especially where experience and story cannot be separated (Sims, 2003). Sims (2003: 1198) develops this further by suggesting that "our relationship with our stories is less under our control and less utilitarian on our part than the 'sense-making' tag might suggest. There is always a tingle of uncertainty, which gives spice to our storied lives, an aleatoric element". Beyond this, there is also the question of meaning, and how we interpret stories. Is meaning the product of the author's intentions, or the creative experience of the reader? In regards to this, we attempt to produce a Derridian inspired reading of these stories (after Derrida, 1998) where order is disordered and thus meaning is contestable, indeterminate, and open. Such an attempt to deconstruct allows for an unfixing of the meaning of the stories by creating a space that opens up multiple, plural, and contradictory possible interpretations. So we work within the spaces surrounding the stories, spaces that tend to be glanced over in more objective methods; and in this way we hope to reveal something of the alterity that surrounds the experience of being unemployed. Having embarked in this approach, it is altogether possible to describe the interpretations produced as an open work (after Eco, 1962/1989), intertexual (Kristeva, 2002), or even something more akin to literary theory (after Eagleton, 1996).

INTERVIEWING

An interview is literally an inter view, an exchanging of views (Kvale, 1996). They allow for the parsing of an interaction between people (Silverman, 2001) revealing how discourse is co-constructed (Mishler, 1986). Also, and in perhaps a less rationalisable way, interviews create a space for people to present themselves and their social world in what Elliot (2005) fetchingly describes as a social collaboration. And so when we go seeking the exchange of views in the course of a study, raising the implied questions of 'who are you', 'account for yourself', and 'what is it you do', we cannot separate the inquiry from the inquirer and from the inquired upon, a point well made by Boje (2001) in his fetching terms teller and co-tellers and co-listeners. Indeed, Butler (2005) suggests that all accounts of the self are fundamentally incomplete, and performatively re-create subjective identity; as such interviewers must exhibit tact and care, allowing ambiguity and polyvalence rather than demanding a clear 'authoritative' account. Certainly to the unemployed, raising questions about doing and identity is to re-iterate the questions they are habitually asked by state institutions. In this way the interviewer is not an interrogator or detector of facts (Benjamin, 1968), but is more fellow-traveller, empathising, encouraging, and filling in the blanks for themselves (Gabriel, 1995). Indeed, even to choose a person for interview based on the fact that they are currently unemployed is to follow the idea that doing is very much more important than being.

DATA GATHERING

In the fieldwork collected for this study 16 unemployed people shared their stories with us telling us both about their own experience of being unemployed and the experience as lived out in particular days. This research was undertaken as part of a summer school research programme called Waterford Unemployment Experiences Research Collaborative (WUERC). To produce a plurivocal response, we gathered a panel of interviewers, who in turn sourced two interviews each, which they then conducted. These interviewers were drawn principally from recent graduates, all of whom were presently unemployed, and many of whom had a longer history of unemployment. As a result, each interview was carried out by researchers with varied subjective experience and understanding of unemployment. Interviewees were selected based on convenience and thus they are examples of unemployed people, representations rather than representative, offering comprehension rather than comprehensiveness. Each interview has its own character and colour, but all were strongly tethered to the core theme of the research. All interviews were recorded and transcribed.

The 16 interviewees were relatively evenly split in terms of gender, but in terms of age, they clustered around the age groups of 20 to 35 and over 50. This emerged due to the relative ages of our collaborative group and the ages of those who they found accessible to interview. In our assessment, this clustering is not problematic, but even useful because it allows us to consider the relative significance of age for the experience of unemployment. In particular, we noticed that the older cohort evinced a stronger adherence to the 'work ethic', which made their experience of unemployment more severe. However, the older group also tended to produce a more coherent story of unemployment as the result of economic conflicts between workers and factory owners, having been made redundant after decades of skilled service in a landmark industry. By contrast, the younger cohort tended to either have left college, been engaged in precarious employment, say in call centres, or to have been construction workers made redundant in Ireland's recession (2008–2013).

The ages and genders of the interviewees are summarised in Table 6.1 for convenience, and briefly noted alongside quotes in our discussion sections.

Table 6.1   Research participants—age and gender.

ID	1	2	3	4	5	6	7	8	9	10	11	12	13	14	15	16
Sex	M	F	M	F	F	M	F	F	M	F	M	M	F	M	M	M
Age	21	22	23	24	26	28	30	32	36	40	53	54	55	56	57	58

DATA AND DISCUSSION

In this section we present our interpretations of the stories told and untold on the experience of being unemployed. These interpretations are based on our readings of the interview transcripts and from repeated listening to the audio recordings of those meetings. Sometimes our analysis is based on the overall tone of the interviews, while in some instances we present story extracts and narratives to support the conclusions we arrive at. All of the interviews can be characterised as intense, fractured, and emotional, with lots of repetition, contradiction, and obfuscation. No interviewee produced a coherent, well-fettled narrative of their experience. What we really encountered was a refusal or an inability to narrate their lives and attendent efforts to essentialise their experience—as though not working spoke for itself as a difficult and alienating experience; which demonstrates that the deprivation theory of unemployment now circulates within popular discourse on unemployment. This section focuses on the talk of nothingness and the corresponding silence around story within the text of the narratives.

Not in the Real World

Each interviewee struggled to present stories from what it is that they do. Many revisited the act of being made unemployed, as if this was their last story of doing, and others allowed the gap in story to start to emerge.

> Interview 1 (Male 21): I was sacked on a workday, it was a Tuesday, I'm fairly sure. So I wasn't quite sure what to make of it, I was thinking to myself, like, is this a day off? Is this a weekend? Is this a summer holiday from school? What the hell am I meant to do now? I felt like I was completely lost. So I just back into my room and sat down on my bed, I wasn't really sure what to do . . . I think I was there for a few hours at least.

This story conveys experience reasonably coherently, as a 'redundancy story' with place, space, character, and action, yet at the same time the core of the story is the respondent's incapacity to make sense of what has happened to them. Effectively it trails off into uncertainty and indeterminate time. As mentioned later by the interviewee, one of the peculiarities of modern society is that the world of work is referred to as the 'real world' and in these terms, they have lost their footing in the real world. To be unemployed is to enter a curious in-between world, neither a day off, nor a 'day on'. This becomes a chronic problem of giving meaning to the cycle of day and night:

> Interview 6 (M 28): I made my own hours, made my own rules and on the very last day we all drank rum in the car park, it was great like. It

was really good ya know and then a couple of days later it starts to like, sink in.

Many interviewees demonstrated ambivalence about losing their jobs. In this case, there is an initial euphoria at the liberty of knowing that redundancy is coming; this leads through a certain period of license at work to the camaraderie of drinking with work mates in the park, but eventually to the realization that unemployment is problematic experience. Yet, what exactly starts to 'sink in' is scarcely explicated; indeed the 'it' which 'sinks in' is the essentialised experience of unemployment, which the interviewee and interviewer are implicitly supposed to understand. This inchoate understanding certainly existed, as interviewers had their own experience of unemployment. However, this essentialised experience can scarcely be expressed, it is sensed intuitively, but almost unnameable.

Unemployment has been well theorised as an alienating deprivation of structures (c.f. Jahoda, 1982). This stripping of identity leads into the limbo world of 'doing nothing'. Paradoxically, this is a time within which everything is possible, and yet nothing really happens. Status, social contact, time structure, collective purpose, and regular activity are all lacking as unemployment takes hold of a person's life.

> Interview 5 (F, 26): Some days are as long—like two years in a day, like. I try to be good, I do try and ehm, I couldn't just get up and sit around and do nothing, but some days that is just what I do.

Most storytellers, talked at length about the challenge of doing nothing, as though they were in some way reduced to nothing by not having a job. However, no interview really dwelt at length on the experience of doing nothing—perhaps because the method involved encounters between strangers, who could not be expected to reveal the details of precisely how they did nothing. Many interviews detailed the various activities which supplanted doing nothing; taking walks and photographs, doing DIY or cooking. What remains at the vanishing point of these narratives is the sense that unemployment somehow rendered all of these activities as pointless and uninteresting, merely treading water and marking time.

> Interview 7 (F, 30): If you have good things by working, if you don't work then you have nothing.
> Interview 8 (F, 32): I was leader of my line and can't believe I went from that to nothing!

These two quotes directly express the opposition of working and unemployment, of something and nothing. Clearly, the world of work can be narrated and explained, and fills the gap in the interviewees description of their current situation; it is the presence against which absence is measured. To have good things, to be leader of a line has content and meaning, but against this is positioned an inexplicable yet essential nothingness.

Being Undeserving

Work is not just remembered as a strenuous physical or mental activity which brings remuneration, but as a means to become deserving. The meaning of consumption and home are transfigured by work, so that they are rightfully enjoyed; those who are unemployed are implicitly undeserving in this schema, and if they accept it, cannot enjoy these elements of everyday life as they did when employed:

> Interview 3 (M, 23): There's nothin' sweeter than slobbing in front of crap TV after a hard day's work . . . There is nothing worse than slobbing in front of crap TV after a hard day's nothing.
> Interview 11 (M, 53): You come home after a hard day's work like you know you're after working and like, you can sit down and you can relax or even after a hard week you can go and you can sit down and eat or you know what I mean on a Friday and go and have a few pints like and you can feel you are after putting in a week's work, you're entitled to have a few pints.

Whether work is or was experienced as enjoyable, it facilitates the enjoyment of life. Many interviewees reported that this experience of doing nothing seeped into other aspects of their life, so that no matter what their material conditions, health, financial or family situation, life itself is not enjoyable.

> Interview 4 (M, 24): I mean you just feel so kinda beat down and down trodden and everything becomes a chore and the only thing ya can do is then try to escape from it. Sometimes the only way to escape from it is from fuckin getting pissed.

Another interviewee, whose partner was in employment, expressed this experience of meaninglessness in regard to caring for his children:

> Interview 9 (M, 36): I'm stuck at home now, I'm a stay at home dad, something I didn't want to be, something I don't want to be. [. . .] It gets monotonous, you're only there, you know you have to be there with your kids . . . but you're only there . . . it's not because of choice.

What is most significant is the way in this interviewee's reasonably comfortable financial and physical circumstances—married with two children, home-owner—do not translate into a good quality of life. Unemployment is reflexively experienced as a deprivation, so much so that the interviewee has become depressed and scarcely enjoys his time with his children. If the world of work is the real world, then non-work must be purgatory. The experience of unemployment is limbo, a life without structure or purpose without any clear end-point. Rather than being a lower status than work, it is more like the absence of status.

Madness and Depression

Many other themes emerge from the interview corpus, such as a decline in social contacts, financial difficulties, and so forth. Another is the theme of subjective suffering, often described in terms of 'depression' but usually separate from clinical diagnoses of depression. Since the experience of doing nothing is not articulated directly, it is sometimes described in terms of incipient madness or insanity:

> Interview 5 (F, 26): it drives me mad, like, finding, like something to do.
> Interview 10 (F, 40): You have nothing to do, but I'm good with time, I have hobbies and interests . . . because otherwise you'd go insane.

What is important here is that the attempt to describe unemployment occurs through a very vague metaphor. Madness or insanity is not reported on in detail, but appears as the limit of experience, perhaps even as the abyss to which the unemployed are brought, and stave off through hobbies and interests.

This state of 'depression' is stasis and limbo, connected to the difficulty of 'doing nothing'. Petersen (2011) argues that capitalism valorises action, within the market and the workplace, sometimes leading to subjective exhaustion, which is medicalised as 'depression' but is symptomatic of the pathological excesses of contemporary working conditions.

> Interview 12 (M, 54): But it hits ya, getting up every morning sitting on your arse. . . . Filling time is the killer now. It is now. I think I'd say, there's more people become depressed and down and feeling worthless, and I do mean worthless, because they ain't got a job. . . . All you have to do is talk to some people and they're so down and depressed about doing absolutely nothing.

In unemployment, the absence of activity itself leads to a sense of alienation in Blauner's sense (1964) of powerlessness, meaninglessness, social isolation, and self-estrangement. Interviewees expressed a feeling of powerlessness before the 'labour market' with some older workers arguing that 'they'd never work again'. Social isolation clearly emerged in terms of declining socialisation and the loss of 'the craic' at work. The alienation of self-estrangement and meaninglessness is more complex, and is distinctly connected to the difficulty of 'doing nothing'. Indeed, 'doing nothing' was almost indescribable or even unspeakable.

DEPRIVATION THEORY: THE GENERAL SOCIAL THEORY OF UNEMPLOYMENT

This reading of unemployment is builds on the existing work on the experience of being unemployed particularly Jahoda and Zeisel (2002), Burman and Rinehart (1990), Letkemann (2002), Ezzy (2001), Howe (1990), and Gabriel, Gray, and Goregaokar (2010, the study which inspired this work); and more general journalistic work on the phenomenon (such as Paddy O'Gorman's book (1994) and radio programme *Queuing for a Living*). As one would expect, this literature tends towards the sociological imagination (Mills, 1970), examining private troubles and public problems. Taken together, this literature reflects a 'deprivation theory' (Edgell, 2012) of unemployment where the experience of unemployment is considered a state of anomie at the absence of meaningful work.

Becoming unemployed is firstly a movement from a definite status into a 'statusless' status. The norms governing behaviour are suspended, so that many people begin to adopt or create unusual lifestyles. As noted earlier, one of the aspects of unemployment was a decline in social contacts, a sort of withdrawal from the community. Both physically and socially, the person becomes less visible, because they are not technically part of the world of work but also because they are socially unrecognisable. Media reports and popular culture describes the 'masses' or 'ranks' of the unemployed or the 'dole queue', imagining a vast undifferentiated social body devoid of proper individuality. Persons without status in the world of work have no recognisable identity; they are even defined in terms of what they lack or what they have lost, even naming themselves thus 'an ex-plasterer' or suchlike. States of being, such as being a 'qualified architect', are undermined by the fact that they are not doing, that is, a 'practicing architect'.

In the absence of structure, which prescribes certain tasks and behaviours, and proscribes others, every moment can be a choice. When one wakes, eats, drinks and sleeps becomes a matter of choice, open to endless revision. Hence, many respondents recall an initial response to redundancy of reversing night and day. Similarly, recreation and social interaction are released from any pattern, so that recreation may be constant, yet unfulfilling, and social interaction constantly postponed as there is no rush. Filling the day becomes a problem, which sounds trite, but what it effectively means is that life itself becomes a problem. The scarce commodity of time becomes a burden.

Below are citations where individuals more directly describe the problem of time, firstly through the widely recognised difficulty of 'getting up to face the day', and secondly in terms of another familiar phenomenon where night and day are reversed:

> Interview 9 (M, 36): Cos you've no work your independence is gone. Like it's very very hard to motivate yourself first thing in the morning to get out of bed. It's like today, this is another day. Very hard, so.
>
> Interview 6 (M 28): You do start to develop cabin fever, you get stuck in the door. . . . Em, my sleeping hours, fuck I was a full vampire like, sleep all day, wake up at night and watch Star Trek on Sky One and sleep again like, it was horrible, it was a very very depressing time. . . . Maybe it wasn't even a year, it just feels like that.

In each case, these are widely recognised problems around unemployment. What is significant in the first case is the difficulty in actually describing the problem; categorical statements about self-esteem, work, and independence lead into the difficulty of motivation, getting out of bed, and another day. Yet the connection between these statements remains unstated; they are assembled together elliptically as the subjective suffering that flows from the absence of work. These 'psychological' consequences of unemployment are well documented; but more difficult to assess is the effect on personal stories. Haydn White (1996) argues that modern events caused by impersonal social forces beyond anyone's ability to conceptualise or understand are characterised by the incapacity to give a satisfactory meaning to experiences, prompting silence or meaningless clichés and chatter. Unemployment as a widespread or economic or structural problem has subjective consequences that are literally 'unspeakable', leading to silence or trivialities.

The second quotation gives a more precise and dramatic description of 'doing nothing' whereby the de-structured limbo of unemployment leads to an inversion of typical sleeping patterns. Waking up as the conventional 'working-day' ends and going to sleep just before it begins could even be seen as a strategic avoidance or even rejection of the structured world of work. Yet, this would be to ignore the reported subjective consequences; "horrible . . . a very very depressing time". The inverted demi-monde of unemployment might seem appealing at first, and perhaps for a short time it is, but eventually, the absence of structure and purpose become an affliction. Yet, this experience of 'doing nothing' proves almost impossible to narrate. Indeed, there is no doubt that each interviewee filled their day with a variety of activities; the real sociological problem is not activity or inactivity, but the way in which individuals reflect on their experience as a void or non-entity.

> Interview 8 (F, 32): God I hate it. This is no existence; I keep saying it's only temporary! But two years is far from temporary.

The difficulty of unemployment emerges with some clarity here; it is defined in terms of the 'world of work' as a temporary interval between jobs (Foucault, 2008). However, as this interval stretches out, it is a void or limbo which is hated, and it is experienced as no existence at all.

BEYOND THE GENERAL SOCIAL THEORY OF UNEMPLOYMENT

This sets the scene for the next section, where we re-consider all the various silences and ellipses we encountered within the interviews. Whilst some talk is always superficial, silence is never superficial (Love, 2005). Silence and incoherent talk suffuses the text; but beyond acknowledging it, we have little by way of precedent on how to go about conducting an analysis. Although often unacknowledged, there is a natural tendency to project meaning onto the silence. But emboldened by Nietzsche's observation that if we stare into the abyss, the abyss stares back at us, the substance of our analysis is a consideration of various silences we encountered. Indeed, the problem of the deprivation theory of unemployment is that it is not a theory of unemployment but a theory of the absence of work. It pays insufficient attention to the changing situation of the unemployed, and refuses to engage with the experience itself, rendering it simply as a lack or absence. Deprivation theory ignores the abyss. The silences of the unemployed tend to be conflated into one thing—the absence of work; ellipses rationalised, and even marginalised as a reluctance to discuss something troubling. However, in attempting to take some sense out of the silence, we should respect that it is an inherently speculative act, the dominant voice echoing back from the research is that of the researchers; yet mediated now through Kafka and Beckett, highlighting the Kafkaesque and the Beckettian in the ordinary and pervasive story of the experience of meaninglessness.

ON SILENCE

What we really encounter in the stories is a rich landscape of silence—where attempts to narrate experience are more notable for the absence of story. This is a hidden silence, because so much text is produced, text which is largely silent about the object of the research. Thus, it is useful to interpret the silences and narrative ellipses both within and without our attempts to gather stories about the experience of being unemployed. Blimes (1994) usefully suggests how discourse can monopolise the field of talk, displacing or silencing other possible discourse. As a result, hidden silence may not be the unit of analysis, but it can be noticed or even created by the researcher (Blimes, 1994). In Jaworski's (1993) terms it can be described as an absence of something that we had expected to hear and so assume it is there, even if it remains unsaid.

THE TRIAL OF UNEMPLOYMENT

It is natural in organization studies to think of such silences as arising from unequal relations of power and dominant discourses (Gramsci, 1971; Foucault, 2008; Spivak, 1988; Clegg, 1989; Calás & Smircich, 1991; Grint, 2010). In this line of thinking it might well be the case that our approach silenced the interviewees, where the interviewer might have been found to exercise control over the discourse (Eades, 2000; Scollon, 1985); simply put, we might not have been good enough at researching the unemployed to get the story from reluctant narrators. Or, perhaps wider discourses around the absence of work exercise power over the interviewees. A variant to this way of thinking is to consider the silence that emerges in the data as a resistance to having to make sense, a resistance to the interpellation of ideology (cf. Althusser, 2006, an example of refusing to acknowledge the voice of a law) that might come from their story. As such the silence might even be a form of protest.

In this line of thinking we draw on Kafka's work to unpick the impenetrable obscurity and implacable absurdity that can arise in dealings with bureaucratic systems, something which many interviewees raised regarding their interaction with the social welfare system. *The Trial* is not just about bureaucracy, which is inscrutable within the novel, but about the experience of supplicants within it. In particular, it narrates the story of Joseph K. and his 'case', where he is accused of an unspecified crime, and the whole book plays out the protagonist's incapacity to make sense of the situation. The case is absolutely unknowable "For the proceedings were not only kept secret from the general public, but from the accused as well" (Kafka, 2000: 109). And over time the case comes to consume him: "The thought of his case never left him now" (Kafka, 2000: 107). Technically, the unemployed are not accused of anything, yet their time is not leisure, but the constant tending of the position of 'job-seeker', and their claim within the office is literally a 'case'. Interview quotes above reflect the constant unease of this position but reflect little of the labour of unemployment.

Kafka, similarly to Beckett, is concerned with waiting; indeed *The Trial* is a series of underwhelming incidents where K. waits for information, advice, or clarification but is continually disappointed or distracted. Initially self-confident, K. asks another man in the court's offices "What are you waiting here for?", and the eventual reply is revealing;

> 'I'm waiting—', the man started to say, but could get out no more. He had obviously begun by intending to make an exact reply to the question but did not know how to go on.
>
> (Kafka, 2000: 62)

All the man can say is that he has handed in certain documents; beyond that, making sense of his situation is impossible. Equivalently, people attain the status of 'unemployed' by handing in documentation, but their personal 'case' awaits judgement—will they be employed swiftly or long-term unemployed? In the interim they are waiting, and this experience is ambivalent, inscrutable, and impossible to narrate. Without judgement—by the court or the labour market, representing the self coherently is problematic, as K. finds:

> Now two people were already after him, it wouldn't take much to bring all the officials down on him, demanding an explanation of his presence. The only comprehensible and acceptable on was that he was an accused man and wished to know the date of his next interrogation, but that explanation he did not wish to give, especially as it was not even in accordance with the truth, for he had come only out of curiosity or, what was still more impossible as an explanation of his presence, out of a desire to assure himself that the inside of this legal system was just as loathsome as its external aspect.
>
> (Kafka, 2000: 65)

Despite the resistance intended by K. here, he falters, feels faint and cannot articulate himself, and retreats in confusion. The system is particularly exhausting in that it offers no means of self-presentation to the accused other than in its own terms. Similarly, to present oneself at the social welfare office means having to explain one's presence in its terms. For instance:

> Interviewee 3 (M, 23): . . . I missed my signing on date . . . well what actually happened was . . . they changed my signing on date and on the little slip you get in the post office it kept on saying the week before I was meant to sign on, so I was out there two weeks in a row for about three months and then I just said- Ah- screw it now I'll just go the week after it says on the thing but in the end I ended up going out on the Thursday and signing on.
>
> . . . you know, the girl behind the counter said 'look your money will be there for you Tuesday no bothers', because I always sign on time anyway but eh, . . . she said it would be 'there for you' on Tuesday. So I went to the dole, or went to my post office Tuesday the money wasn't there so I rang them, they says it'd be there Friday, it wasn't there, . . . so I called straight out to them, and then like, 'I have a small child I can't afford to be without money like, you know what I mean, have to pay maintenance, I've credit union bills, I've insurance for the car, I have petrol for the car you know, I have to put food on the table'.
>
> So I went out there then and I was talking to a girl and everything was all pleasant, and she was telling me . . . 'look your money will be there on for you on Tuesday'. I said 'look I need money like today like, I can't afford to go another four days without, without money like because the money isn't there like'.

And in the end then a woman walked over, a big burly butch woman came over and just started being very blunt with me like, and telling me that tough look, it's my own fault, and I asked her to check the time I signed on at and what day and she said yeah well 'that's not our fault', and I said well obviously it's your fault because your meant to sign on two days later if you are after missing your signing on date and I was after missing it on the Tuesday, it was on the Thursday when I signed on, . . . your one was just completely ignorant to me but I suppose she probably had people coming in all day giving out to her like, so, . . . you probably couldn't blame her either at the same time.

This is a richly dull narration of a Kafkaesque situation, told in halting detail, expressing negative experiences yet coming to no great conclusion. Nonetheless it reflects a similar experience to Joseph K. The narrator is bound to a system that they don't fully understand, they resist it, resent it, struggle with it, but when it affects them adversely, there is little that can be done about it. All the while, the system significantly constitutes and regulates their life.

The penultimate chapter of *The Trial* is particularly absurd. It concerns K. arranging to meet an Italian he cannot comprehend at a Cathedral which is too dark to be viewed, to hear a preacher tell a story about a pointless Kafkaesque wait of a client at the door of a law held by a guardian of the law; and this story itself simply cannot be interpreted definitively and has no clear bearing on K.'s case.

He was too tired to survey all the conclusions arising from the story, and the trains of thought into which it was leading him were unfamiliar. . . . The simple story had lost its clear outline, he wanted to put it out of his mind.

(Kafka, 2000: 204)

The preacher's story initially seems like a re-capitulation of the whole novel, expressing in a nutshell K.'s own experience. Yet, as K. attempts to set forth the meaning of the story, he is undermined by the preacher's numerous possible and mutually exclusive interpretations. This has meta-reflective implications for readers of *The Trial*, particularly that the problem is not just the absurdity of the system itself, but also the absurdity of attempts to make sense of that system. *The Trial* itself is absurd, and is far from a reliable or close account of modern bureaucracy. What it does achieve is an illumination of the experience of meaningless waiting, where life itself becomes a 'case' or a 'claim'. Kafka himself considered *The Trial* unfinished, and it is perhaps necessarily incomplete and elliptic. Yet, through Kafka this experience is in itself raised for reflection, thereby providing a literary theoreticisation of the problematic situation of doing nothing.

WAITING FOR JOBS

Silence is itself a part of communication as important as speech (Enninger, 1987; Jaworski, 1993; Tannen & Saville-Troike, 1985). Silence has been studied from perspectives as varied as semiotics, pragmatics, sociolinguistics, social psychology, and anthropology. But such an approach to thoughtful silence can be best found in Beckett's play *Waiting for Godot*, a play in which 'nothing happens twice'. Much of Beckett's work concerns situations where action is non-existent or futile, and for the purposes of this chapter, we interpret his work as an extended meditation on 'doing nothing' in modern society. Beckett addresses the widespread alienation, anomie, and disenchantment with both religious convictions and the modern project of progress, but also the concrete situation of interminable waiting and incomplete communication.

Waiting for Godot centres on two tramp-like characters, Vladamir and Estragon, who wait in a desolate landscape for Godot, a character who never appears, and whom they might not even recognise if he did arrive. All of their actions are pointless, in both a trivial and profound way. For instance, the opening line "Nothing to be done" (Beckett, 1998: 1) both sums up the play, but also remarks upon Estragon's incapacity to remove his boots. Or later, when Estragon finally articulates his despair and incapacity to continue, Vladamir diverts him into triviality; "Would you like a radish?" (Beckett, 1998: 63), and Estragon's reply "Is that all there is?" can be taken as an existentialist lament of the absence of meaning, or an enquiry seeking other vegetables. And there are turnips!

Amidst the torment of endlessly waiting, Vladamir and Estragon frequently misunderstand each other and talk at cross-purposes. Neither has a good memory, and even when Vladamir attempts to recall better days, his speech is halting:

> Vladamir: But we were there together, I could swear to it! Picking grapes for a man called . . . [He snaps his fingers] . . . can't think of the name of the man, at a place called . . . [Snaps his fingers] . . . can't think of the name of the place, do you not remember?
>
> (Beckett, 1998: 57)

Despite the superfluity of time granted to them they cannot quite manage to fully express themselves. Yet, their incapacity itself speaks volubly:

> Estragon: Yes, now I remember, yesterday evening we spent blathering about nothing in particular. That's been going on now for half a century.
>
> (Beckett, 1998: 61)

Here, Estragon gives us either a trivial gloss of the first half of the play, or a profound diagnosis of modern life. Frequently there is a tension between the trivial and profound meanings of the dialogue, and it is from this incomplete signification that silence becomes articulate: There is something unspeakable and indescribable about doing nothing.

The profundity of trivialities and the triviality of profundity as illuminated by Beckett enables us to make better sense of the silences and ellipses of the stories of the unemployed. Indeed, their words could form the text of the play:

Estragon sits, filling out a form for welfare benefits. Stops. Scratches head. Writes. Rubs out. Writes. Rubs out. Puts down form. Waits. Enter Vladimir:

Vladimir: [*Brightly*] Today, this is another day.
Estragon: This is no existence;

Vladimir: Filling time is the killer now.
Estragon: It drives me mad, like, finding, like something to do.

Vladimir: Everything becomes a chore
Estragon: It gets monotonous, you're only there, you know you have to be there.

Vladimir: Some days are as long—like two years in a day ... [*pause*] Maybe it wasn't even a year, it just feels like that.
Estragon: After a hard week you can go and you can sit down and eat ...

Vladimir: I went from that to nothing
Estragon: What the hell am I meant to do now?

These lines, even if they lack Beckett's compact lyricism, capture the profound triviality of waiting and how a pervasive sense of meaninglessness makes trivial all profundity. The stories of the unemployed are halting and elliptical, replete with common places, and assume that the interviewer implicitly understands the experience of 'doing nothing'. Yet re-interpreted through Beckett it becomes clear that these stories are necessarily meditations on peculiarly modern states of perpetual waiting, unemployment in particular, and more philosophically on the problematic relationship of doing and being and the threat of nothingness.

Beckett's play diagnoses the modern world in general, and is relevant to all those who have plenty to do, including busy scholars who write papers for academic profit, but also to stave off the nothingness that emerges from their free-time/research day. But the relevance is closer to those who are unemployed. Beckett's tramps make articulate the faltering speech about nothing, less through occasional 'profound' statements, than through elliptic, confused speech which can scarcely articulate the peculiar torment of waiting.

> Interviewee 6 (M 28): If you've got nothing to do yourself to keep yourself occupied you'll go 'round the twist. Which you would, you know?

The dangling rhetorical question here covers a vast unspoken and untold story played out by Beckett over 2 hours. This 'you know?' can scarcely be answered definitively, for who really knows? Not all experiences of unemployment are the same, and not everyone goes 'round the twist'. However, modern tendency to translate life into things which we do in order to keep the 'nothingness' at bay is the real insight of Beckett's plays. ("That passed the time. / It would have passed anyway. / Yes, but not so rapidly.") Whether unemployed people develop a reflexive awareness of this is a moot point. Indeed, our own analysis could be compared to the occasional attempts at profundity within *Waiting for Godot*, our use of literature as theory can appear as a faltering, a mere gesture towards another text which might give a satisfactory explanation, and even then, we have chosen most ungraspable texts. However, given the alternative explanation of being as doing, the centrality of action in Western culture, including the deprivation theory of unemployment, which renders non-work as an absence, it is possible to consider silence, incompleteness, and metaphor as a resistance to a metanarrative. Just as *The Trial* refuses to name K's crime, just as Godot never appears and is not defined as God, the experience of nothingness cannot be explicitly defined here. It remains a story, expressed in faltering inarticulate speech, ellipses, and silence. Thus, this chapter 'cannot go on', and even without a conclusion, falls again into silence, as readers and authors return, again, to the existential challenge of doing nothing.

REFERENCES

Althusser, L. (2006). Ideology and ideological state apparatuses (notes towards an investigation). In S. Aradhana, & G. Akhil, (Eds.), *The Anthropology of the State: A Reader* (pp. 86–111). Oxford: Blackwell.

Beckett, S. (1998). *Samuel Beckett: The Complete Dramatic Works*. London: Faber.

Benjamin, W. (1968). *Illuminations*. London: Random House.

Bilmes, J. (1994). Constituting silence: Life in the world of total meaning. *Semiotica*, 98(1–2): 73–88.

Blauner, R. (1964). *Alienation and Freedom: The Factory Worker and His Industry*. Chicago: University of Chicago Press.

Boje, D.M. (1991). The storytelling organization: A study of story performance in an office-supply firm. *Administrative Science Quarterly*, 36(1): 106–126.

Boje, D.M. (2001). *Narrative Methods for Organizational & Communication Research*. London: Sage.

Boje, D.M. (2008). *Storytelling Organizations*. London: Sage.

Burman, P., & Rinehart, J. (1990). *Killing Time, Losing Ground: Experiences of Unemployment.* Toronto: Thompson Educational Publishing.

Butler, J. (2005). *Giving an Account of Oneself.* New York: Fordham University Press.

Calás, M., & Smircich, L. (1991). Voicing seduction to silence leadership. *Organization Studies*, *12*(4): 567–601.

Clegg, S. (1989). *Frameworks of Power.* London: Sage.

Connelly, F., & Clandinin, D. (1990). Stories of experience and narrative inquiry. *Educational Researcher*, *19*(5): 2–14.

Czarniawska, B. (1999). *Writing Management: Organization Theory as a Literary Genre.* Oxford: Oxford University Press.

Czarniawska-Joerges, B. (2004). *Narratives in Social Science Research.* London: Sage.

Derrida, J. (1998). *Of Grammatology.* Baltimore, MD: JHU Press.

Eades, D. (2000). I don't think it's an answer to the question: Silencing aboriginal witnesses in court. *Language in Society*, *29*(2): 161–195.

Eagleton, T. (1996). *Literary Theory: An Introduction.* Minneapolis, MN: University of Minnesota Press.

Eco, U. (1989). *The Open Work* (A. Cancogni, Trans.). Cambridge, MA: Harvard University Press. (Original work published in 1962).

Edgell, S. (2012). *The Sociology of Work: Continuity and Change in Paid and Unpaid Work.* London: Sage.

Elias, N. (2000). *The Civilising Process.* Oxford: Blackwell.

Elliott, J. (2005). *Using Narrative in Social Research: Qualitative and Quantitative Approaches.* London: Sage.

Enninger, W. (1987). *What Interactants do with Non-talk across Cultures. Analyzing Intercultural Communication.* Berlin: Mouton de Gruyter.

Ezzy, D. (2001). *Narrating Unemployment.* Aldershot: Ashgate.

Forster, N., Cebis, M., Majteles, S., Mathur, A., Morgan, R., Preuss, J., Tiwari, V., & Wilkinson, D. (1999). The role of story-telling in organizational leadership. *Leadership & Organization Development Journal*, *20*(1): 11–17.

Foucault, M. (1984). *The Foucault Reader.* London: Penguin.

Foucault, M. (2008). *The Birth of Bio-Power: Lectures at the College de France, 1973–1974.* London: Palgrave.

Gabriel, Y. (1991). Turning facts into stories and stories into facts: A hermeneutic exploration of organizational folklore. *Human Relations*, *44*(8): 857–875.

Gabriel, Y. (1995). The unmanaged organization: Stories, fantasies and subjectivity. *Organization Studies*, *16*(3): 477–501.

Gabriel, Y. (2000). *Storytelling in Organizations: Facts, Fictions, and Fantasies.* Oxford: Oxford University Press.

Gabriel, Y. (2004). *Myths, Stories, and Organizations: Premodern Narratives for Our Times.* Oxford: Oxford University Press.

Gabriel, Y. (2012). Under new management. *Nouvelle Revue de Psychosociologie*, *13*(1): 241–264.

Gabriel, Y., Gray, D., & Goregaokar, H. (2010). Temporary derailment or the end of the line? Managers coping with unemployment at 50. *Organization Studies*, *31*(12): 1687–1712.

Geertz, C. (1973). *The Interpretation of Cultures: Selected Essays.* New York: Basic Books.

Giddens, A. (1991). *Modernity and Self-identity: Self and Society in the Late Modern Age.* Stanford: Stanford University Press.

Gramsci, A. (1971). *Selections from the Prison Notebooks* (Q. Hoare, & G.N. Smith, Trans.). New York: International Publishers.

Grint, K. (2010). The sacred in leadership: separation, sacrifice and silence. *Organization Studies*, *31*(1): 89–107.

Heidegger, M. (2002). '. . . poetically man dwells. . .'. *Canadian Journal of Psychoanalysis*, *10*(2): 233–236.

Honneth, A. (1993). *The Critique of Power: Reflective Stages in a Critical Social Theory*. Cambridge: MIT Press.

Howe, L. (1990). *Being Unemployed in Northern Ireland: An Ethnographic Study*. Cambridge: Cambridge University Press.

Jahoda, M. (1982). *Employment and Unemployment: A Social-Psychological Analysis* (Vol. 1). Cambridge: Cambridge University Press.

Jahoda, M., & Zeisel, H. (2002). *Marienthal: The Sociography of an Unemployed Community*. London: Transaction Publishers.

Jaworski, A. (1993). *The Power of Silence: Social and Pragmatic Perspectives*. Newbury Park, CA: Sage.

Kafka, F. (2000). *The Trial*. London: Vintage Classics.

Kristeva, J. (2002). *The Portable Kristeva*. New York: Columbia University Press.

Kvale, S. (1996). *Interviews: An Introduction to Qualitative Research Interviewing*. London: Sage.

Letkemann, P. (2002). Unemployed professionals, stigma management and derivative stigmata. *Work, Employment and Society*, *16*(3): 511–522.

Love, C. (2005). Contextualizing silence. *The American Benedictine Review*, *56*(2): 152–166.

Mills, C. W. (1970). The contribution of sociology to studies of industrial relations. *Berkeley Journal of Sociology*, *15*: 11–32.

Mishler, E. (1991). *Research Interviewing: Context and Narrative*. Cambridge, MA: Harvard University Press.

Mishler, E. G. (1986). *Research Interviewing*. Cambridge, MA: Harvard University Press.

O'Gorman, P. (1994). *Queueing for a Living*. Dublin: Poolbeg.

Petersen, A. (2011). Authentic Self-realization and depression. *International Sociology*, *26*(1): 5–24.

Ryle, G. (1971). Thinking and reflecting. *Collected Papers 2* (pp. 465–479). London: Hutchinson.

Scollon, R. (1985). The machine stops: Silence in the metaphor of malfunction. In D. Tannen, & M. Saville Troike, (Eds.), *Perspectives on Silence* (pp. 21–30). Norwood: Ablex.

Silverman, D. (2001). *Interpreting Qualitative Data: Methods for Analysing Talk, Text and Interaction*. London: Sage.

Sims, D, (1999). Organizational learning as the development of stories: Canons, apocryphas and pious myths. In M. Easterby-Smith, J. Burgoyne, & L. Araujo (Eds.), *Organizational Learning and the Learning Organization* (pp. 44–58). London: Sage.

Sims, D. (2003). Between the millstones: A narrative account of the vulnerability of middle managers' storying. *Human Relations*, *56*(10): 1195–1211.

Spivak, G. (1988). Can the subaltern speak? In C. Nelson, & L. Grossberg, (Eds.), *Marxism and the Interpretation of Culture* (pp. 271–313). Basingstoke: Macmillan.

Tannen, D., & Saville Troike, M. (Eds.). (1985). *Perspectives on Silence*. Norwood: Ablex.

Weick, K. (1995). *Sensemaking in Organizations*. London: Sage.

White, H. (1996). The modernist event. In V. Sobchack, (Ed.), *The Persistence of History: Cinema, Television, and the Modern Event* (pp. 17–38). New York: Routledge.

7 Stories Gone Cold
An Analysis of Untold Organizational Stories among Reference Librarians

Mónica Colón-Aguirre

INTRODUCTION

Society values communication (Bruneau, 2009), particularly in organizations where it is the way in which valuable ideas, information and knowledge are passed on and innovation started (Dalkir, 2005; Hislop, 2010). Sharing stories is one way in which humans communicate, and in organizational settings storytelling has been recognised as a way in which people make sense of their jobs, and also a way in which they transfer knowledge (Boje, 2008; Orr, 1990, 1996). This is a study of organizational stories, however the focus is not on the stories that are passed on and shared among members of an organization, but those that never made it out of the individual's mind, those that died on the lips of the storyteller; the stories that went cold. They all had promising beginnings, a colleague told a story to another colleague, an incident was witnessed by an individual, or a decision was made by the supervisors. But these stories were kept in silence, only to be uncovered by the researcher under the cover of anonymity provided by purposeful research. The organizations researched here were academic libraries; organizations that, like many others, have been deeply affected by technological changes and are under constant change and reinvention.

Parting from the premise that organizational stories offer real contributions to the development of innovation and transfer of knowledge in organizations; this study focuses on identifying the circumstances under which stories are left untold. Which are these circumstances and which factors contribute to stories among reference librarians working at the reference desk to not be shared? How does the untelling of stories occur among reference librarians? Understanding these factors may help develop systems in which employees are encouraged to share stories which contribute to expanding existing knowledge as well as creating new knowledge in a collaborative environment. These processes of sharing and collaboration can hold the key to developing strategies that can help librarians thrive in the current information environment. The topics explored here can also provide insights into other not-for-profit organization management; that is, organizations which create and provide services for a group but does not generate a profit from these activities (Moran, Stueart, & Morner, 2013). Nowadays these organizations have constant pressures related to staying relevant and providing superior services to their clients in a volatile environment driven by fast changing technology, changing expectations, and evolving social order.

ACADEMIC LIBRARIES AND REFERENCE LIBRARIANS

Academic libraries in the U.S. began almost at the same time as the first universities and during the second half of the 19th century started to be recognised as a critical factor necessary to support the curriculum and the research of both students and faculty affiliated with each academic institution (Rubin, 2004). Academic libraries are complex organizations, with both internal and external organizational structures.

According to Martin (1996) the internal organizational structure is similar across all libraries; the main feature is the bureaucratic division of labour into departments with specific functions within it. These departments can include specific positions such as: acquisition librarians, catalogers, reference librarians, and circulation staff. The second part of the organizational structure of academic libraries pertains to its place in the academic institution in which it operates. The academic institution is known as the 'parent organization' and the place the academic library occupies there is not standardised. In many academic institutions the head of the library has the position of Dean of Libraries; this gives the library a place among the higher levels of the organizational hierarchy but this is not necessarily the only place in the organizational structure where the library can be found.

One of the most outstanding departments in the academic library is the reference department. Reference librarians are those who assist patrons with queries and are the main representatives of the library (Cassell & Hiremath, 2011). They are in charge of activities that include: overseeing and guiding reference transactions, and "the creation, management, and assessment of information or research resources, tools, and services" (Reference and User's Services Association, 2008: para. 2). A reference transaction itself includes "information consultations in which library staff recommend, interpret, evaluate, and/or use information resources to help others to meet particular information needs" (Reference and User's Services Association, 2008: para. 1). In academic institutions reference librarian positions include a wide variety of tasks including: supervision, academic department liaison work, acquisitions as well as promotion and marketing the library's services and collections, among many others (Detmering & Sproles, 2012).

In the U.S. a professional librarian possesses the terminal degree of master's in library and information science from a program accredited by the American Library Association (ALA) or from a program in a country with a formal accreditation process as identified by ALA's Human Resource Development and Recruitment Office (Association of College and Research Libraries, 2011). There are other groups of employees that work in academic library settings other than professional librarians, these include but are not limited to: library staff members (also referred to as para-professionals, or those individuals who do not possess a terminal degree but work in the library), Student Library Assistants (SLAs), and Graduate Assistants (GAs). This last group is generally recognised to be students who are in the process of getting their degree in library and information science.

Nowadays all libraries function in a constantly changing environment. These changes are mainly driven by technological advances that threaten to make library services obsolete in the eyes of some (Herring, 2005, 2008). Free, online search engines have revolutionised information seeking processes and given individuals the freedom to access information at their convenience, fast and economically and also have exacerbated the need to gather further understanding regarding the processes of information creation and maintenance. These processes have been historically the purview of libraries (Herring, 2005, 2008; Kaufman, 2007). Academic libraries, in particular, are mainly concerned with providing the necessary tools for advancing educational goals and fomenting scholarship among its member's.

As places that acquire, store, organize, and disseminate information to different groups of people within a larger organization, academic libraries can be considered knowledge organizations (Hislop, 2010; Martin, 1996). The job of an academic librarian is in most aspects that which has been described as the job of a knowledge worker in that it is primarily intellectual, creative and non-routine in nature, and it also involves both the utilisation and creation of knowledge both theoretical and abstract (Hislop, 2010). At the same time, reference librarians are part of an organization that must find ways to deal with and excel over its competitors. In this case the competition is mainly free online search engines. These are the main tools that students and professors use when collecting information necessary to do their school work and research (Lim, 2009; Head & Eisenberg, 2010). In such a volatile environment, academic libraries would greatly benefit from exploiting the ideas proposed by many that relate to knowledge management and the role organizational storytelling has in it.

KNOWLEDGE MANAGEMENT AND ORGANIZATIONAL STORYTELLING

With the recognition of a new economic system that focuses on services rather than on physical products, the management literature turned its attention on people, as members of organizations, as the focus of value creation in organizations (Hislop, 2010). During the 1990s the management literature focused on knowledge creation and transfer in organizations and many attempted to understand and explain the processes that enabled organizations to learn and to constantly improve by innovating, and learning from past mistakes or replicating past successes (Dalkir, 2005; Hislop, 2010; MacMorrow, 2001).

One of the main ways of understanding these processes is represented in Figure 7.1 by Nonaka and Takeuchi's (1995) SECI model in which knowledge—mainly of two types: explicit and tacit—was transferred through processes that included: socialisation, externalisation, combination, and internalisation. Tacit knowledge is that which is deeply rooted in action, hard to formalise, and difficult to communicate while explicit knowledge is that which has already been coded in words, diagrams or mathematical formulas (Dalkir, 2005). According to this model, knowledge always starts at the individual level in a person's head and through socialisation processes the individual shares this tacit knowledge with others (Nonaka, 2007; Nonaka & Takeuchi, 1995).

To exemplify this process Nonaka and Takeuchi used the case of Matsuchita Electric Company, which in the 1980s had a group of engineers working on designing a new home bread-making machine. Despite all the group's efforts, the machine was not kneading the dough properly and

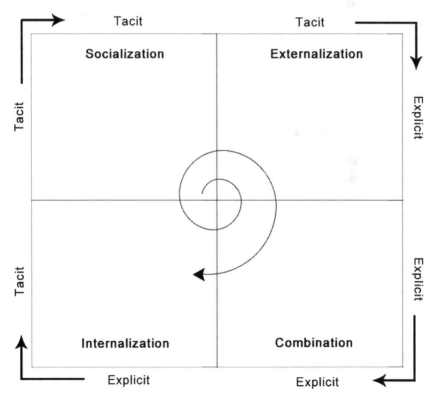

Figure 7.1 SECI Model. (Nonaka & Takeuchi, 1995).

therefore producing inferior quality bread. One of the software developers suggested becoming an apprentice baker at the Osaka International Hotel, which at the time had a reputation of making the best bread in Osaka. The idea proved to be a successful one, the software developer learned from the head baker how to knead the bread dough and prepare bread. Then came back to the Matsushita and communicated the lessons learned to other organizational members, which resulted in a reworking of the machine to adapt to the kneading techniques.

In the socialisation processes knowledge that is tacit is passed on to others also in tacit form; as when a software developer becomes the apprentice of a baker in order to learn the process of bread making, that she will try to adapt in the creation of a bread making machine (Nonaka, 2007). The process of externalisation implies tacit knowledge becoming explicit knowledge; as when the software developer is able to articulate the lessons she learned about bread making and communicates them to her team. The process of combination implies a process of putting together explicit knowledge with more explicit knowledge in order to create something new; such as when a comptroller collects information from different departments of the organizations and puts together a financial report. Internalisation includes a process through which knowledge that is explicit becomes tacit as when employees learn from information provided by the organization and adapt it to their own tacit knowledge for later application in their day to day work.

Chun Wei Choo (1998) added a third type of knowledge in organizations which he called *cultural knowledge*. This includes the affective and cognitive structures that are used habitually by organizational members to perceive, explain, evaluate, and construct reality. These structures take the form of shared beliefs, norms, and values which form the framework in which organizational members construct reality and assign value to new information.

The processes described both in Nonaka and Takeuchi's SECI model and in Choo's writings have been applied to other processes of organizational studies and social relationships in organizations; particularly Weick's *Sensemaking* (1995) connected the processes indicated in the SECI model to the social and cultural aspects of organizations (Choo, 1998). Organizations, as social systems, come to be when roles are institutionalised; this process of institutionalisation of roles is mainly the product of communication processes among different organizational members (Berger & Luckmann, 1966). Seen this way, knowledge becomes organizational once individuals draw upon a corpus of generic rules produced by the organization (Tsoukas & Vladimirou, 2001). Stories are central to this process, since the process of institutionalisation, as explained by Berger and Luckmann (1966) includes several explanatory schema—including narrative forms—which are transmitted in poetical forms; these poetical forms include legends and folk tales, and other narratives. Stories are ways in which cultural reality are reflected and also distorted; they can contribute to social cohesion or weaken social structures and that can function as social control, social criticism, or escape mechanisms (Georges, 1969).

The relationship of human social life and narration, including storytelling, is so close that Fisher (1984: 6) proposes the metaphor of *homo narrans* to present the essential nature of human beings. According to this point of view, recounting and accounting stories (the ones we tell ourselves and each other) is how humans establish a meaningful life-world. And as explained before, it is at the center of organizational life, from the process of knowledge creation, to sense-making in organizations to the creation of organizational culture itself. When identified in organizations, there is a need for a more specific and articulated definition of storytelling, in order to allow the study of something so ingrained in the human experience. Gabriel (2000) defines stories as:

> ... narratives with plots and characters, generating emotion in narrator and audience, through a poetic elaboration of symbolic material. This material may be a product of fantasy or experience, including an experience of earlier narratives. Story plots entail conflicts, predicaments, trials, coincidences, and crises that call for choices, decisions, actions, and interactions, whose actual outcomes are often at odds with the characters' intentions and purposes.
>
> (emphasis in the original, Gabriel, 2000: 239)

According to Connell (2006), one of the most valuable aspects of organizational stories is that they are rich in tacit knowledge which is stored through retelling. This is particularly important because, due to its personal nature, tacit knowledge is harder to extract and use (Nonaka & Takeuchi, 1995). In the explanation of the SECI model, organizational storytelling is essential for the externalisation process. This is the part of the process in which tacit knowledge becomes explicit. The current organizational storytelling literature focuses on what specific knowledge is transferred from one member of the organization to another through stories, which includes: sense-making, communication, learning/change, politics and power, and identity and identification (Rhodes & Brown, 2005).

Orr (1996) examined the stories shared among photocopier technicians and how these stories helped disseminate knowledge by allowing other technicians to identify complex problems encountered while fixing a machine. Another study by Boje (1991) at an office supply company identified the main purposes of the stories told at meetings as: sensemaking, introducing change, and gaining of political advantage. A more recent study by Musacchio Adorisio (2009) revealed that storytelling is a very important factor in the employee's life in the organization as stories provided a central contribution to the process of creating collective memory that can later impact the organization's decision-making process (Musacchio Adorisio, 2009).

SILENCE AND ORGANIZATIONAL STORIES

The literature on silence is not as abundant as that relating to other areas of communication, including organizational storytelling. However, it is still an important consideration since for all that organizational stories represent in organizations, these are sometimes suppressed. Organizations are not just places were stories happen, as in other social systems; they also are places in which silence thrives.

A working definition of silence involves elements of a physical nature, such as Baker's definition of it as situations in which "speech breaks down or words become irrelevant" (Baker in Johannesen, 1974: 30); or sociolinguistic aspects that characterise silence as a nonlinear brain processes and closely ties it to processes of silencing, which in turn refer to restricting speech and expressions of ourselves and/or others (Bruneau, 2009). Silence is more widely studied in relation to cultural perceptions of silence in social interaction; particularly contrasting how Western cultures tend to disregard silence as worthless and socially disagreeable, whereas it is perceived as valuable and expected in other cultures (Johannesen, 1974; Ramsey, 1998).

Kurzon (2007) created a typology of silence, as it occurs in social interactions, which includes four main types: conversational, thematic, technical, and situational. Conversational silence covers situations of silent answers to a question and non-participation in a conversation, which can happen for a multitude of reasons, and can be either intentional or unintentional. Thematic silence is that which relates directly to a specific theme, topic, or subject. Here the person will keep silent on a specific topic deliberately. According to this typology, occasions in which an individual keeps silent and just reads a particular, pre-arranged or written text, as is the case of a person who reads a book in a library or silent reading time in a classroom setting are known as technical silence. The last type of silence is what Kurzon describes as situational silence; this refers to that which is observed by people in a large group in response to a particular situation, such as when observing a minute of silence.

Silence can also be viewed in the dimension of occasions of social interactions in which it is expected, as is the case of secrets. Erving Goffman (1959), points out this concept when he discusses the importance of secrets in team performance. According to Goffman a team is ". . . a set of individuals whose intimate co-operation is required if a given projected definition of the situation is to be maintained" (p. 104). Secrets involve controlling information about an individual or group. The secrets which a team keeps are classified as: dark, strategic, and inside. Dark secrets are facts about the team which are incompatible with the image of self the team wants to present to the audience. Strategic secrets involve intentions and capacities which the team conceals from the audience as they might interfere with the state of affairs that the team wants to bring about. Inside secrets are those that mark an individual as a member of a team and help differentiate the members of the team from others.

RESEARCH METHOD

This research presents the results of 20 interviews of librarians in four different institutions in the southeastern region of the U.S. All the libraries were members of the Association of Southeastern Research Libraries (ASERL) and were chosen based on a grouping of the staffed service points for each library system; which is a place where patrons can get service in a library. The chosen libraries had numbers of staffed service points that ranged from 17 to 22.

The librarians interviewed in this research all had a master's degree in library and information science, or equivalent, and worked at the reference desk as part of their job responsibilities. The researcher requested permission to contact qualified participants for the research from the library directors at each institution. After the participants had accepted the invitation to be part of the research project, the researcher scheduled individual meetings with each one of them. Participation in this research was voluntary and it involved interviews conducted face-to-face in a setting chosen by the participants. Each of the participants received a very small remuneration for their participation in the form of a gift card, which was given to each one of them at the end of the interview.

The interviews were conducted until redundancy, or the point of saturation was reached. This means that additional interviews were not providing new information, but rather just confirming the information gathered from previous interviews (McCracken, 1988; Morrison, Haley, Sheehan, & Taylor, 2002; Patton, 1990). The interviews lasted anywhere from 30 minutes (shortest interview) to 76 minutes (longest interview). The researcher used a semi-structured questionnaire based on questions specifically intended to elicit organizational stories modeled after those suggested by Yiannis Gabriel (2000). All the interviews were digitally recorded and the researcher did all the transcription and purged any personally identifying names, including names of institutions, specific job positions, and both library and academic departments. The clean transcripts were sent to each respective participant for their final approval.

After the participants approved the transcripts the researcher coded the information using both open coding and axial coding. These processes involve the initial separation of the data into meaningful groups and the grouping of related codes to each other according to relationships that the researcher identified (Corbin & Strauss, 2008). The researcher then arranged the categories identified in this process into a research narrative (Corbin & Strauss, 2008; Dey, 1993), the results of which are presented here.

RESULTS

This study focuses on the stories that the participants indicated they had not shared before they shared it with the researcher as part of the research interview, these will be referred to here as the untold stories. In addition the stories that the participants shared with the researcher and admitted to only sharing with selected members of the organization or their social circle are also analyzed. Here examples of the stories will be provided along with the reasons the participants gave not to share them, or to share them with only a selected group of individuals.

UNTOLD STORIES

One of the factors that seemed to inhibit the act of sharing organizational stories among reference librarians was the physical proximity to their colleagues. As indicated by Librarian 8 when she points out that sharing stories with her colleagues is hard because it would require them to make special plans to meet due to the way their offices are located in the building. This specific building has multiple floors and reference librarians have offices located in different floors throughout the building. When asked if there were any common areas in the library building where the personnel could meet, Librarian 8 pointed out that they did have a staff lounge but that it was mainly ". . . dismal looking and a lot of people just don't use it". This participant went on to explain that in the past, while working on another department in the same library, the flow of communication in general was easier since they were all in the same office:

> . . . we were all sitting in the same area and so there was much more, just kind of everyday chit chat, discussion in our talk about things going on in the department that I feel like we do not 'cause we're physically separated.
>
> (Librarian 8)

This situation repeated itself throughout the study and points to organizational storytelling as form of communication which is usually conducted as part of face-to-face interaction. Although this is not the only way participants shared organizational stories (some mentioned calling specific individuals or sending electronic mail to share certain stories about their organization) the absence of a common space was one of the reasons reference librarians identified for not sharing stories with their colleagues. This contrasts with those who explained that they do share stories with their office mate or the person on the office next door, in some cases as soon as an incident took place, as is the case of Librarian 3 who indicated that:

I mean usually [it's] just the people that are sitting closest to me, prox-imity wise I think. But yeah I mean I think we are pretty tight knit group so I think we all pretty much get along really well so it's not that I wouldn't tell anybody because I didn't, I wasn't friends with them or anything like that, but probably because the people I sit close to are the people that I talk to the most I guess.

This point is an important factor to take into consideration when analys-ing untold stories in the academic library. In academic settings it is common to find a main library building and multiple smaller branch libraries that operate in a different location on campus. Some of these libraries are affili-ated to a specific academic school or department and some are separated due to their special purpose, the special need of a collection or lack of space for a big department in the main building (Alire & Evans, 2010; Martin, 1996). A setting in which librarians are spread out in different physical locations presents itself as a reason not to share stories; if they cannot see each other, librarians will be less likely to share stories. This can also affect who shares stories with whom, since those who are isolated in a different building or specific area of a building will be less likely to hear the stories.

Another reason cited for not sharing stories with colleagues is forget-ting to do so. These lapses in memory were fairly common occurrences. In this category are classified the stories that the participants shared with the researcher when asked about specific events or stories related to events that took place in the library, but that the librarians did not share with colleagues. For example, when the researcher asked about traditions or special celebrations in the library, Librarian 7 shared a rather interesting story about a generic birthday card that use to be passed around among the colleagues in the department, each of whom would keep it until it was another colleague's birthday. This story could be interpreted as an impor-tant consideration of the organization's culture and to someone unfamiliar with the organization, or even to the specific department, it might provide an opportunity to learn more about the social rules that existed there. When asked if Librarian 7 had shared the story, the reply was: "No [laughs] I actually just now thought of it when we were talking about it, I completely forgot about it actually".

Lapses in memory when it comes to communicating, or telling an orga-nizational story with colleagues, can be affected by many factors. Among the most salient is that the participants did not seem to think there was any particular importance or urgency to share the story. Many of the stories that were not shared, and therefore remained untold, were the lighthearted and amusing type; these characteristics may also have contributed to the conscious or unconscious decision of the participants to keep silent and not share the stories with others. But the fact that a story is lighthearted, funny, or amusing does not mean that it is less valuable (Snowden, 1999). The most obvious value that can be pointed out here is for the new members of the organization who are trying to familiarise themselves with their new work environment. Lapses in memory can be a real enemy of a story, particularly if valuable knowledge about the organization—whether cultural, tacit or explicit—is carried in it. Another factor to consider in the lapse in memory is the nature of the interview method itself. Here organizational members were explicitly asked questions designed to elicit storytelling related to their organization, this condition is a rather unnatural one that is not necessarily going to manifest itself in the day-to-day activities in most organizations.

The opposite of a lapse in memory was the intentional omission of a story. Here an intentional omission of a story refers to situations in which a participant made a conscious decision not to share certain stories with their colleagues. For example, Librarian 6 expressed apprehension to sharing negative stories, or those which involved "voicing frustration". According to Librarian 6: ". . . I don't really want to [share negative stories], I mean overall it's a good place to work. . .". Here Librarian 6 expresses reluctance to share stories that reflected a negative view of the work environment, particularly with newer members of the organization. This action reflects issues of trust, where Librarian 6 does not feel safe sharing stories with people who do not have known social connections in the organization; those who have not entered the circle of colleagues yet. It can also be a situation in which Librarian 6 wants to protect the newer colleagues from the negative stories in an attempt to shield them from any negative interactions in their new job, or does not want to "bring people down" (Librarian 6). This last point is better explained in the assertion that the library is "a good place to work" so silence here can be justified as a face saving mechanism utilised with newcomers who are still not fully socialised into the organization. The same negative stories however, are shared freely with another colleague ". . . who's been here a while. . .". according to Librarian 6.

Many stories were not shared because the participants thought that it was not needed, since the events were not stories per se according to their view. The main misconception was that a story did not need to be shared with others because it was "fact based" (Librarian 9), because everybody knew about it (Librarian 17) or because nobody was affected (Librarian 9). In the first case, Librarian 9 was referring to a specific incident that involved locating equipment outside of the library and how she relayed the story of what had happened to a group of students who were going to work at the reference desk from the group of librarians who initially had to find out a way to locate the equipment on campus. In the interview Librarian 9 informed the researcher about the incidents that had proven particularly challenging at work:

> . . . there were some students for a class who were supposed to have
> a video camera and we don't have those here but somebody told them

that we did so we found out who on campus actually had that and then sent it out to make sure that everyone knew 'Refer them to this office, we don't have one'.

When asked to give more details about the story of how they came about the information of where to locate the video cameras on campus, Librarian 9 explained that this was not a story because it was "fact based". This aligns with a modern interpretation of events in which storytelling is "silenced by facts" (Gabriel, 2000: 15). Librarian 9 shared a story of how they came to find the material they were searching for, but does not recognise the narration of the events as storytelling because what was being communicated were hard facts. The perception is that stories belong to the realm of fantasy, contrary to what is told to the researcher. Here Librarian 9 communicates the process to her colleagues as non-negotiable facts and that leaves no room for interpretation by others; negating in this process the existence of storytelling.

Similarly untold stories identified in this research were stories that are just not recognised as untold because there were other witnesses to a specific event. This is the case of Librarian 17 who had a disagreement with a supervisor which descended into a very loud and public argument. These events took place right in the front door of the library:

Interviewer: And have you ever shared that story with somebody else?
Librarian 17: No, not really. Everybody knew about it, this happened right out of, we were walking into the building and it was pretty loud.

Here the story was not told to anyone else, and therefore becomes and untold story, because other people were witnesses to the events that took place. Since plenty of people saw the incident unfold the retelling of the story is seen by Librarian 17 as redundant and unnecessary. What Librarian 17 does not acknowledge is that, although this incident took place many years ago, he is still not telling the story of what happened to newer members of the organization who were not part of it when the original events took place. In this case it seems like Librarian 17 is keeping this story secret from other members of the organization who are not aware of these events as a face saving mechanism in order to avoid embarrassment (Goffman, 1967). This however, was not indicated in the interview, and the story was shared with the researcher as a fun, amusing incident that had taken place many years ago and that reflected the stresses of the job, not as a story shared with colleagues.

Another incident that became an untold story had to do with a technical malfunction at the library that happened during Librarian 9's shift at the reference desk. Despite making mention of it to other colleagues at the reference desk, Librarian 9 indicated that since others were not affected there was no need to share the story of the incident. ". . . I shared it with the people who were at the desk with me but not with anybody else because it ended being resolved by the end of the hour". In this case, Librarian 9 indicates that since the problem was solved early and with apparent minimal consequences, there was no need to share the story with colleagues. The story, in a way lacked a 'story', since the complication that produced the short lived crisis was solved immediately by the technical team and did not have major consequences for the library's operations.

> . . . because it didn't end up affecting anybody else I did call down to our technology [lab] on the [library floor] level to see if they were affected and they weren't. I guess our [branch], library [name] too; [branch] library called to see if our [computer network] was down too and it was just, it seems like it was an entire system problem.
>
> (Librarian 9)

SILENCED STORIES

Untold stories were not only initiated by or as part of the decision process for the individuals who participated in this research. In some cases the participants had been silenced by their organizations, or they later learned of stories that had been silenced by other members of the organization. In one case in particular the silencing was mainly due to the intention of keeping a colleague's privacy regarding a very delicate health issue. In this case Librarian 20 reported a situation with a supervisee that was not widely shared among colleagues: ". . . I think [a story] fewer people know about is that one of our colleagues . . . tried to commit suicide; only a few of us knew the complete circumstances. . .". According to Librarian 20:

> . . . she had [degenerative disease], she didn't show up at work for a couple of days and we finally heard, we were worried about her, because we had no word from her and then we found out that she was in hospital and that she was on suicide watch and that they found her in her home passed out.

Librarian 19 found out about the colleague's illness and consequent suicide attempt from a third party, but decided to keep silent about the situation:

> Well I think first of all I was [supervisory position] at the time [for] our department and the [department head] at the time decided that it was a personal issue and that if she wanted to tell people about what happened she could . . .

In this case, both Librarian 19 and the department head decided to keep silent about the situation and not share the story with other colleagues because this was a personal matter and so the decision to tell the story should be made by the person affected. This was described by Librarian 20 as a "very sad" situation and one that the few people who knew about it did not share any details other than telling colleagues that this person was hospitalised. The decision to keep silent on the matter in this case stems from both Librarian 19's position as a supervisor and agreement with a superior's decision. This aligns with research that points to silence on a matter as a reflection of concern and intention not to hurt another individual and commanding silence as a component of authority (Glenn, 2004).

Another compelling case was that of Librarian 4, who was silenced by her superiors when there was a major change in hours of operation in her library. This particular library had staffing issues that had forced a reduction in hours of operation during the week, imposing a late night closing time. According to Librarian 4, this was motivated due to the lack of personnel available to work the remaining hours.

> So this was the middle of the fall semester a couple of years ago, the [head of the library] decided to go ahead and reinstate 24 hour service, as head of the [library department] I was told, and I was told not to tell the staff, for whatever reason. This person wanted to disseminate that information. And she did but did not told [sic.] the [library department].

As a result of the administrator's decision to not allow Librarian 4 to disseminate the information regarding the new hours of operation, the library department in charge of staffing the library during those hours did not learn about the change after the new schedule had been agreed upon by the administration. Since this situation took place in the middle of the semester, new hires had to be done in a very short period of time when finding suitable candidates for the job was the hardest. Librarian 4 also explained "I felt horrible. I did. As a manager, because I knew what was going to be going on and I was put in the position not telling my people about it. . .".

Here Librarian 4 was expected to keep silent about the changes and not tell her own supervisees in order for the head of the library to make the announcement. The problem was that by not allowing Librarian 4 to make the announcement, the staff under her supervision had no participation in a decision that directly affected them. Here forcing Librarian 4 into silence turned into a case of the authority figure exerting their power (Glenn, 2004). By silencing her regarding the news of the change of schedule, the story Librarian 4 told her employees changed; it became a story of how the superiors exercised their authority by requiring her silence on a matter, while she was powerless against their decision.

SELECTIVELY SHARED STORIES

In addition to the untold stories, some stories were selectively shared. These stories where shared with specific groups of colleagues or carefully picked individuals only. Sometimes the nature of the story itself made it a delicate manner that lends itself to be shared only with people who are affected by the events it depicts. This was the case expressed when Librarian 10 only shared the story of a former colleague with a new colleague because of noticeable similarities in each colleagues' experiences. The story involved a former director of the department who would not renew an employee's contract. The general understanding, according to Librarian 10, was that the reason was that the employee suffered from a minor disability. Librarian 10 expressed that upon learning that the director was not planning on renewing his contract, the aforementioned colleague confronted the director and informed that if the reason for this decision was his disability he was going to notify the human resources department and would even consider legal action. This employee later left the job for unrelated reasons, but when another employee with a different disability joined the department, Librarian 10 started noticing this new employee was having a similar experience to that of the former colleague. At this point Librarian 10 made the decision to tell the story of what had happened between the former colleague and the supervisor to this new colleague.

When the researcher asked Librarian 10 the reason for this decision, Librarian 10 replied:

> . . . because I wanted to let him know that if there was, if he felt like that was going to happen to him and if he felt like he needed me to help him in anything uhm or anything like that I would [support his claim].

In this case, Librarian 10 did not indicate mentioning the story, of which she thought was unfair treatment of a former colleague, with other employees with the exception of the one employee that was involved in a similar situation. According to Librarian 10's own account, the act of sharing the story with the new colleague was to make this person more cognizant of the work environment: ". . . there's [sic] a lot of things that might have happened that he might have just blown off but instead he knew to pay attention to them".

Some stories were not shared with any other organizational member but with other reference librarian's as illustrated in this exchange with Librarian 15:

> Interviewer: So have you shared what happened to you? Have you told other people?
> Librarian 15: Oh yeah. Everything that happens to me unless it's truly embarrassing and makes me look bad, I'm probably going to tell them; even if it does make me look bad, I'm probably going to tell them.

Interviewer: Why?

Librarian 15: I don't know uh, why do I tell people those stories? I don't know, I mean who else is going to appreciate it [the embarrassing moments] other than another librarian. Or maybe I feel bad and I want to expiate myself with something that's personally embarrassing, but uhm you know it just, it depends.

The embarrassing moments that Librarian 15 refers to in this exchange are the kind of story that members of a group share with each other in what Goffman (1959) defines as the team. Here, "another librarian" is a member of the team and sharing embarrassing moments can be categorised as sharing a dark secret. This type of secret is kept from the audience but is shared among members of the team in order to maintain ". . . the quality and consistency of the performance that is staged for [library] users" (Quinn, 2005: 337); that is, the performance of the knowledgeable, self-composed librarian. The embarrassing moments Librarian 15 talks about in this interview excerpt are not going to be shared freely with everyone because they are embarrassing, and this would involve a loss of face (Goffman, 1967), but they are likely to be shared with members of the team as a secret to be kept from the audience, in this case the library users and other library employees.

In a similar case there were some stories that were shared with colleagues from the same department, but they were not shared with colleagues from other departments in the library. For example, Librarian 12 pointed out that the stories about a specific period of time when the reference department was doing a search for a new head were shared only among members of the reference department, excluding other colleagues at the library. The main reason for keeping the stories only to members of the same department according to Librarian 12 was:

I don't think, you know, I don't [think] it went ever, 'cause I don't think it was so traumatic that we felt like we had to share it you know, and I suppose there's some sense, there's no sense in the, you know, the [reference department] crap being spread [laughs] throughout the whole organization.

The act of spreading the reference department's 'crap' throughout the whole organization could be seen as a dark secret (Goffman, 1959). Here, revealing the conflicts and disagreements the group had while searching for the new department head was mainly a way to maintain an image of a well-adjusted team that had members working together in order to find the right individual for the job, someone that was to be ". . . a first among equals. . ." (Librarian 12). This image was inconsistent with the reality of working in an organization that might just appoint somebody who just ". . . very clearly wants to be a supervisor. . ." (Librarian 12) without consulting with the rest of the team. By keeping the stories regarding the search for the new supervisor as a team secret, the reference department in this institution, presented themselves as accepting of their organization's decisions; however, there was a lot of resistance to bring someone new to the department who was not approved by the team members. Librarian 12 even expressed that the team had already chosen who they wanted as their new department head: ". . . we all had a person in mind that we thought would be really good".

Some stories were shared exclusively with people from outside of the organization. This is the case of Librarian 20 who reported sharing a story of an administrative possible decision to close a library branch with a fellow librarian who does not work at the organization: "I don't know if I really should, but I did talk to a colleague who doesn't work in this institution, who works in another state. Is a librarian colleague and I just happened to tell that person. . .". Librarian 20 shared this information with this other librarian in order to get a feel for what the person thought of the move. This participant indicated that the administration's move to close the branch library was a surprising one, and that it was not taken well by the library employees and the students at the university. Despite the seemingly personal purpose for sharing the information, Librarian 20 still questions the decision to share the information with somebody from outside the organization.

In this case, the stories that were not shared had negative connotations for both individuals and teams; due to this, they were very selectively shared excluding entire groups of colleagues from the storytelling process. These stories were shared with some individuals, either because the people sharing the stories thought the addressee was directly affected by the contents of the story and could use it as a lessons learned or because sharing the story would have had a negative impact on the team, particularly damaging their image or breaking their performance and destroying the team's image in what Goffman (1959) refers to as "gaffes" (p. 209).

CONCLUSION

Silence here is seen as the opposite of storytelling. A natural enemy of organizational storytelling, or at least the other side of the storytelling coin. One which needs to be understood in order to fully understand organizational storytelling and all its potential benefits for organizations. Stories which have gone cold here were classified into specific groups: untold stories, silenced stories, and selectively shared stories. There were two main circumstances that contributed to untold stories: lack of physical proximity among colleagues and lapses in memory. Proximity is a recognised inhibitor for organizational narratives of all types; according to Gabriel (2004) organizations' control of multiple factors including movement and space are at the root of this issue. Lapses in memory mainly belonged to three types of situation: no urgency to tell the story due to its seeming lack of importance, light hearted nature of the story itself and the fact that the participants were being requested to produce stories as part of a research interview which would be a situation unlikely to be faced in their day-to-day activities in the organization. The lack of a sense of urgency has been discussed previously as a factor that contributes to silence (Glenn, 2004), while the lighthearted nature of stories in organizations has been excluded as an indicator of a story's lack of value for organizational purposes (Snowden, 1999; James & Minnis, 2004).

Other factors that contributed to a story going cold included intentional omissions due to confusing the story with hard facts, the perception by the participants that the story was so widely known that there was no need to repeat it, and not recognising the generalisability of the story due to the contained nature of the incident which can be seen as not affecting anyone. These omissions are part of the narrative contract in which the storyteller is allowed by the audience to include a number of poetic interventions, including silencing events that interfere with a specific storyline, in the name of providing an experience of storytelling (Gabriel, 2008). The relationship between stories and hard facts has been a conflicted one that has been recognised as a reason for not studying organizational stories in the past and its fairly recent inclusion in the organizational literature and is rooted in modernity (Gabriel, 2000).

Some stories went cold really early in their development, as is the case of the silenced stories. These stories were not untold because the participants' own will, but other factors that influenced the decision to keep silent. The most common reasons for this dealt with silence as a way to avoid hurting another individual and being committed to silence regarding an event in order for a supervisor to ascertain their authority (Glenn, 2004). These stories become part of the power structure in the organization, its bureaucratic division of labour and hierarchical structure of power.

In addition to untold stories and silenced stories, some stories were selectively shared by the participants. This selectivity means that individuals will not freely share all stories with all members in their organization, but will pick and choose who they share stories and which parts of the story they share with very specific colleagues, instead of uniformly with all members of the organization. A discussion of organizational stories must also recognise that individuals present their own versions of a story in the organization and stories that may imply a loss of face or produce embarrassment are likely to be omitted; the omission acting as a way to save face (Goffman, 1959, 1967). Stories were also treated as secrets that were shared only with certain members of the organization, most specifically members of the same team; in some cases the reference department acted as a team, and in some cases the team was located outside of the department and even the library as was the case of those participants who shared their stories with members of other organizations. The relationship between storytelling and face saving was also pointed out as one of the most direct reasons for a story to be selectively shared.

In general, the negative stories or those with bad connotations both for the individual and the organization were the least likely to be shared or to be shared only with a selected group of colleagues. Because of this situation, the contributions of organizational storytelling should be reconsidered; studies such as those by Geiger and Antonacopoulou (2009) point to organizational stories' potential for promoting organizational inertia by constructing a self-sustaining frame of reference which prevents organizations from questioning the principles underlying its past successes. This in turn leads to the organization's silencing or ignoring any divergent narratives, which potentially limits the capacity of organizations to deal with change, specifically adapting to a changing environment. This is of paramount importance for organizations which depend heavily on innovation in the face of constant change. In this case, silence can be a deterrent to processes of organizational knowledge creation particularly because it obstructs the process of knowledge externalization.

These implications are not only valid for libraries, but equally apply to other types of organizations which operate in fast changing environments. The need for innovation is generally understood as an essential component for competitive advantage in both for profit and not-for-profit organizations (Hislop, 2010). Therefore silence becomes a common threat, by disrupting the process of knowledge transfer and knowledge creation.

Organizational stories are not criminal cases to be solved, there are no culprits to be identified and brought to justice; however, some organizational stories deal with the unjust, the unethical, even the illegal, and also the embarrassing. The organizational stories discussed here were neither crimes nor criminal investigations; but just as criminal investigations can remain inconclusive and be swallowed by oblivion and silence, so can stories remain untold, and just like a cold case, can be reignited if the right elements come together.

REFERENCES

Alire, C. A., & Edward, G. E. (2010). *Academic Librarianship*. New York: Neal-Schuman Publishers.

Association of College and Research Libraries. (2011, May 11). *Statement on the Terminal Professional Degree for Academic Librarians*. Retrieved from http://www.ala.org/acrl/standards/statementterminal.

Berger, P. L., & Luckmann, T. (1966). *The Social Construction of Reality: A Treatise in the Sociology of Knowledge*. New York: Anchor Books.

Boje, D. M. (1991). The storytelling organizations: A study of story in an office-supply firm. *Administrative Science Quarterly*, 36(1): 106–127.

Boje, D. M. (2008). *Storytelling Organizations*. Thousand Oaks, CA: Sage.

Bruneau, T. (2009). Silence, silences and silencing. In S. W. Littlejohn & K. A. Foss (Eds.), *Encyclopedia of Communication Theory* (pp. 881–886). Thousand Oaks, CA: Sage.

Cassell, K. A., & Hiremath, U. (2011). *Reference and Information Services in the 21st Century*. New York: Neal-Schuman Publishers.

Choo, C. W. (1998). *The Knowing Organization: How Organizations use Information to Construct Meaning, Create Knowledge, and Make Decisions*. New York: Oxford University Press.

Connell, N. A. D. (2006). Organizational storytelling. In D. G. Schwartz, (Ed.), *Encyclopedia of Knowledge Management* (pp. 721–727). London: Idea Group Reference.

Corbin, J., & Strauss, A. C. (2008). *Basics of Qualitative Research: Techniques and Procedures for Developing Grounded Theory*. Thousand Oaks, CA: Sage.

Dalkir, K. (2005). *Knowledge Management in Theory and Practice*. Burlington, MA: Elsevier.

Detmering, R., & Sproles, C. (2012). Forget the desk job: Current roles and responsibilities in entry-level reference job advertisements. *College & Research Libraries*, *73*(6): 543–555.

Dey, I. (1993). *Qualitative Data Analysis: A Use-friendly Guide for Social Scientists*. London: Routledge.

Fisher, W. R. (1984). Narration as a human communication paradigm: The case of public moral argument. *Communication Monographs*, *51*(1): 1–22.

Gabriel, Y. (2000). *Storytelling in Organizations: Facts, Fictions, and Fantasies*. Oxford: Oxford University Press.

Gabriel, Y. (2004). The narrative veil: Truth and untruths in storytelling. In Y. Gabriel (Ed.), *Myths, Stories and Organizations: Premodern Narratives for Our Times* (pp. 17–31). Oxford: Oxford University Press.

Gabriel, Y. (2008). Seduced by the text: The desire to be deceived in story, memoir and drama. *Tamara—Journal for Critical Organizational Inquiry*, *7*(2): 154–167.

Geiger, D., & Antonacopoulou, E. (2009). Narratives and organizational dynamics. *The Journal of Applied Behavioral Science*, *45*(3): 411–436.

Georges, R. A. (1969). Toward an understanding of storytelling. *Journal of American Folklore*, *82*(326): 313–328.

Glenn, C. (2004). *Unspoken: A Rhetoric of Silence*. Carbondale: Southern Illinois University Press.

Goffman, E. (1959). *The Presentation of Self in Everyday Life*. New York: Anchor Books.

Goffman, E. (1967). *Interaction Ritual: Essays on Face-to-Face Behavior*. New York: Pantheon Books.

Head, A. J., & Eisenberg, M. B. (2010). How today's college students use Wikipedia for course–related research. *First Monday*, *15*(3). Retrieved from: http://firstmonday.org/ojs/index.php/fm/article/view/2830/2476.

Herring, M. Y. (2005). A gaggle of Googles. *Internet Reference Services Quarterly*, *10*(3–4): 37–44.

Herring, M. Y. (2008). Fool's gold: Why the Internet is no substitute for a library. *Journal of Library Administration*, *27*(1/2): 29–53.

Hislop, D. (2010). *Knowledge Management in Organizations* (2nd ed.). Oxford: Oxford University Press.

James, C. H., & Minnis, W. C. (2004). Organizational storytelling: It makes sense. *Business Horizons*, *47*(4): 23–32.

Johannesen, R. L. (1974). The functions of silence: A plea for communication research. *Western Speech*, *38*(1): 25–35.

Kaufman, P. (2007). It's not your parent's library anymore: Challenges and opportunities in the new webs of complexity. *Journal of Library Administration*, 46(1): 5–26.

Kurzon, D. (2007). Towards a typology of silence. *Journal of Pragmatics*, 39(10): 1673–1688.

Lim, S. (2009). How and why do college students use Wikipedia? *Journal of the American Society for Information Science and Technology*, 60(11): 2189–2202.

MacMorrow, N. (2001). Knowledge management: An Introduction. *Annual Review of Information Science and Technology*, 35: 381–422.

Martin, L.A. (1996). *Organizational Structure of Libraries*. Lanham, MD: The Scarecrow Press.

McCracken, G. (1988). *The Long Interview*. London: Sage.

Morrison, M.A., Haley, E., Sheehan, K.B., & Taylor, R.E. (2002). *Using Qualitative Research in Advertising: Strategies, Techniques, and Applications*. Thousand Oaks, CA: Sage.

Moran, B.B., Stueart, R.D., & Morner, C.J. (2013). *Library and Information Center Management* (3rd ed.) Santa Barbara, CA: Libraries Unlimited.

Musacchio Adorisio, A.L. (2009). *Storytelling in Organizations: From Theory to Empirical Research*. New York: Palgrave Macmillan.

Nonaka, I. (2007). The knowledge-creating company. *Harvard Business Review* (July–August): 162–171.

Nonaka, I., & Takeuchi, H. (1995). *The Knowledge-Creating Company: How Japanese Companies Create the Dynamics of Innovation*. New York: Oxford University Press.

Patton, M.Q. (1990). *Qualitative Evaluation and Research Methods*. Newbury Park: Sage.

Orr, J. (1990). Sharing knowledge, celebrating identity: Community memory in a service culture. In D. Middleton, & D. Edwards (Eds.), *Collective Remembering* (pp. 169–189). London: Sage.

Orr, J. (1996). *Talking about Machines*. Ithaca, NY: Cornell University Press.

Quinn, B. (2005). A dramaturgical perspective on academic libraries. *Libraries and the Academy*, 5(3): 329–352.

Ramsey, S.J. (1998). Interactions between Americans and Japanese: Considerations of communication Style. In M.J. Bennett (Ed.), *Basic Concepts of Intercultural Communication: Selected Readings*, (pp. 111–130). Boston: Intercultural Press.

Reference and User Services Association. (2008, January 14). *Definitions of Reference*. Retrieved from http://www.ala.org/rusa/resources/guidelines/definitionsreference.

Rhodes, C., & Brown, A.D. (2005). Narrative, organizations and research. *International Journal of Management Reviews*, 7(3): 167–188.

Rubin, R.E. (2004). *Foundations of Library and Information Science* (2nd ed.). New York: Neal Schuman Publishers.

Snowden, D. (1999). Storytelling: An old skill in a new context. *Business Information Review*, 16(1): 30–37.

Tsoukas, H., & Vladimirou, E. (2001). What is organizational knowledge? *Journal of Management Studies*, 38(7): 973–993.

Weick, K. (1995). *Sensemaking in Organizations*. Thousand Oaks, CA: Sage.

8 Story-Spaces and Transformation
The Caravan Project

Maria Daskalaki, Alexandra Saliba,
Stratis Vogiatzis, and Thekla Malamou

INTRODUCTION

The narrative paradigm with a long-standing tradition in sociology, literary theory, psychology, and hermeneutics primarily claims that individuals make sense of experiences through narratives, stories or performances (Fisher, 1985; Goffman, 1959; Ricoeur, 1988). Narratives and stories are relational and collective accounts of events (Boje, 2011; Boje, Rosile, & Gardner, 2007; Gabriel, 2000; Czarniawska, 1998, 1999, 2004; Czarniawska-Joerges & Guillet de Monthoux, P. 1994; Gabriel, 2013; Gabriel & Connell, 2010). Each narrative level entails multiple, interacting narratives that may overlap or be contradictory (Hawkins & Saleem, 2012).

Narratives are not always deliberate and coherent; they can be spontaneous acts of interpretation, improvised, situated, contested, fragmented, incomplete, and embodied performances (Boje, 2011; Cunliffe & Coupland, 2012). Social narratives are embedded in personal stories (Gabriel, 2000), the journeys that individuals embark in order to make sense of their experiences. Thus, stories provide a platform for shared meaning of what is happening, has happened or is going to occur and a shared platform for action. Stories do not represent a 'reality out there' but imaginative constructions or 'fabulations' (Ricoeur, 1988), outcome of performance, co-construction, and interaction. More importantly, the field of relational storytelling studies has provided attention to "key research foci: specifically current concerns for intertextuality, heteroglossia, materiality and flux" (Hitchin, 2014: 59).

Yet, unlike stories and narratives, that have been studied as unfinished, fragmented, and intertextual phenomena, space has been predominantly examined like a fixed and permanent physical structure, with limited studies exploring how the "public domain comes into being in flux, often extremely temporarily" (Hajer & Reijndorp, 2001: 14; see also Massey, 2005). In this chapter, we discuss the co-construction of temporary spaces that emerge when stories become re-territorialised. Space and stories, we will suggest, are entangled and co-construct story-spaces.[1] These are emergent territories that are constituted through irregular, temporary and 'mobile practices' (Thrift, 2000; Cresswell & Merriman, 2011).

We build upon the dialogue on territoriality and organizing (Marechal, Linstead, & Munro, 2013) and explore the process of re-territorialisation of stories and the spaces of transformation that emerge. By adopting the concept of transformative creativity—adapting Boden's (2003) work—we discuss an artistic, creative initiative namely, the *Caravan Project*[2] that helps us explore story spaces in the making. We will suggest that creative initiatives, when re-enacted in diverse social contexts, have the capacity to co-produce spaces that elicit untold stories. Story-spaces, in turn, are a product of a co-constitutive process that can lead to a new way to connect, relate, and organize social relations.

We focus on a social context in flux—namely, the ongoing financial crisis in Greece—where a radical redefinition of values, needs, and lifestyles occurs. Rising unemployment, poverty, deprivation, and social inequality are having direct effect on relationships with the self and others as well as the collective definitions of culture and society. In a context like this, individuals and groups enact and modify existing narratives, try to create new meanings, ante-narratives, and meta-narratives in the living moment (Boje, 2011). Through character-based, short documentaries, *The Caravan* gathers and diffuses everyday life stories that have the power to unsettle relations and interactions, and co-construct spaces of collective reflection and transformative social experiences. These spaces of transformation give voice to the marginalised, often voiceless communities that persistently remain underrepresented in recent accounts of the financial crisis.

Thus, in situations of acute change, we are wondering: how can the impulse of telling untold stories be enhanced? How can we create new spaces, or transform spaces so they can maintain their potential to elicit untold stories? The chapter is structured as follows: first, we discuss the *Caravan Project* and the processes through which it co-constructs spaces of transformation. Secondly the methodological approach of our work is presented, stressing the impact of documentary filmmaking in eliciting untold stories. Finally, we present the first instances of the re-territorialisation of the *Caravan* stories, the untold story-spaces that emerged and conclude with the challenges and opportunities presented when studying stories as transformative socio-spatial events.

UNTOLD STORIES AS SPACES OF TRANSFORMATION: THE CARAVAN PROJECT

In this section, we present the *Caravan Project* as an instance of transformative creativity, a 'mobile practice' (Thrift, 2000) that changes rigid and fixed spaces allowing for untold stories to emerge. Recognising the intertextuality of stories (Izak, 2014), we view them as open invitations to 'the Other', a creative process that involves the transformation of something into something else.

Figure 8.1 The Caravan Project Documentaries: A Collage of Images (Photographs and Collage by the Caravan Project).

THE CARAVAN PROJECT

The *Caravan Project is* a visual ethnography consisting of a series of documentaries that narrate stories of people who despite the crisis continue to dream and creatively deal with the harsh realities of their everyday life. Employing portrait and landscape photography, field-recordings, texts, and predominantly documentary filmmaking, the *Caravan Project* team has been travelling all over Greece to collect stories from cities and islands to the most isolated geographically areas in the country. We embarked on this journey in 2011 aiming to give voice to stories that are neglected by the mainstream media. A caravan vehicle was our principle means of transport but also a research tool that kept our practice mobile enabling 'an ethnographic journey' to locate characters and unveil stories.

Once the documentaries were completed, we decided to move beyond established modes of distribution (theatrical release, national and international television broadcast, festival run, or DVD sales) and screen our work in 'temporary autonomous zones' (Bey, 2011) including isolated village squares and co-operative cafes, universities, schools, and several social centres. Evidently, audience engagement is a key component in a process during which newly co-constituted spaces attain a transformative capacity. Below we explain further our conceptualisation of untold stories in relation to spaces of transformation.

UNTOLD STORIES: SPACES OF TRANSFORMATION

Although, according to Boden (2003), working within an existing space can produce interesting outcomes (exploratory creativity), a higher form of creativity can only result from making changes to space. Radical, qualitative changes describe transformational creativity that challenges established and well-defined boundaries. Transformation extends the conceptual space out by devising a new poetic form. If transformation is to occur, the conceptual space must be embedded within a broader system of possibilities. The 'transformation of spaces', Boden (2003) continues, highlights a practised form of creative artefacts (in our case, the *Caravan* films) as these become part of diverse contexts.

Thus, we propose, spaces of transformation, "are not objective, predetermined structures, but processes of social construction and meaning creation, wherein social order is negotiated" (Hardy &Phillips, 1998: 218). For example, when the stories are shared in places such as city squares, spontaneous gatherings, or community/public spaces, they enact story-spaces. These story-spaces are constantly re-constituted and re-enacted every time they become temporarily inhabited (as shown below, the two school story-spaces and the prison story-space) by the creative artefacts and the various audiences. In this respect, they remain always in the making, allowing untold stories to emerge.

Hence, we pursue an approach towards the irregular and the unexpected, another way to theorise organizing by expanding approaches to account for unbounded and ephemeral sites of intra-connectivity, sites of 'intra-action' (Barad, 2003). These sites re-order organizational practices as temporary territories that constitute encounters of flows and fixities. We thus move away from statically relating entities in stories stressing the importance of the mutually constituting element of relationships, dynamically forming each party of the relationship through ongoing intra-play of discourses and materiality. This process is both dynamic and strategic with the latter being as important as the former, for it is precisely what captures

> the potentiality of potentiality, by deriving a portfolio of the various ways of inducing the efficacy to operate which also describe new states. And some of these states will be new hybrid actors, glimpsed for the first time at the beginning of the runway as they prepare to go about their work.
>
> (Thrift, 2006: 145)

Institutions should not be fixed structures but creative spaces where change is embedded in processes and interactions. Untold stories—due to their intertextuality (Izak, 2014; Hitchin, 2014)—can inspire and allow for this change, co-constituting platforms where boundaries are challenged. Encouraging open and fluid social engagements, we thus stress that story-spaces

> inspire creativity and enhance possibility through emergent . . . territories and inhabitation of emergent identities. In essence, the stories of new formations have not yet been written, they float in the absence of any formalised communities and can be 'narrated' in a creative exploratory state of becoming.
>
> (Daskalaki & Mould, 2013: 14–15)

The *Caravan Project,* a non-institutionalised community, co-constructs emergent territories, changing the spaces, which it inhabits. In the following sections, we will discuss three of these spaces, a prison and two educational settings and describe how untold stories surfaced in these contexts. Before this, however, we present our documentary filmmaking perspective.

METHODOLOGY: DOCUMENTARY FILMMAKING

In this section, we explain how we filmed in marginalised spaces in Greece (remote areas, grassroots movements, excluded communities, and so forth) and our approach to co-constructing new story-spaces where the untold can be triggered. That is, we explain how by sharing the film documentaries in unusual dissemination platforms (such as prisons and schools), we enable spaces of transformation to be co-constituted and re-constituted as the stories of the films become (re-)territorialised.

Our guiding principle was the intimacy of the relationship that we developed with the individuals and the collectivities that we encountered while on the move. The documentaries that we shot were the result of an intense experience with the people we met.[3] This bonding with our main characters defined our narrative structure and cinematography. We were not observing a reality; we became an active part of it, a joint and almost intuitive decision. Essentially, our documentaries were the result of an intense sharing and this was what gave a naturalistic touch in our films and opened a window in an alter reality of our character(s).

Visually, we focused on the hidden details that carry central meanings associated to both the emotional and intellectual worlds. Inspired by the writings of Paul Valery (1962), we envisioned the coordination of the soul, the eye, and the hand and ultimately fashion the raw material of experience, on our own in a solid useful and unique way (Benjamin, 1936/1968). The uniqueness of the characters' experiences and their values (such as freedom, creativity, solidarity, equality, and diversity) convey the narrative hook in our films.[4] In each of these films, the inciting incident is not a special event or an action but the most casual routine of an alter reality. "An inside story, a transcript, an interview, a film, and a recurrent story can be acted on to provide a shape that is both generative and suitably complex. . . . It's all there if you take the time to look and feel" (Weick, 2012: 150). It is this artistic yet ethnographic approach to documentary filmmaking that constructs the *Caravan's* films as incidents of transformative creativity.

FINDINGS: CO-CONSTRUCTING STORY-SPACES

In this chapter, we employ three contexts, a prison, a 'second chance' (adult) school and finally, a school at a socially deprived area of Piraeus to demonstrate the re-territorialisation of artistic artefacts and the co-constitution of story-spaces. To begin with, we screened the documentary *The Blind Fisherman* (2011a)[5] at the drug detoxification unit at a correctional prison. This documentary is about a fisherman, Mr. Yiannis, who at the age of 11, lost his vision and his left arm after an accident. Through the fisherman's story the audience met a vibrant character who has not lost his passion for fishing at the age of 84. He narrates:

> Just imagine that you are blind with no arms and you are alone in a boat rowing and fishing. One would say 'where are you going?', thinking that I cannot see . . . I go wherever I want with my boat. I go fishing. I even surprised myself often wondering how did I get here alone without eyesight, something quite hard to do. . . . I always dream and my dreams are always related to the sea. It brings me joy and fulfills my life.
> (Another World is Here, The Caravan Project, "The Blind Fisherman", 2011a)

The screening venue was packed and everyone remained silent, concentrating on the story. After the screening the inmates participated in a vibrant dialogue, which lasted more than an hour. "For the first time we had the opportunity to watch a documentary based on a personal story and talk to the filmmakers for issues like the meaning of life . . . which we only discuss with our therapist" (Participant A). The audience wanted to learn more and discuss the story of this man and our relationship with him during the shooting of the documentary.

It was clear from the discussion that followed that the element of self-surprise, that characterised Mr. Yiannis' story, captured the audience attention. An inmate repeated Mr. Yiannis' words: "I don't really know how I do it, I have a map inside my head . . . I can go anywhere I want to go . . . I am not afraid" (Participant B). Driven by that, another man cried out "he can manage his life being blind and without a hand and we cannot manage a bag of 'white dust' . . ." (Participant C). Some members of the audience expressed their gratitude after the screening and told us how this story "is definitely going to change them" (Participant D).

Another event involved a 'second chance' school for adults. The audience consisted of returning high school students from different classes, aged from 18 to 60 years old. All of them were facing serious difficulties making a living as well as trying to graduate. Their teachers have been trying to keep them motivated and inspire an interest in school education. Yet, "they are only interested in playing football and nothing else . . ." (teacher). Three different documentaries were shared: first, *The Blind Fisherman* (already mentioned above); second, *The Boat Carpenter Paporias* (2011b)[6] which is about a ship carpenter who is struggling to preserve and spread the knowledge of his craftwork; third, *Black Land*, Black Land (2012a)[7] the story of an Egyptian immigrant, Mohamed, who during the forest fires in the island of Chios volunteered to help in fire-fighting. Mohamed explains:

> I feel connected to this place. What can one do? Your village is on fire. You must act. You might burn alive but you will die as a human.
> (Another World Is Here, The Caravan Project, 2011b)

The students were clearly moved by his commitment to a place that he now consider 'his own village'. His devotion to fire-fighting, the students commented "clearly challenges extreme right wing discourses that discriminate and marginalize immigrants" (Participant, E) and shows that "when it comes to natural disasters we are all equally affected; we feel the pain and we react, it does not matter where one was born" (Participant F).

In *The Boat Carpenter Paporias*, the carpenter explains:

> Crafts, crafts open up your mind. A craft is not just about survival. Crafts are also about the concept of creativity, and the feeling that the craftsman feels after all. It makes you more patient, okay? It teaches

you to complete things, you know? I mean, you won't leave anything unfinished. . . . I believe that it is completely irresponsible and reprehensible, for this to be happening to Greece (eradication of traditional occupations), to a land like this, where half of Greece is made up of islands. Where half of its civilization is islands, and half of its economy is islands. You are breaking apart from a person's feelings; you are breaking apart from what one needs.

(Vogiatzis & Malamou, 2011)

After this, a student confessed to us: "It's unbelievable some of us would sit in class for more than 10 minutes without a cigarette break" (Participant G). A 45-year-old man started talking about his struggle with depression and another, clearly upset by the story of *Paporias*, commented "greed has led people to abandon their villages . . . traditional knowledge is getting lost" (Participant H).

Clearly, a traditional educational setting became an interactive platform where untold stories were shared raising contemporary societal issues and challenging social and cultural values, enriching through this, the educational process. The school space changed for the students—from a place that they could not see how it related to their everyday life, experiences, and concerns to a story-space where they could reflect on their relationship with self, others as well as values about life. The *Caravan* started transforming the educational space, altering its potential for inspiring a new form of learning for all participants involved.

A third instance of embedding was at a school at a downgraded neighborhood in Piraeus. The audience was a class of 20 high schoolers aged 16–17 years old. The documentary we screened was about a couple *Fred & Dana*[8] who left their previous lives and moved to the island of Mytilini in search of a self-sufficient lifestyle:

I have an ideology, how can I put it . . . ? You must learn to make things by yourself. If you don't have money you must do it yourself. . . . How many things do we need to live on? What we like very much is going away with a backpack. Ultimately our lives are a journey.

(Vogiatzis & Malamou, 2012)

The reactions to this story underlined an opposition to what the high school students are being taught in school regarding the social concept of success. The educational system, their families, and their broader social entourage have all been encouraging them towards neo-liberal, capitalist lifestyles failing to enquire after their true concerns, desires, or emotions. For most of the students, it was the first time that they were introduced to different values. They started talking about the need to change societal values, linking social change with the need for creativity and self-determination: "This is very different to what we are used to consider as a life choice after we finish school . . . it is very encouraging to see that people choose to live a life so different in every respect . . ." (Participant I).

Hence, these specific schools/prison spaces became story-spaces, temporary territories, with a potential to enact untold stories. Following Deleuze and Guattari (1987), story-spaces can be seen as rhizomes, "part of a fluid system of connections and tensions, changes and flows that constantly transform the mode of their political activity, constructing new platforms for urban engagement . . . constantly unsettled, unpredictable and heterogeneous" (Daskalaki & Mould, 2013: 8). Eliciting original and unexpected interactions, the *Caravan* unveiled contestations and associations in ways that in other circumstances may have not become visible. Accordingly, emerging story-spaces (*Caravan*-school, *Caravan*-prison, *Caravan*-square, and so on) become inhabited by untold stories. During this process, audiences remain "complex, disparate and hidden storytellers" and story-interactions "operationalize otherness" (Hitchin, 2014: 70).

A story-space, like art, is dialogical and social encounter that predominantly produces relations that provoke moments of sociability and belongingness, spark new thoughts, and enact alternative values for entire communities (Nenonen & Storbacka, 2010). In this respect, transformation is an imminent change, anticipated and in that respect, constituted but also co-constitutive of future re-enactments. This process enables unique connections and provokes a collective experience, a common place for dialogue and reflection. Widening audience involvement and participation and promoting multiplicity of social interactions, the *Caravan* co-constituted story-spaces where transformation may occur (*multiplicity*).

Thus, rhizomatic story-spaces reproduce and re-territorialise institutions, identities, and social relations. *Caravan* achieved a departure from fixed stagnated identities towards new territories, a movement that can capture the untold element of stories (*mobility*). The *Caravan* will soon move to another space, create conditions of original, unexpected, and heterogeneous interactions and through that enact other story-spaces.

Movement of assemblages (artists, residents, activists, audiences, visitors) is responsible for temporarily constituting a new territory that has unexpected qualities. The networked relationships are a crucial feature creating new systems of interaction, feedback loops, and mediated settings for social interaction (Daskalaki, 2014).

Following this, the story-spaces described here and *Caravan's* subsequent territorialisations (e.g., future screening of the films in other social contexts or their integration into new artistic/cultural or educational platforms) are permeable thus allowing alternative story modes to emerge (*permeability*). Moreover, in contrast to centred (or polycentric) systems with hierarchical modes of communication and pre-established paths, these story modes including the untold, stay a-centred, and non-hierarchical.

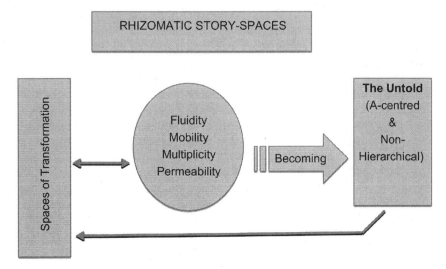

Figure 8.2   Rhizomatic Story-spaces, Transformation, and the Untold.

Thus, as Figure 8.2 summarises, rhizomatic story-spaces remain transformative due to their three properties namely, mobility, multiplicity, and permeability.[9] Being mobile, multiple and permeable, story-spaces remain in the making, always imminent, incomplete—in a state of becoming. This state enacts the 'yet to come' (Deleuze & Guattari, 1987; Bloch, 1995) potential of story-spaces and, at the same time, elicits the 'untold'. In the last section, we conclude, by exploring some of the potentialities and challenges for projects similar to the *Caravan*.

CONCLUSION AND IMPLICATIONS FOR FUTURE RESEARCH

In this chapter, we proposed that the *Caravan*, as an artistic storytelling platform, co-constructs alternative spaces of interaction and elicits the untold element of stories. In times of crisis and uncertainty, stories can contribute to the development of a creative dialogue between various social entities. The focus is thus shifted towards the ways in which creativity has the capacity to change the values and relations (as well as organizations) for the better. With reduced public spending for schools, local authorities, and remote communities, artistic interventions can become a catalyst in a process of change. Exposing established institutional settings to marginalised stories and excluded voices (screening the films in a prison, for example), we invite change and hope to inspire alternative organizational arrangements.

Story-spaces could challenge fixed, ineffective institutional-organizational forms (by bringing different fields together, such as art and education) and allow for untold stories to be released. In practical terms, the constitution of story-spaces with rhizomatic qualities requires the following: (a) Embedding creative projects (like the *Caravan*) into already established organizational processes; in other words, linking creative initiatives with organizational practices (such as training or management development programmes); (b) Creating fab labs or co-lab spaces where a network of artists, social entrepreneurs, and grassroots projects can work together—that is, allow for heteroglossia and heterogeneity which in times of crisis can provide creative solutions; (c) Providing or constructing new spaces where co-production can occur—that is, facilitating the (re-)construction of (existing) institutional structures (e.g., educational, artistic) and community-based relationships so alternative forms of organizing can emerge; (d) Transforming existing spaces where communities can reclaim art and storytelling as (self) transformative processes (for example, through urban redesign programmes).

Undoubtedly, emerging story-spaces also face challenges. How can spaces for transformation re-arrange power structures, challenge established organizational practices or contribute to the emergence of new ones? Future studies could explore how creative projects can remain outside the ordering system to enable the (trans)formation of spaces in the future. For example, a mix of strong and weak interpersonal ties could enhance creative collaborations and promote ongoing transformation (Daskalaki, 2010). Furthermore, despite the emancipatory potential of such projects, market-oriented ideology and profitability encourage homogeneity. We suggest that ensuring involvement with the unexpected and the unpredictable, creative communities ought to involve emergent, self-organized or temporary spaces which allow participants to challenge pre-existing norms and values and "the power relations that they entail, constructing new creative potentialities" (Daskalaki & Mould, 2013: 13). Self-organized or temporary spaces could provide this and claim a marginal but nonetheless significant use, nurturing experimentation and transformative creativity (Landry, 2000; Temel, 2006).

Finally, there are inequalities associated with access to information and participation and hence capacity to participate in the co-production and transformation process. It is important when devising these temporary and emergent platforms to ensure diversity, minimise exclusion, and offer opportunities for heterogeneous linkages. Again, mobility of stories (see also Hitchin, 2014) across locations, multimedia entanglements including online platforms as well as temporary, or spontaneous spaces for social engagement are proposed as potential conditions for ensuring diversity, inclusion, and multiplicity.

Hence, from an organizational perspective, it is the process through which story-spaces emerge or change that we ought to focus upon during our exploration of the untold. We therefore encourage more studies on how heterogeneous and unbounded territories are co-constituted but more importantly, how these territories are disrupted by spontaneous, ephemeral, and temporary artistic initiatives, breaking away from traditional forms of interaction (for example induction training programmes) and thus eliciting the untold element during organizing. Future organizational storytelling research, for example, can focus upon different assembling configurations among artists, urban activists, freelancers, and project-based professionals as well as academic communities/disciplines and numerous other mobile subjects and explore the conditions and the processes through which they have the potential to dis-order established yet ineffective organizational practices. "If location and situation are untold storytellers (or editors)— theoretical and methodological attention should turn to consider the implication of this for both organizational storytelling and storytelling studies . . . tracing both stories and situations on the move becomes an imperative" (Hitchin, 2014: 70).

Participation in diverse sociocultural and political contexts is what makes transformative spaces visible and what creates new organizational potentialities (Daskalaki, 2014). These organizational potentialities signify an invention. If transformation in organizing is to occur, new story-spaces that entail autonomous, open/participative, nomadic, multimodal, collective, emergent, and performative storytelling have to be created. Concluding, this chapter discussed the processes through which film documentaries can release untold stories and initiate a process of space transformation. While screening the *Caravan*'s stories in one location, we participated in a process that resulted in a unique territory, conducive of the unique untold stories it elicited. Discussing untold stories along with transformative creativity, we viewed artistic initiatives as co-constructing agents of territories, previously unknown, where one has the potential of becoming-Other. This was our story, a voyage into *Another World*, which, though subtle, *is Here*.

NOTES

1. According to Boje (2007), 'story space' is the co-mingling of narrative, ante-narrative, story, and terse story. We don't refer to this conceptual story space here. Instead we use the term to denote the socio-spatial space that is co-constituted though storytelling events.
2. The project is solely funded by SNFCC (Stavros Niarchos Foundation), http://www.snfcc.org/default.aspx. We would like to express special thanks to the Foundation for their support. The title of the project in which the *Caravan* belongs is 'Another World is Here'.
3. Trailers of all documentaries can be viewed at: http://www.anotherworldishere.com.
4. We would like to thank all five characters of the documentaries we have included in this work for the stories and experiences that we shared.
5. Another World is Here, The Caravan Project, "The Blind Fisherman" (2011a), https://vimeo.com/93360203, for the trailer of the documentary.
6. Another World is Here, The Caravan Project, "The Boat Carpenter Paporias", 2011b, https://vimeo.com/97094476, accessed June 2014.
7. Another World is Here, The Caravan Project, "Black Land", 2012a, https://vimeo.com/95014454, accessed June 2014.
8. Another World is Here, The Caravan Project, "Fred and Dana", 2012b, https://www.youtube.com/watch?v=KmaCWtELLdU, for the trailer of the documentary.

9. Deleuze and Guattari (1987) also discuss the principles of the rhizome, including elements of multiplicity, heterogeneity, connectivity, and rupture along
   the same lines that we propose here. For a full discussion of how these are
   performed by alternative social formations, see Daskalaki and Mould (2013).

REFERENCES

Another World Is Here, The Caravan Project, (2011a). *The Blind Fisherman.*
Screened at 14th International Documentary Festival of Thessaloniki. Retrieved
from http://vimeo.com/groups/248392/videos/94736941 .
Another World Is Here, The Caravan Project, (2011b). *The Boat Carpenter Papo-
rias,* Retrieved from http://www.youtube.com/watch?v=BMJWi-wHlv8.
Barad, K. (2003). Posthumanist performativity: Toward an understanding of how
matter comes to matter. *Signs: Journal of Women in Culture and Society, 28*(3):
801–831.
Benjamin, W. (1968). The work of art in the age of mechanical reproduction. In
H. Arendt (Ed.), *Illuminations* (H. Zohn, Trans.). New York: Schocken Books.
(Original work published 1936).
Bey, H. (2011). *The Temporary Autonomous Zone.* Seattle, WA: Pacific Publishing
Studios.
Bloch, E. (1995). *The Principle of Hope.* Cambridge, MA: MIT Press.
Boden, M. A. (2003). *The Creative Mind* (2nd ed.). London: Routledge.
Boje, D. M. (2007). *Storytelling Organization.* London, Sage.
Boje, D. M. (2011). *Storytelling and the Future of Organizations.* London: Routledge.
Boje, D. M., Rosile, G. A., & Gardner, C. L. (2007). Antenarratives, narratives and
anaemic stories. In N. Taher, & S. Gopalan (Eds.), *Storytelling in Management*
(pp. 30–45). Hyderabad, India: The Icfai University Press.
Cresswell, T., & Merriman, P. (2011). Introduction: Geographies of mobilities—practices,
spaces, subjects. In T. Cresswell & P. Merriman (Eds.), *Geographies of Mobilities:
Practices, Spaces, Subjects* (pp. 1–15). Farnham: Ashgate Publishing Limited.
Cunliffe, A., & Coupland, C. (2012). From hero to villain to hero: Making experi-
ence sensible through embodied narrative sensemaking. *Human Relations, 65*(1),
63–88.
Czarniawska, B. (1998). *A Narrative Approach in Organization Studies.* Thousand
Oaks: CA Sage.
Czarniawska, B. (1999). *Writing Management: Organization Theory as a Literary
Genre.* Oxford: Oxford University Press.
Czarniawska, B. (2004). *Narratives in Social Science Research.* London: Sage.
Czarniawska-Joerges, B., & Guillet de Monthoux, P. (1994). *Good Novels, Bet-
ter Management: Reading Realities in Fiction.* Reading, CT: Harwood Academic
Press.
Daskalaki, M. (2010). Building bonds and bridges: Linking tie evolution and network
identity in the creative industries. *Organization Studies, 31*(12): 1649–1666.
Daskalaki, M. (2014). Mobility and urban social events: Towards organizational
transvergence. *Culture and Organization, 20*(3): 215–231.
Daskalaki, M., & Mould, O. (2013). Beyond urban subcultures: Urban subversions
as rhizomatic social formations. *International Journal of Urban and Regional
Research, 37*(1): 1–18.
Deleuze. G., & Guattari. F. (1987). *A Thousand Plateaus.* Minneapolis: University
of Minnesota Press.
Fisher, W. R. (1985). The narrative paradigm: An elaboration. *Communication
Monographs, 52*(4): 347–367.

Gabriel, Y. (2000). *Storytelling in Organizations: Facts, Fictions and Fantasies*. London: Oxford University Press.

Gabriel, Y. (2013). Researchers as storytellers: Storytelling in organizational research. In M. Gotti, & C. Sancho Guinda, (Eds.), *Narratives in Academic and Professional Genres* (pp. 105–122). Bern: Peter Lang.

Gabriel, Y., & Connell, N.A.D. (2010). Co-creating stories: Collaborative experiments in storytelling. *Management Learning*, *41*(5): 507–523.

Goffman, E. (1959). *The Presentation of Self in Everyday Life*. New York: Doubleday.

Hajer, M., & Reijndorp, A. (2001). *In Search of New Public Domain*. Rotterdam: Nai Publishers.

Hardy, C., & Phillips, N. (1998). Strategies of engagement: Lessons from the critical examination of collaboration and conflict in an interorganizational domain. *Organization Science*, *9*(2): 217–230.

Hawkins, M., & Saleem, F. (2012). The omnipresent personal narrative: Story formulation and the interplay among narratives. *Journal of Organizational Change Management*, *25*(2): 204–219.

Hitchin, L. (2014). Fabricating methods: Untold connections in story net work. *Tamara—Journal for Critical Organization Inquiry*, *12*(1): 59–73.

Izak, M. (2014). A story-in-the-making: An intertextual exploration of a multivoiced narrative. *Tamara—Journal for Critical Organization Inquiry*, *12*(1): 41–57.

Landry, C. (2000). *Creative City: A Toolkit for Urban Innovators*. London: COMEDIA & Earthscan.

Marechal, G., Linstead, S., & Munro, I. (2013). The territorial organization: History, divergence and possibilities. *Culture and Organization*, *19*(3): 185–208.

Massey, D. (2005). *For Space*. London: Sage.

Nenonen, S., & Storbacka, K. (2010). Business model design: Conceptualizing networked value co-creation. *International Journal of Quality and Service Sciences*, *2*(1): 43–59.

Ricoeur, P. (1988). *Time and Narrative* (Vol. 3). Chicago: University of Chicago Press.

Temel, R. (2006). The temporary in the city. In F. Haydn, & R. Temel, (Eds.), *Temporary Urban Spaces: Concepts for the Use of City Spaces*. Basel, Switzerland: Birkhauser.

Thrift, N. (2000). Afterwords. *Environment and Planning D: Society and Space*, *18*(2): 213–255.

Valery, P. (1962). *The Outlook for Intelligence*. New York: Harper & Row.

Vogiatzis, S., & Malamou, T. (Directors) (2011). *Black Land*. Produced for The Caravan Project: Another World Is Here Another World Is Here. Retrieved from http://vimeo.com/95014454.

Vogiatzis, S., & Malamou, T. (2012). *Fred and Dana*. Produced for The Caravan Project: Another World Is Here Another World Is Here. Retrieved from http://www.anotherworldos here.com/en/features-en/fred/

Weick, K. (2012). Organized sensemaking: A commentary on processes of interpretive work. *Human Relations*, *65*(1): 141–153.

9 "I Just Want a Job"
The Untold Stories of Entrepreneurship

Lucia Garcia-Lorenzo, Lucia Sell-Trujillo, and Paul Donnelly

> Those who do not have power over the stories that dominate their lives, power to retell them, rethink them, deconstruct them, joke about them, and change them as times change, truly are powerless because they cannot think new thoughts.
>
> *(Rushdie*, 1992: 432)

INTRODUCTION

Despite increasing recognition of entrepreneurship as a diverse phenomenon (Shane & Venkataraman, 2000; Venkataraman, 2002), most research on this area still assumes that entrepreneurship is a positive behavioural quality or state to aspire to (Calás, Smircich, & Bourne, 2009; Carland & Carland, 1991, 1992; Dey & Steyaert, 2010, 2012). Thus, entrepreneurship is generally portrayed as that positive, elusive competence individuals need to develop, and organizations and institutions need to foster, to increase creativity, innovation, and the possibilities of finding employment in times of economic instability (Drucker, 1985; Perren & Jennings, 2005).

Recent research has attempted to critically assess the area of entrepreneurship studies (e.g., Imas & Weston, 2012; Ogbor, 2000; Özkazanç-Pan, 2009), providing alternative views on entrepreneurship that go beyond the wealth and business creation focus of much of the managerial literature. This type of research outlines a view of entrepreneurship more as a process than an ideal state to be reached. Within this tradition, a discursive and narrative approach to entrepreneurship studies has been suggested by a number of scholars (Cornelissen, Clarke, & Cienki, 2012; García & Welter, 2013; Holt & MacPherson, 2010). The aim is to capture the multi-voiced representations of entrepreneurship, as well as to provide more contextualised knowledge of the process, thereby providing an alternative to the predominant ambition in much entrepreneurial research to describe the ideal 'entrepreneur' and to explain and predict individual entrepreneurial behaviour (Cornelissen et al., 2012; Steyaert & Bouwen, 1997). Thus, our aim here is to contribute to this emerging, alternative tradition.

In this chapter, we will focus on a number of situated entrepreneurial stories of people in Spain and Ireland. During 2013, we used qualitative research methods to collect in-depth interviews, documents, and digital narratives in the aforementioned countries. We have found that both the Spanish and Irish governments, as well as the media, are encouraging people—through a particular type of narrative—to become more entrepreneurial as a possible way out of unemployment. However, our interviewees do not recognise themselves in this institutionalised narrative of entrepreneurship as the empowered, creative and independent individuals who go on a 'quest' to 'put an innovative product in the market'. It is necessity, rather than opportunity (Hessels, Van Gelderen, & Thurik, 2008), that is pushing, rather than pulling (Amit & Muller, 1995; Gilad & Levine, 1986; Storey, 1982), them to become self-employed. This chapter aims to make explicit the untold stories about their transitory state. By collecting these alternative stories of the entrepreneurship process, we hope to "access deeper organiz[ing] realities, closely linked to [people's] experiences" (Gabriel, 1999: 270), as well as to complement the dominant narrative of entrepreneurship as a 'quest' present in most research, institutional, and media contexts.

The chapter is structured as follows. The first section explores the concept of entrepreneurship and the research being done on entrepreneurial narratives. The second section looks at stories, both told and untold, as ways to manage in drifting and ambiguous contexts. The third section explains the methods of data gathering and analysis used to handle the data material. The fourth section describes the dominant narrative in entrepreneurship: the quest. Section five looks into the untold stories that lead to that narrative and that get pushed aside as redundant or not fitting, but that show the struggle of the forced entrepreneurs to find new anchors within a transitory situation.

NARRATIVES ABOUT ENTREPRENEURSHIP

There does not seem to be a clear agreement among researchers about what *entrepreneurship* is. The common definition, however, seems to revolve around wealth and business creation by motivated individuals and the factors that might support or enable that process (Gartner, 2010). For instance, Kirzner (1973) defined entrepreneurship as the ability to perceive new opportunities and to exploit them, whereas for Shane and Venkataraman (2000: 218) entrepreneurship is the study of "how, by whom, and with what effects opportunities to create future goods and services are discovered, evaluated, and exploited". Intellectual capital is considered important and factors such as education and previous experience in work are seen as influencing the entrepreneur's capacity to understand, interpret and apply new information in a way that others cannot (Shane & Venkataraman, 2000). Social capital and networks are also considered critical, as they provide and support the entrepreneur's understanding of his 'market' (Cope, Jack, & Rose, 2007; De Clercq & Voronov, 2009; Lin, Ensel, & Vaughn, 1981; Portes, 1998). Yet, the narrative tends to be very much about an individual, motivated to create wealth and able to discover and exploit new opportunities. Indeed, it was Schumpeter (1939) who first emphasised the role of entrepreneurs in economic theory, endowing them with a drive to power and an intuitive insight that he saw as instinctive.

Yet, as Gartner (2008: 359) suggests, there is not "'an' entrepreneurial type. Variation is, inherently, a fundamental characteristic of entrepreneurship". Mitchell (1997) also describes the shortcomings of this type of research: apparently no 'typical' entrepreneur exists. The array of contradictory studies only adds to the mythical status of entrepreneurs and to the consequent difficulties that non-entrepreneurs have in understanding the practitioners of this most unique profession (Mitchell, 1997: 123). And yet, most of the stories we hear about entrepreneurs focus on the exemplar individual who, as hero or jester (Anderson & Warren, 2011), achieves success and wealth. This can lead to a sense of failure when potential entrepreneurs struggle to live up to that ideal, especially in economically uncertain times (Trethewey, 2001).

There is, however, an emergent research tradition that sees entrepreneurship as a socially constructed process (Kenny & Scriver, 2012). For instance, Drakopoulou-Dodd and Anderson (2007: 343) strongly criticise the myth of the asocial individual entrepreneur, stressing that the very phenomenon of entrepreneurship is 'socially constructed'. Radu and Redien-Collot (2008) have also illustrated how the public sphere, in the form of the French press, constructs images of French entrepreneurs and how these influence the perception of entrepreneurship's social desirability (entrepreneurship as an attractive career option) and social feasibility (entrepreneurship as an accessible and realistic career option). A similar phenomenon is reported in the British press by Nicholson and Anderson (2005). Anderson, Dodd, and Jack (2009) also looked into the different metaphors used to describe entrepreneurship in different business schools in Europe and their potential consequences in shaping entrepreneurship education. All this research indicates a growing interest in the phenomenon of entrepreneurship as a collective process situated in particular historical and social contexts, rather than just dependant on individual motivations, cognitions, or behaviours. As Holt and Macpherson (2010) argue, entrepreneurship is not a state, but a process based on the collaborative and on-going reconciliation of multiple views and voices. Going further, Jones and Spicer (2005: 236) have described the 'entrepreneur' concept as an empty signifier, an 'absent centre', whose function is to be constantly articulated. Entrepreneurship might not even be an ideal condition to aspire to, as Marris (1986: 121) indicates, suggesting a different perspective on the process, as "no one would surely undertake so uncertain and stressful endeavour unless they were excluded from easier ways of realising themselves".

In line with this perspective, a number of researchers (Cornelissen et al., 2012; García & Welter, 2013; Holt & MacPherson, 2010; Neergaard & Ulhoi, 2007; Steyaert & Bouwen, 1997) have suggested that a narrative approach can make a constructive contribution to entrepreneurship research by introducing enhanced conceptual, epistemological, and methodological reflection. In line with this research area, the following section explores the use of stories and narratives during transitional situations, such as the ones necessity entrepreneurs in Spain and Ireland are experiencing.

THE UNTOLD STORIES OF ENTREPRENEURSHIP: FACING ANXIETY AND UNCERTAINTY.

The increasing amount of uncertainty and fragmentation in our organizations and communities (Bauman, 2000; Beck, 2000) makes it difficult to generate enduring collective meanings and coherent personal identities. It is an increasing challenge to maintain trust in traditional institutional arrangements, as well as a coherent personal narrative, in a context where risk and uncertainty are the norm (Sennett, 1998; 2006).

When it comes to entrepreneurship, and in the context of the current European financial crisis, increasingly, as Bauman (2013) says, "state functions [have been] . . . shifted sideways, to the market . . . or dropped downwards, onto the shoulders of human individuals, now expected to divine individually, inspired and set in motion by their greed, what they did not manage to produce collectively, inspired and moved by communal spirit". While this might encourage growth, it also "undermines the basis of trust and reciprocity on which economic relationships rely" (Marris, 1996: 145).

And yet, against this incessant fragmentation and becoming, narrative spaces allow us to find and negotiate continuity. As an inherently social psychological endeavour, narratives support our efforts for community building, as well as for developing our personal and social identities. As Bruner (1990) suggests, narratives help to institutionalise social practices by giving legitimacy to the known and expected. Yet, narratives are also the way in which we are able to incorporate the fragmented, the extraordinary and the unintelligible into the register of the possible. They are, therefore, a favoured tool to cope with change and potential loss (Garcia-Lorenzo, 2010; Marris, 1993). It is partly through the telling of stories that we try to contain uncertainty—by allowing the connection between the unknown and the familiar narratives to provide us with a 'potential space' (Winnicott, 1971) where we can safely set new bounds to previously unfamiliar situations.

It is partly this drive for sensemaking, for the completion of the narrative, for constant re-enactment until the 'new' finds itself 'familiar' in the configuration of the 'old', that might drive away the stories of necessity entrepreneurs, those individuals who are, in employment terms, "neither here nor there; they are betwixt and between the positions assigned and arrayed by law, custom, convention and ceremony" (Turner, 1995: 95). There are few stories told about the 'liminal period' of forced transition between being an employee and having to create employment. Most necessity entrepreneurs find themselves going through a period where the social and community structure they know is dissolving (Jahoda, 1982), where they are perceived as potentially dangerous or become invisible and are pushed to find 'structure' by themselves, since the institutions they used to rely on (e.g., government or employers) find it difficult to provide one for them. Yet, this is also the period where unlimited possibilities for a new structure or narrative also exist (Turner, 1995).

Indeed, in this chapter, we see entrepreneurship as both a storytelling and a story-making process, emphasising both the communicative and the persuasive, constraining aspect of narratives. Looking at how the stories of entrepreneurs come to be made, we stress the importance of cooperation and reflection, aspects of entrepreneurship that contrast with the idea of entrepreneurship as just storytelling. Yet, both processes shed light on entrepreneurship as a dynamic, on-going process. Indeed, in terms of performative functions, there is a clear role for storytelling in conveying and articulating the entrepreneurial experience. Obviously, storytelling is closely related to how the entrepreneur makes sense of what s/he does, and how s/he relates to others, recognises opportunities, and gains experience. The identification of the role of storytelling thus enables a richer, fuller understanding of how entrepreneurs learn about themselves and the entrepreneurship process, as well as gain experience.

METHODOLOGY

This section describes the research methods used to gather the data for the analysis of the entrepreneur stories. The research strategy involved a qualitative methodology to gather both personal entrepreneur narratives, as well as public sphere representations of entrepreneurs, both in Spain and Ireland.

In our research, we look for both the micro-interaction between the entrepreneurs and their situation (Cornelissen et al., 2012; Holt & MacPherson, 2010), as well as at the macro-representation of entrepreneurs in the institutional and public sphere (Anderson et al., 2009; Radu & Redien-Collot, 2008). As such, we have collected narratives from necessity entrepreneurs through eight in-depth and face-to-face interviews, as well as employing digital blogs and media in what Murthy (2008) calls 'digital ethnography' to collect media stories illustrative of public narratives of entrepreneurship in Ireland and Spain. We have also used publicly available documents, such as government and international organization reports (e.g., Global Entrepreneurship Monitor) to gain an appreciation for the cultural understanding of entrepreneurship in both countries. Our aim is to straddle the micro-macro boundary, looking at the development of personal narratives of self and entrepreneurial identity within particular social and historical contexts that shape how the individual narratives are developed, told or kept implicit.

Several authors have stressed the importance of the media's effects on entrepreneurial desirability and feasibility (Nahapiet & Ghoshal, 1998; Swedberg, 2000). Through framing, exposure, and interpretation, the media tends to portray entrepreneurship as a more or less desirable condition. At the same time, media renders entrepreneurship as more or less feasible, due to its impact on (i) the efficient dissemination of information about available institutional support and (ii) portrayal of the personal skills required to become a successful entrepreneur. The stories we have collected in the media show positive portrayals of entrepreneurship, considered as vital to stimulating entrepreneurial career choices, as they convey perceptions that obstacles to success can be overcome, and failure can be transformed into a learning opportunity (Nicholson & Anderson, 2005; Radu & Redien-Collot, 2008). The use of different methods enabled the inclusion of different viewpoints to refine our understanding of the phenomenon under study (Flick, 1992).

The narrative analysis followed Parker (2005) in looking for the different story elements (e.g., scene, purpose, actors, etc.). The narrative analysis sought to capture the process of entrepreneurship as lived by the necessity entrepreneurs in both Ireland and Spain, as well as the representations of entrepreneurship in the public sphere.

The analysis of the data was accomplished in two different steps. The first step sought to identify the activities, experiences, and transition processes the necessity entrepreneurs go through from employment to unemployment to entrepreneurship. It consisted of multiple readings of the interview transcripts, field notes, and documentation for the identification of everyday activities, experiences, and events. These were initially coded according to three main areas: the historical narrative of their transition between employment and creating their own job; their main activities as entrepreneurs; and their self and social image as entrepreneurs.

The second step involved comparing these non-public narratives with the analysis of the public narratives on entrepreneurship. The most common narrative identified has been that of the 'Quest' (Booker, 2004). When applied to the 'necessity entrepreneurs', we have found that it presents the following abridged structure:

1 **The call:** Life has become intolerable and the hero realizes he can only change matters through making a long difficult journey, e.g., unemployment and its results.

2 **The journey:** The hero sets out across hostile terrain, encountering a series of life-threatening ordeals. They include monsters to overcome and temptations to resist (e.g., abandon or accept precarious, but dead

end jobs), but also periods of respite with the help of, for example, 'wise old men' (e.g., for the government this translates as education; for the necessity entrepreneurs it translates as friends or family.)

3 **The goal:** After the last escape from death, the prize, kingdom, treasure, etc., is finally achieved. Renewed life is assured to stretch 'ever-after'. Thus, once the company is set up, employment and salary are ensured.

This was clearly the framework in the public narratives of entrepreneurship both in Ireland and Spain. While our analysis shows that the lived, unstructured experience of necessity entrepreneurs in both countries is not yet as clearly structured or formulated, it also shows that many of the stories of that transitional phase seem to be either 'edited out' or suppressed in the final 'edited' public narrative. The consequence is that the narratives of entrepreneurship circulating in the public sphere, and being used to shape necessity entrepreneurs experiences, represent the entrepreneurship ideal to be attained, rather than the real experience that is being lived. The next two sections contrast the public and private narratives.

THE ENTREPRENEURIAL NARRATIVE IN THE PUBLIC SPHERE: THE QUEST

When it comes to unemployment, the critical economic and social situation of southern Europe, as well as Ireland, has been widely publicised (Standing, 2013). One of the solutions suggested to come out of the crisis is the encouragement of entrepreneurial activity among the unemployed. As the most recent Global Entrepreneurship Monitor report for Spain (Hernández et al., 2013: 20) declares, "a quarter of the [entrepreneurial] activity continues to be driven by necessity and the high level of unemployment in Spain", yet this type of entrepreneurship is still considered of lesser value, resulting in the "composition of the entrepreneurial initiatives [being] more heterogeneous than before the crisis in terms of quality". This perspective reinforces the narrative of the entrepreneur as a developer of initiatives. Indeed, for the Spanish press, the 'entrepreneur' is seen as

> a person who perceives the opportunity, has confidence in her/his idea, has a higher than average ability to gather and convince people around her/him, knows how to sell ideas and, overall, has the ability to offer results. Entrepreneurial spirit is synonymous with innovation, change, company start-ups and risk taking.
>
> (Marketing Partners, 2013)

Even when traditional portrayals of entrepreneurship are not valid, the press actively transforms the characters into standard entrepreneurial heroes, who, on top of fighting economic adversity, have to overcome cultural defamation and family rejection:

Table 9.1 The necessity entrepreneur's journey: Complete framework for narrative composition.

Transition over time / Story elements	[Un]Finishing employment	Disorientation	Seeking alternatives	The on-going construction of employment position
Scene and purpose (where and why)	Becoming unemployed and initiating the search for paid employment	Trying to understand the recurrent unemployment situation	Looking for possible work alternatives	Working within the unstructured job situation
Who (actors)	The (ex) employee Organizations and institutions	The unemployed	The unemployed/ entrepreneur, family, friends and institutions	The 'necessity entrepreneur' and his/her stakeholder community
Act/Actions (what and how)	Job search in the same area/industry Use of contacts and networks	Continued job search Looking for viable alternatives	Accepting odd jobs Developing a job idea Looking for financial/ social support	Generating own jobs Maintaining the network of stakeholders Supporting other with similar needs
Transition	Fighting to maintain the status quo	In betwixt	In betwixt	On-going construction of new employment condition

Sitting at the bar, with their jeans and long hair, no one would guess that Pepita Marín and Alberto Bravo are two ruthless businessmen. In full economic wastelands, these two 25 year-olds have achieved €150,000 in funding for their brand "We are knitters". . . . It was 2010. The crisis had already hit Spain. And the families of these two economists could not believe they were about to leave their promising careers to become "grandmother weavers". Especially because they had never picked up a needle. "We had to learn on YouTube. In Spain there is no entrepreneurship culture. In the States we would be heroes, but here, they just saw us as crazy or wayward brats".

(Mañana, 2013)

The press works hard to adapt the entrepreneurial language to reflect the cultural repertoire of Catholic Spain. Headlines, such as "Seeking angels to launch businesses" (Fernández, 2013), introduce entrepreneurial activities as short of miraculous deeds in need of divine intervention:

One of the things that is needed is the professionalization of this activity. Most business angels are unaware that they are [angels] and are investing in friends and families' projects, often pressured by the future entrepreneurs themselves. They are unsure they chose the best project to allocate their savings, as they act following emotional ties without analysing the feasibility of the project.

(Fernández, 2013)

Becoming an entrepreneur is presented not only as a story of bravery and success, but also as the only way 'from the dole to self-employment' as one Spanish newspaper puts it:

Nearly 12,000 professionals each month are in transit through the uncertain path leading from unemployment to self-employed. Four hundred unemployed people every day are trying to find their own autonomy. It is not easy. When you are burned out, there are two options: resign or start a difficult and arduous journey, passing through the hell of unemployment, but exploring a hypothetical path to exit the tunnel . . . The only way out of the Spanish labour market debacle.

(Mármol, 2013)

Thus, the entrepreneur is portrayed as someone with an innate drive to wealth and power, and an almost intuitive insight to identify 'opportunity', while the entrepreneurial process becomes a 'quest' (Downing, 2005; Linstead, Fulop, & Lilley, 2004). It is through this journey that the unemployed person becomes an adventurer who challenges a bad situation and a negative personal status quo, and, despite setbacks, ultimately achieves the goal of job creation, achieving freedom. Governmental institutions are expected to support this 'great adventure' through a series of financial backings. The Spanish government, for instance, has recently passed the "Law of Entrepreneurs" (BOE, 2013), taking some steps to increase the ability of Spanish nationals (and foreigners who could be granted nationality) to take the uncertain road of labour emancipation and entrepreneurship.

The public narrative in Ireland presents entrepreneurship as the new frontier in the country's economic development, for the country can no longer rely on foreign direct investment alone, nor on the folly of home-grown property bubbles (*Irish Times*, 2009; O'Keefe, 2013; Ward, 2008): Thus, "it is necessary to promote indigenous entrepreneurial skills; without entrepreneurs who have the motivation, capacity and resources to establish businesses and who have the courage to take necessary business risks, there can be no economically sustainable long-term jobs" (Power, 2009). Indeed, with one headline heralding "Irish entrepreneurs: Your country needs you" (Hancock, 2013), entrepreneurs are the "heroes" of the hour (*Irish Times*, 2010). Further, according to Ireland's Minister for Jobs, Enterprise and Innovation, "[e]ntrepreneurs are the heroes of the economy, creating businesses, jobs and growth from which the rest of us benefit [and, while the country] has some amazing entrepreneurs, [there are] not nearly enough" (Newenham, 2014).

Thus it is that promoting entrepreneurship and creating an environment that is "entrepreneur-centric" (Horn, 2010) is high on the government's agenda (Department of the Taoiseach, 2010; Hancock, 2013; O'Keefe, 2013). In championing entrepreneurship as the country's potential 'saviour', the government is positioning itself as the driver and supporter in chief of this very saviour (Kenny & Scriver, 2012: 623). Its first Action Plan for Jobs (Department of Jobs, Enterprise and Innovation, 2012: 39) asserts:

> Creating an indigenous engine of economic growth is central to revitalisation of the Irish economy. Entrepreneurship, and the start-up companies that emerge as a result, provides the feed-stock for future exports and employment. Start-ups are one of the means by which new sectors take root in Ireland. They are the lifeblood of local economies and make an important contribution to regional development. . . . In these more challenging times . . . It is critical that we create an environment that supports entrepreneurs and small businesses in every way possible to . . . contribute to our economic growth.

Indeed, as stated by the Taoiseach (Prime Minister), the aim of the government's annual jobs action plan is "that by 2016 we can make Ireland the best small country in the world in which to do business" (Department of Jobs, Enterprise and Innovation, 2012: 3). It is interesting that this aim coincides, and is explicitly linked, with the centenary of the country's 1916 Easter Rising (Department of Jobs, Enterprise and Innovation, 2012: 7), which aim was to end British rule in Ireland and establish an independent Irish Republic. Thus, entrepreneurs are cast as the patriots of the present, being called to action to regain the country's economic independence, and articulated with the patriots and the nationalist fervour of a century earlier, when the fight was for independence from the British.

Notwithstanding this public narrative, the crisis has dented the public's view of entrepreneurship. While successful entrepreneurs continue to be well regarded in Irish society, the past decade has seen entrepreneurship as a good career choice consistently fall from a high of 70% in 2006 to 45% in 2012 (Fitzsimons & O'Gorman, 2012). This trend has translated into the proportion of the population aspiring to be entrepreneurs falling from a high of 12.6% in 2005 to 8% in 2012, which is lower than the average for the OECD (14.4%) and EU (14.8%) (Fitzsimons & O'Gorman, 2012).

Equally, the perception of media coverage of entrepreneurs being supportive has fallen from a high of 84% in 2006 to 61% in 2012, albeit this is an increase over 2011 and it is higher than the average across the OECD (52%) and EU (50%) (Fitzsimons & O'Gorman, 2012). Paradoxically, the death of the Celtic Tiger coincided with *Dragon's Den* (where budding entrepreneurs pitch their ideas to a panel of potential investors) appearing on national television and capturing the public's imagination, while giving entrepreneurs an increased media profile and making celebrities of the team of 'dragon' investors (*Irish Times*, 2010).

The media narrative largely focuses on the opportunity entrepreneur and on stories of success, albeit there is recognition that "becoming an entrepreneur has always been difficult" (Lynch, 2012) and that the journey involves "self-doubt, failures, successes, self-questioning and more than a few dark nights of the soul" (O'Brien, 2011b). Despite the perception that there are fewer opportunities to start a business in a recession (Fitzsimons & O'Gorman, 2012), "a vibrant entrepreneurial culture is thriving beneath the tough economic reality" (Lynch, 2012), so much so that there are "Celtic Tiger orphans" whose undiminished "entrepreneurial spirit" has them on a quest to go from "bust to boom" (Cunningham, 2009).

The media narrative addresses the "born or made" argument and declares that entrepreneurs are both, thereby suggesting that anyone can be an entrepreneur (Ahlstrom, 2009; *Irish Times*, 2009; Ward, 2008); all that is needed is "passion" (O'Brien, 2011a). Hence, there are some stories of people who, following redundancy, "see the crisis as an opportunity to reinvent themselves and start new enterprises" (Holmquist, 2010), but these are few and far between. The majority of stories are about people who always seemed destined to start their own business and who are always motivated by opportunity.

Despite necessity being the principal motivator of a sizeable minority of early stage entrepreneurs in recent years—with 28% of those starting a new business in 2012 motivated by perceived necessity, compared with 6% in

2007, higher than average across the OECD and EU, including Spain (Fitzsimons & O'Gorman, 2012)—necessity entrepreneurs remain relatively invisible in the national narrative. For the few Irish media articles that tell the stories of necessity entrepreneurs (e.g., Kerr, 2013), the narrative is very much one of overcoming adversity, typically linked with redundancy, to carve out one's own success story as the owner of one's own business and future.

THE UNTOLD STORIES: THE ON-GOING CO-CONSTRUCTION OF AN EMPLOYMENT SITUATION

The narrative analysis of the Irish and Spanish necessity entrepreneur material presents some clear commonalities with the existing media analysis for those respondents who engage in the entrepreneurial 'Quest' narrative. They do take on similar institutional/organizational discursive elements: they do take a path and it is a story of strife and struggle. However, as Table 9.1 shows, when they describe their journey as necessity entrepreneurs, the tale becomes less linear, more ambiguous, and less full of hope than the public narratives presented so far.

Furthermore, these stories are difficult to elicit. They come on the 'asides', that is, breaks in the talk or interview, or at the end once the recorder is switched off, which is not surprising, as these stories tend to be suppressed and reluctantly told because they generate feelings of shame or 'difference'.

[UN]FINISHING EMPLOYMENT

The narrative of the necessity entrepreneur's journey rarely starts with a 'call' or a bright idea that needs implementation. It tends to start with a tale of sorrow and regret, with a break down: the unemployment condition. In some cases, this comes as a surprise, in some others it is presented as expected. Yet, the heroine finds herself falling from full employment due to external circumstances, generally outside her control, e.g., the crisis, the market:

> My husband . . . had his own business and when the crisis came, he was the first to go . . . A lot of debts and there is no way of finding a job, especially in his area . . . the building sector [was the first to go], and on top of it . . . lots of foreign competition. (Marisa, Spain)
>
> Well, now [there] are . . . more consultants . . . a dentist . . . solicitors . . . people that we've never had [asking for support to start their own business] in the last 15 years; they're coming in now from the crash. . . . They find it very hard, very difficult.
>
> (Geraldine, Ireland)

In some cases, there is talk of a 'wrong doing', a personalisation of the reasons for the fall:

> So, the family business was started by my dad when he was very young
> . . . and that was going well . . . But, we made the mistake of joining
> with other partners, and then trouble began. . . . My father still thinks
> that it was his fault, and he wants to start all over again, but we don't
> let him. He is very old, we don't have money, and, obviously, we were
> just unlucky with the partners . . .
>
> (Javier, Spain)

There are, however, a number of similar elements in these stories: suffering and strife are the main emotions associated with the narrative followed by hope of success and a potential comeback due to hard work. The journey as 'salaried employee' is also presented as unfinished. There is a desire to retake the path and, therefore, the tale starts recounting the strategies that need to be followed in order to do so—job searches, activating business networks, and seeking institutional support to be back where they left. Disbelief and pity are the emotions associated with this part of the narrative.

DISORIENTATION

For those who have lost their safe employment and cannot find a similar employment situation, this is a moment of disorientation, as the old structures do not seem to hold, but no new alternatives can be found or thought of. To frame life differently, with a new employment condition and new social and institutional relationships, becomes too disturbing a task to undertake. As Marris (1986: 104) says, "our instinct of survival pulls us the other way, to protect our sense of identity and the setting which has moulded it" thus, to keep on searching for secure, stable employment. It is in this stage of the narrative that necessity entrepreneurs start expressing the loss of a secure situation of full employment. Yet, becoming an entrepreneur is still not seen as 'real':

> I had a year or two in the wilderness [before becoming an entrepreneur]
> . . . 18 months with no money.
>
> (Tony, Ireland)

> We are now trying to get sorted by starting our own company, which
> right now is not happening—so far I'm just knocking on doors, but no
> one is answering. . . . This thing of being an entrepreneur is not real.
> Everything is already thought up . . .
>
> (Espe, Spain)

The reaction is to go back to employment, any kind:

> People around me would tell me not to even try to work on what I want
> as a psychologist because there is nothing . . . my colleagues who were
> in the same situation have gone to work on anything . . . I started to
> work as a shop assistant; I wanted a salary, to get a paycheck, frankly,
> with anxiety and shame . . . but you need the payslip every month to
> feel you are OK.
>
> (Ines, Spain)

The common themes in this stage of the narrative are the dreams of
returning to full employment, while at the same time there is a slow acceptance of the condition of unemployment and the difficulty of finding a job
that might maintain the previous status quo. Self-questioning regarding
alternatives and considering other people's views starts, but there is difficulty in seeing beyond the 'full employment' possibility.

SEEKING ALTERNATIVES

This is very much a betwixt stage in the narrative, when one is not yet an
'entrepreneur', but more 'odd jobs' are being accepted as the only way to
survive. There is a common element to how the respondents construct and
make sense of their struggles in finding a way to gain resources to keep living. They are still in between searching for salaried employment, but also
engaging in the entrepreneur journey. As such, most of them struggle when
trying to make sense of their position in society. They report feelings of
vulnerability, define themselves as being cheated by 'the system' or see themselves outside of 'the normal social expectations':

> I feel alone. I have my family. . . . But, in terms of support, something or
> somebody to help us out. . . because if there are no jobs, you go to the
> social worker at the town hall and she just says, "there is nothing for
> you". So, yes, in that sense, I feel alone, at risk. . . unprotected, that's
> the word (Desiré, Spain)
>   I'm 45, then there's nobody going to give you a job, and if they do
> it'll be €9 an hour, and if I have, please God, 30 years left in me, I want
> to have a decent holiday once a year, have a half decent car, nothing
> extravagant . . .
>
> (Tony, Ireland)

Some of the respondents react by using the small, remaining social benefits they might have as a sort of basic income to start something new within
a parallel system of accountability. To explain these endeavours as business
or entrepreneurial activities within the black market would be misguided,

as the respondents perceive themselves as marginal to a social system that has clearly failed them. Instead of expressing guilt for the violation of widely held norms, respondents express their distrust for institutional and organizational bodies. They are not 'free-riding', but creatively engaging in activities to be able to feed their family or pay their debts. In a social climate where political corruption is becoming visible, the respondents feel empowered by playing outside the system:

> Since I finished my degree as an architect . . . I've been job pecking, here and there. If something as an architect comes out, I take it. If it is as a teacher, or in an association, let's do it . . . the thing is to keep on moving, never stopping . . . Instead of a fixed job, as it does not come out, so I have to look for anything, small jobs through different places. Alone or with others as a company . . . Sometimes they take too long to pay me back, but I know they . . . are going through a bad patch and . . . like a nursery school I did up—there are so many illegal nurseries that they are really struggling. To become legal, they have to pay a lot of taxes, and so they have higher fees, so they don't get enough students . . . so yes, they are a little tight and they are paying little by little. So, well, I just have to wait a bit, no?
>
> (Osset, Spain)

And engaging in creative initiatives to overcome fragmentation:

> So, at the beginning, I made up a business that was . . . called Divine-Divine. So, you come because you have an event to go to. I dress you up, you give me some money, go with the clothes and, eventually, you return it. It was a good idea . . . the business had the underlying philosophy of responsible consumerism and I started working with Mercedes, a very honest and hard working person . . . and then I started another business. See, so from one idea, many others start coming. So, I thought I could start a private cooking school with local products, organic products. I tried to get a space through the town hall, and, well, I was just shooting in the dark, going around and around . . . but always learning . . . because there was no other alternative, I have a €1,200 mortgage. (Pilar, Spain)
>
> Yes, I did 33 years of working for 'the man'. So, I thought, "That's it. No more excuses". . . . I was laid off on October 23rd, 2009 . . . in 2008 I was one of only three employees who were awarded the highest level bonus . . . then not 12 months later I'm suddenly surplus to requirements. So, I'd look at P&L for profits and go: "Why I am I doing this for Mr. [company]? Why am I not doing it for me?" . . . So, I decided to go [for it].
>
> (John, Ireland)

And, ultimately, being able to put some food on the table:

The only time that I have asked for food, it's been through the barter-ing page—I kind of cook meals and keep half of it. So, that is the only thing that I published in the webpage. And then, two ladies brought me one day some food, as a surprise. Because they were surprised that I've offered the service, that I wasn't asking for money or anything, but food—or not even, just my services in exchange for keeping half of it . . . so I cook, I make meals and keep half for my family, that way I have something good to give my kids.

(Marisa, Spain)

One of the very strong themes coming out of the stories in this phase of the journey is the lack of 'structural' support from both society and institu-tions. Indeed, respondents perceive social reciprocity as the means of social exchange that uses economic and/or symbolic currency to maintain social equilibrium—where altruistic and egotistical needs combine (Kets de Vries, 2011). As Marris (1996) claims, people have always understood that a frame-work for social reciprocity is crucial to maintaining functioning societies. Yet, the stories of entrepreneurship we have uncovered tell of an increasing heavy burden on those with the fewest social and economic resources (Mar-ris, 1996), who are at once marginalised and constrained. Thus, social reci-procity becomes replaced in their tales by a brutal meta-narrative of struggle in an unprotected and extremely uncertain environment.

THE ON-GOING CONSTRUCTION OF A NEW 'EMPLOYMENT' CONDITION

Another common theme in the necessity entrepreneurs' narratives is the sense of 'incessant becoming' (McKenna, Garcia-Lorenzo, & Bridgman, 2010). Necessity entrepreneurs seem to be dealing with the constant strug-gle to define their self and their new 'employment conditions'. The questions are constant: Who am I? What are my skills? What can I sell that makes me different from the rest? These are common questions among all necessity entrepreneurs we interviewed. As Paula says:

When I started to think about setting up my own company, I realized that I had to go to my core, to what makes me different, to my own expertise and my experience. I had to reach there and have a clear plan based on that, building on that. You have to reinvent yourself . . . to understand what is it that you can provide . . . what kind of value can you add? And check that constantly to see if you are able to provide that.

(Paula, Spain)

It is what Miller and Rose (1990) call the rise of the 'enterprising self', in which the self has to invest in itself in order to improve its self constantly.

For the necessity entrepreneurs, this takes the form of a brutal and constant process of self-evaluation and appraisal:

> . . . the selection process did not come through, so what now? And then I asked myself, "OK, so what do I have? Which path shall I take? Right?" . . . it was then a moment of looking inside myself and saying, "Come on, Pilarita, what do you have, my dear? What do you have, on top of need and want?" So then I started working on the house I have at the beach. I did it up, a beautiful house in front of the beach, and I put it on the Internet.
>
> (Pili, Spain)

During this period, in which most of the necessity entrepreneurs we interviewed find themselves, the struggle is to keep on generating jobs and money, to maintain a business network of stakeholders, as well as to support others that have joined the new company or have similar needs. There is no sense of 'Goal' achieved, or sense of 'epiphany or dawning' (Beech, 2011); rather, there is a sense of constantly having to reinvent oneself. The 'Goal' is elusive and the journey continues:

> The problem we have now, we've grown to ten employees, we've now reached the threshold for the County Enterprise Boards, so, theoretically, our next point of contact is Enterprise Ireland, and frankly, they are just not interested. We're not sexy . . . [not] what they call the 'high potential start-up', which can be the next this or that, they get sucked into that 'high potential', whereas I was a bit more, let's be honest, 'plodding', really, by nature, just getting there. We've tried . . . [but Enterprise Ireland] are more trouble than they're worth. (John, Ireland)
>
> Look, we have been working for already like three years and I call potential clients and I say we are a company . . . we even have a name and a website . . . but we are still getting to become a limited society, etc. . . . It is hard. There is not enough volume of businesses to make sense for us to start paying all those taxes. It is coming, but not yet . . . so it is better to remain as self-employed almost . . . I don't know. It is a constant conversation among us . . . and Kika has a small girl now. I don't know, we'll see . . . so, maybe we are not a company yet, but an association?
>
> (Patty, Spain)

As in the example above, the classical 'liminal transition' is not completed, as there is no sense of recognition by the 'outside', as Beech (2011: 64) outlines. The necessity entrepreneurs find themselves trapped in a constant transition with very few social structures recognising them as entrepreneurs.

CONCLUSIONS

The chapter has looked into the stories of necessity entrepreneurs in Spain and Ireland, those that are in the public domain and those that relate experiences of uncertainty and transition, and that are, to a certain degree, untold.

The interest driving this research was to generate greater insight and understanding into both necessity entrepreneurs and the entrepreneurial process from an empirical perspective, while at the same time contributing to advance theory in the areas of entrepreneurship and work transitions. The chapter contributes to this endeavour in four different ways.

First, necessity entrepreneurs are very much under-researched in academic literature, not to mention practically ignored by the media and policy makers. We have, through exploring the stories and experiences of those engaging in entrepreneurship out of necessity, tackled an area of study that has remained at the margins of academic research.

Second, in moving away from a focus on static aspects of entrepreneurs and entrepreneurship, this chapter has engaged with the problem of representation in extant literature, very much questioning the dominant view inherent in the 'holy trinity' of the entrepreneur (Weiskopf & Steyaert, 2009): the strong figure of the entrepreneur and the entrepreneurial self; scientific methods to uncover the secret to success; and optimistic policy making grounded in the entrepreneur's role in economic success. Through the journeys of Irish and Spanish necessity entrepreneurs from unemployment to entrepreneurship, we question these assumptions. In their stories, the entrepreneurs do not portray themselves as strong heroic figures, rather, they come across as engaged in a process of constant doubt and self-questioning. Furthermore, their stories tell of a transition where the social and institutional structures necessity entrepreneurs used to rely on are dissolving, rendering them 'invisible' in the job market and pushing them to create 'structure'—in the form of a new job—by themselves. This is a threatening situation with both self-identity and social status undefined and in flux; necessity entrepreneurs find themselves 'betwixt and between' the positions assigned and arrayed by norms and custom. Yet, this is also the period where innovations in job identities and narratives emerged.

The narratives presented open up further the study of the entrepreneur and the entrepreneurship process, while allowing for the possibility of re-balancing the interpretation of 'who is an entrepreneur', how they become one (Imas, Wilson, & Weston, 2012) and how to study the phenomenon.

Third, despite the small sample, methodologically, the research has looked at both the micro-interaction between the entrepreneurs and their situation, as well as at their macro-representation in the institutional and public sphere. Our aim was to straddle the micro-macro boundary, looking at the development of personal narratives of self and entrepreneurial identity within particular social and historical contexts, rather than just focus on individual motivations, cognitions, or behaviours.

Fourth, we have shown how entrepreneurship is both a storytelling and a story-making process. The public narratives presented convey and articulate a particular version of the entrepreneurial process. Yet, we have also seen how the necessity entrepreneurs' experience does not fit neatly within this particular narrative, so 'other' untold stories need to be elaborated. Those are the stories where necessity entrepreneurs make sense of what they do, how they relate to others, recognise opportunities, and gain experience.

The narratives presented reach their function primarily within social interaction. Narratives are constitutive components of on-going relationships, essential for maintaining the intelligibility and coherence of social life, useful in drawing people together, creating distance, and so on. A story, even when 'untold', is itself a situated action, a performance with illocutionary effects. It acts to create, sustain, or alter worlds of social relationships (Donnelly, Gabriel, Özkazanç-Pan, 2013; Garcia-Lorenzo, Nolas, & de Zeeuw, 2008; Gergen, 1994). Our entrepreneurs create their reality and make sense of their journey from unemployed to entrepreneur through the retrospective stories that they tell about their experience of work and through future-oriented stories that they create as a path for action, for developing their own jobs. These conversations establish the context in which our entrepreneurs act and thereby define themselves and their actions (Schrage, 1989).

As such, stories both told and untold, play a vital part in the sense-making process, where apparently disconnected elements become related parts of a whole. It is the concreteness of narratives that allows our entrepreneurs to understand events in a specific context through the organization of their experiences in the form of narrative (Bruner, 1991).

At the same time, we have seen how story lines are powerful frames of reference by which individuals come to rationalise or legitimise what goes on in their work related lives. The media and government narratives provide a clear outline of what an entrepreneur 'should be'. These narratives, however, are not only ways to make sense of the employment-unemployment journey. These are also narratives told with a performative aim, especially in the case of the institutional narratives, so that others might learn from someone else's experience (Garcia-Lorenzo, Nolas, & de Zeeuw, 2007). Thus, they are told to 'educate'. As such, storylines and their plots are, in one form or another, 'vocabularies' or motives in which the descriptions of entrepreneurship behaviour or the path to becoming an entrepreneur are not necessarily derived by the individuals being described, but are imputed to them by the media or those producing the accounts.

These storylines become, then, a 'vocabulary' of power (Linstead et al., 2004: 31). The descriptions of entrepreneurship distributed by institutions and the media, for instance, become a discursive resource or capability that ensures the potential entrepreneurs fit the role. Those who do not conform run the risk of being excluded from the narrative of success, the story of bravery, and hence they should not rely on institutional backing (such as financial subsidies) and would then be silenced by the media.

And yet, we have seen how a key process is the journey from a stable work identity to an internal on-going search focused on 'identity work', which describes the on-going mental activity that an individual undertakes in constructing an understanding of self that is coherent, distinct, and positively valued. We consider identities not as fixed, but as developing through narratives, since individuals constantly engage in creating, testing, and living through their stories. Identity thus becomes a product of one's own story making (Bruner, 2003, 2008; Gabriel, 2004). In attempting to make sense of their situation, our individual entrepreneurs are constantly crafting self-narratives, usually by drawing on cultural resources, as well as memories and desires to reproduce or transform their sense of self (Garcia-Lorenzo, 2004; Knights & Willmott, 1989; Sveningsson & Alvesson, 2003).

Both the explicit and the untold narratives have consequences, not only for the development of particular identifications and visions of self in terms of entrepreneurship, but also for policy making. Thus, not only do these necessity entrepreneurs feel inadequate, different and deviant, they are also unable to access the institutional support that is made available for the 'really entrepreneurial' (Drucker, 1985).

Our research on necessity entrepreneurs complements mainstream entrepreneurial research focused mainly on business development, adding a narrative/storytelling dimension that enables a richer, fuller understanding of how entrepreneurs experience the journey. With these untold narratives about becoming an entrepreneur (out of necessity), we aim to expand our understanding of a complex and non-linear process. As such, entrepreneurship needs to be explored from a variety of angles and perspectives. Indeed, with governments seeking to encourage unemployed people to become entrepreneurs, and with policy based on the entrepreneur-as-hero trope, we are in need of a more nuanced view of both entrepreneurs and the entrepreneurial process.

REFERENCES

Ahlstrom, D. (2009, April 6). The real trick is to make would-be entrepreneurs believe: Make them accept this isn't just a pipe dream. *The Irish Times*. Retrieved from http://www.irishtimes.com/business/the-real-trick-is-to-make-the-would-be-entrepreneurs-believe-make-them-accept-this-isn-t-just-a-pipe-dream-1.739217.

Amit, R., & Muller, E. (1995). 'Push' and 'pull' entrepreneurship. *Journal of Small Business & Entrepreneurship*, 12(4): 64–80.

Anderson, A.R., Dodd, S.D., & Jack, S. (2009). Aggressors; winners; victims and outsiders: European schools' social construction of the entrepreneur. *International Small Business Journal*, 27(1): 126–136.

Anderson, A.R., & Warren, L. (2011). The entrepreneur as hero and jester: Enacting the entrepreneurial discourse. *International Small Business Journal*, 29(6): 589–609.

Bauman, Z. (2000). *Liquid Modernity*. London: Polity Press.

Bauman, Z. (2013, May 14). Europe is trapped between power and politics. *Social Europe Journal*. Retrieved from http://www.social-europe.eu/2013/05/europe-is-trapped-between-power-and-politics/

Beck, U. (2000). *The Brave New World of Work*. Cambridge: Polity Press.

Beech, N. (2011). Liminality and the practices of identity reconstruction. *Human Relations*, 64(2): 285–302.

Boletin Oficial del Estado (BOE). (2013) Num 233. Sabado 28 Septiembre de 2013. Sec I. Pag. 78787. http://www.boe.es/boe/dias/2013/09/28/pdfs/BOE-A-2013-10074.pdf.

Booker, C. (2004). *The Seven Basic Plots: Why We Tell Stories*. London: Continuum.

Bruner, J. S. (2008). Culture and mind: Their fruitful incommensurability. *Ethos*, 36(1): 29–45.

Bruner, J. S. (1990). *Acts of Meaning*. Cambridge, MA: Harvard University Press.

Bruner, J. S. (1991). The narrative construction of reality. *Critical Inquiry*, 18(1): 11–21.

Bruner, J. S. (2003). The narrative construction of reality. In M. Mateas & P. Sengers (Eds.), *Narrative Intelligence: Advances in Consciousness Research* (Vol. 46) (pp. 41–62). Amsterdam: Benjamins.

Calás, M., Smircich, L., & Bourne, K. (2009). Extending the boundaries: Reframing 'entrepreneurship as social change' through feminist perspectives. *Academy of Management Review*, 34(3): 552–569.

Carland, J. W., & Carland, J. A. (1991). An empirical investigation into the distinctions between male and female entrepreneurs and managers. *International Journal of Small Business*, 9(3): 62–72.

Carland, J. W., & Carland, J. A. (1992). Managers, small business owners, entrepreneurs: The cognitive dimension. *Journal of Business and Entrepreneurship*, 4(2): 55–66.

Cope, J., Jack, S., & Rose, M. B. (2007). Social capital and entrepreneurship: An introduction. *International Small Business Journal*, 25(3): 213–219.

Cornelissen, J. P., Clarke, J. S., & Cienki, A. (2012). Sense-giving in entrepreneurial contexts: The use of metaphors in speech and gesture to gain and sustain support for novel business ventures. *International Small Business Journal*, 30(3): 213–241.

Cunningham, E. (2009, November 7). Bust to boom. *The Irish Times*. Retrieved from http://www.irishtimes.com/life-and-style/people/bust-to-boom-1.767711.

De Clercq, D., & Voronov, M. (2009). Toward a practice perspective of entrepreneurship: Entrepreneurial legitimacy as habitus. *International Small Business Journal*, 27(4): 395–419.

Department of Jobs, Enterprise and Innovation. (2012). *Action Plan for Jobs 2012*. Retrieved from http://www.djei.ie/publications/2012APJ.pdf.

Department of the Taoiseach. (2010). *Innovation Ireland: Report of the Innovation Task Force*. Dublin: Stationery Office.

Dey, P., & Steyaert, C. (2010). Social entrepreneurship: Critique and the radical enactment of the social. *Social Enterprise Journal*, 8(2): 90–107.

Dey, P., & Steyaert, C. (2012). The politics of narrating social entrepreneurship. *Journal of Enterprising Communities: People and Places in the Global Economy*, 4(1): 85–108.

Donnelly, P. F., *Gabriel*, Y., & Özkazanç-Pan, B. (2013). Untold stories of the field and beyond: Narrating the chaos. *Qualitative Research in Organizations and Management: An International Journal*, 8(1): 4–15.

Downing, S. (2005). The social construction of entrepreneurship: Narrative and dramatic processes in the coproduction of organizations and identities. *Entrepreneurship Theory and Practice*, 29(2): 185–204.

Drakopoulou-Dodd, S., & Anderson, A. R. (2007). Mumpsimus and the mything of the individualistic entrepreneur. *International Small Business Journal*, 25(4): 341–360.

Drucker, P. (1985). *Innovation and Entrepreneurship*. New York: Harper & Row.

Fernández, D. (2013, May 10). Se buscan 'ángeles' para lanzar negocios [Looking for 'Angels' to launch business]. *El País*. Retrieved from http://sociedad.elpais.com/sociedad/2013/05/10/actualidad/1368202220_061094.html.

Fitzsimons, P., & O'Gorman, C. (2012). *Entrepreneurship in Ireland 2011: Global Entrepreneurship Monitor (GEM)*. Retrieved from http://www.gemconsortium.org/docs/2432/gem-ireland-2011-report.

Flick, U. (1992). Triangulation revisited: Strategy of validation or alternative? *Journal for the Theory of Social Behaviour*, 22(2): 175–197.

Gabriel, Y. (1999). *Organizations in Depth: The Psychoanalysis of Organizations*. London: Sage.

Gabriel, Y. (2004). Narratives, stories and texts. In D. Grant, C. Hardy, C. Oswick, & L. Putnam (Eds.), *The Sage Handbook of Organizational Discourse* (pp. 61–77). London: Sage.

García, M.C.D., & Welter, F. (2013). Gender identities and practices: Interpreting women entrepreneurs' narratives. *International Small Business Journal*, 31(4): 384–404.

Garcia-Lorenzo, L. (2004). (Re)producing the organization through narratives: The case of a multinational. *Intervention Research*, 1(1): 43–60.

Garcia-Lorenzo, L. (2010). Framing uncertainty: Narratives, change and digital technologies. *Social Science Information*, 49(3): 329–350.

Garcia-Lorenzo, L., Nolas, S., & de Zeeuw, G. (2007). Stories and the acquisition of knowledge. *Systemica*, 15(6): 177–191.

Garcia-Lorenzo, L., Nolas, S.M., & de Zeeuw, G. (2008). Telling stories and the practice of collaboration. *International Journal of Sociology and Social Policy*, 28(1/2): 9–19.

Gartner, W.B. (2008). Variations in entrepreneurship. *Small Business Economics*, 31(4): 351–361.

Gartner, W.B. (2010). A new path to the waterfall: A narrative on a use of entrepreneurial narrative. *International Small Business Journal*, 28(1): 6–19.

Gergen, K.J. (1994). *Realities and Relationships: Soundings in Social Constructionism*. Cambridge, MA: Harvard University Press.

Gilad, B., & Levine, P. (1986). A behavioral model of entrepreneurial supply. *Journal of Small Business Management*, 24(4): 45–53.

Hancock, C. (2013, June 12). Irish entrepreneurs: Your country needs you. *The Irish Times*. Retrieved from http://www.irishtimes.com/business/sectors/financial-services/irish-entrepreneurs-your-country-needs-you-1.1425018.

Hernández, R., Coduras, A., Vaillant, Y., Batista, R.M., Sosa, S., Mira, I., & Martínez, J. (2013). *Global Entrepreneurship Monitor: Informe GEM España 2012*. Retrieved from http://www.gemconsortium.org/docs/2811/gem-spain-2012-report.

Hessels, J., Van Gelderen, M., & Thurik, R. (2008). Entrepreneurial aspirations, motivations, and their drivers. *Small Business Economics*, 31(3): 323–339.

Holmquist, K. (2010, April 14). Life after redundancy: 'You're not just your old job', *The Irish Times*. Retrieved from http://www.irishtimes.com/life-and-style/people/life-after-redundancy-you-re-not-just-your-old-job-1.651932.

Holt, R., & MacPherson, A. (2010). Sensemaking rhetoric and the socially competent entrepreneur. *International Small Business Journal*, 28(1): 20–42.

Horn, C. (2010, December 17). Rebuilding a changed Ireland. *The Irish Times*. Retrieved from http://www.irishtimes.com/business/rebuilding-a-changed-ireland-1.687975.

Imas, J.M., & Weston, A. (2012). From Harare to Rio de Janeiro: Kukiya-Favela organization of the excluded. *Organization*, 19(2): 205–227.

Imas, J.M., Wilson, N., & Weston, A. (2012). Barefoot entrepreneurs. *Organization*, 19(5): 563–585.

Irish Times, The. (2009, March 2). Growing business. *The Irish Times*. Retrieved from http://www.irishtimes.com/business/growing-business-1.713282.

Irish Times, The. (2010, November 30). Enter the dragons. *The Irish Times.* Retrieved from http://www.irishtimes.com/business/enter-the-dragons-1.683565.

Jahoda, M. (1982). *Employment and Unemployment: A Social-Psychological Analysis* (Vol. 1). Cambridge: Cambridge University Press.

Jones, C., & Spicer, A. (2005). The sublime object of entrepreneurship. *Organization, 12*(2): 223–246.

Kenny, K., & Scriver, S. (2012). Dangerously empty? Hegemony and the construction of the Irish entrepreneur. *Organization, 19*(5): 615–634.

Kerr, A. (2013, February 22). Banker, barista—breadwinner. *The Irish Times.* Retrieved from http://www.irishtimes.com/life-and-style/people/banker-barista-breadwinner-1.612097.

Kets de Vries, M. F. K. (2011). *The Leader on the Couch: A Clinical Approach to Changing People and Organizations.* Oxford: Wiley.

Kirzner, I. M. (1973). *Competition and Entrepreneurship.* Chicago: University of Chicago Press.

Knights, D., & Willmott, H. (1989). Power and subjectivity at work: From degradation to subjugation in social relations. *Sociology, 23*(4): 535–558.

Lin, N., Ensel, W., & Vaughn, J. (1981). Social resources and strength of ties: Structural factors in occupational status attainment. *American Sociological Review, 46*(4): 393–405.

Linstead, S., Fulop, G. E., & Lilley, S. (2004). *Management and Organization: A Critical Text.* New York: Palgrave Macmillan.

Lynch, S. (2012, February 10). Entrepreneurial spirit hasn't gone away. *The Irish Times.* Retrieved from http://www.irishtimes.com/business/sectors/technology/entrepreneurial-spirit-hasn-t-gone-away-1.460718.

Mañana, C. (2013, May 10). Aprendimos casi todo en Google: De tejer a vender [We learnt almost everything on Google: From Tejera to sell]. *El País.* Retrieved from http://sociedad.elpais.com/sociedad/2013/05/10/actualidad/1368199230_633696.html.

Mármol, C. (2013, May 12). Del paro al autoempleo: Guía para salir del infierno [From unemployment to self-employment: Guide out of hell]. *El Mundo.* Retrieved from http://www.elmundo.es/elmundo/2013/05/12/andalucia/1368347460.html.

Marris, P. (1986). *Loss and Change.* London: Routledge.

Marris, P. (1993). The social construction of uncertainty. In C. Murray Parkes, J. Stevenson-Hinde, & P. Marris (Eds.), *Attachment Across the Life Cycle* (pp. 78–90). London: Routledge.

Marris, P. (1996). *The Politics of Uncertainty.* London: Routledge.

Marketing Partners. (2013, November 23). ¿Qué es ser emprendedor? [What is being an entrepreneur?]. Retrieved from http://rtrucios.bligoo.com/emprendedor.

McKenna, S., Garcia-Lorenzo, L., & Bridgman, T. (2010). Managing, managerial control and managerial identity in the post-bureaucratic world. *Journal of Management Development, 29*(2): 128–136.

Miller, P., & Rose, N. (1990). Governing economic life. *Economy and Society, 19*(1): 1–31.

Mitchell, R. K. (1997). Oral history and expert scripts: Demystifying the entrepreneurial experience. *International Journal of Entrepreneurial Behaviour & Research, 3*(2): 122–139.

Murthy, D. (2008). Digital ethnography: An examination of the use of new technologies for social research. *Sociology, 42*(5): 837–855.

Nahapiet, J., & Ghoshal, S. (1998). Social capital, intellectual capital, and the organizational advantage. *Academy of Management Review, 23*(2): 242–266.

Neergaard, H., & Ulhoi, J. P. (Eds.). (2007). *Handbook of Qualitative Research Methods in Entrepreneurship.* Cheltenham: Edward Elgar.

Newenham, P. (2014, January 23). Entrepreneurship report urges income tax rate of 15–20%. *The Irish Times*. Retrieved from http://www.irishtimes.com/business/economy/entrepreneurship-report-urges-income-tax-rate-of-15-20-1.1665600.

Nicholson, L., & Anderson, A. R. (2005). News and nuances of the entrepreneurial myth and metaphor: Linguistic games in entrepreneurial sense-making and sense-giving. *Entrepreneurship: Theory and Practice*, 29(2): 153–173.

O'Brien, C. (2011a, June 20). Success is really a collection of failures. *The Irish Times*. Retrieved from http://www.irishtimes.com/life-and-style/people/success-is-really-a-collection-of-failures-1.601315.

O'Brien, C. (2011b, June 21). Fear is all part of the learning experience. *The Irish Times*. Retrieved from http://www.irishtimes.com/life-and-style/people/fear-is-all-part-of-the-learning-experience-1.602088.

Ogbor, J. O. (2000). Mythicizing and reification in entrepreneurial discourse: Ideology-critique of entrepreneurial studies. *Journal of Management Studies*, 37(5): 605–635.

O'Keefe, F. (2013, October 11). Can entrepreneurs bring back prosperity? *The Irish Times*. Retrieved from http://www.irishtimes.com/business/sectors/can-entrepreneurs-bring-back-prosperity-1.1556600.

Özkazanç-Pan, B. (2009). *Globalization and Identity Formation: A Postcolonial Analysis of the International Entrepreneur* (Unpublished doctoral dissertation). University of Massachusetts, Amherst, MA, USA.

Parker, I. (2005). *Qualitative Psychology: Introducing Radical Research*. Maidenhead: Open University Press.

Perren, L., & Jennings, P. L. (2005). Government discourses on entrepreneurship: Issues of legitimization, subjugation, and power. *Entrepreneurship Theory and Practice*, 29(2): 173–184.

Portes, A. (1998). Social capital. *Annual Review of Sociology*, 24: 1–24.

Power, C. (2009, April 6). History repeating itself. *The Irish Times*. Retrieved from http://www.irishtimes.com/business/history-repeating-itself-1.739139.

Radu, M., & Redien-Collot, R. (2008). The social representation of entrepreneurs in the French press: Desirable and feasible models? *International Small Business Journal*, 26(3): 259–298.

Rushdie, S. (1992). *Imaginary Homelands: Essays and Criticism, 1981–1991*. New York: Penguin.

Schrage, M. (1989). *No More Teams! Mastering the Dynamics of Creative Collaboration*. New York: Currency Paperbacks.

Schumpeter, J. A. (1939). *Business Cycles: A Theoretical, Historical, and Statistical Analysis of the Capitalist Process*. New York: McGraw-Hill.

Sennett, R. (1998). *The Corrosion of Character: The Personal Consequences of Work in the New Economy*. London: Sage.

Sennett, R. (2006). *The Culture of the New Capitalism*. New Haven, CT: Yale University Press.

Shane, S., & Venkataraman, S. (2000). The promise of entrepreneurship as a field of research. *Academy of Management Review*, 25(1): 217–266.

Standing, G. (2013, May 21). Job security is a thing of the past—so millions need a better welfare system. *The Guardian*. Retrieved from http://www.guardian.co.uk/commentisfree/2013/may/21/job-security-welfare-flexible-labour-precariat.

Steyaert, C., & Bouwen, R. (1997). Telling stories of entrepreneurship: Towards a narrative-contextual epistemology for entrepreneurial studies. In R. Donckels & A. Miettinen (Eds.), *Entrepreneurship and SME Research* (pp. 47–62). Aldershot: Ashgate.

Storey, D. (1982). *Entrepreneurship and the New Firm*. London: Croom Helm.

Sveningsson, S., & Alvesson, M. (2003). Managing managerial identities: Organizational fragmentation, discourse and identity struggle. *Human Relations*, 56(10): 1163–1193.

Swedberg, R. (Ed.) (2000). *Entrepreneurship: The Social Science View* (Vol. 1). Oxford: Oxford University Press.

Trethewey, A. (2001). Reproducing and resisting the master narrative of decline: Midlife professional women's experiences of aging. *Management Communication Quarterly, 15*(2): 183–226.

Turner, V. W. (1995). *The Ritual Process: Structure and Anti-structure.* New York: Aldine.

Venkataraman, S. (2002). *The Distinctive Domain of Entrepreneurship.* London: Edward Elgar.

Ward, M. (2008, September 5). The next crop of entrepreneurs. *The Irish Times.* Retrieved from http://www.irishtimes.com/business/the-next-crop-of-entrepreneurs-1.936527.

Weiskopf, R., & Steyaert, C. (2009). Metamorphoses in entrepreneurship studies: Towards affirmative politics of entrepreneuring. In D. Hjorth, & C. Steyaert, (Eds.) (2009). *The Politics and Aesthetics of Entrepreneurship: A Fourth Movements in Entrepreneurship Book.* Cheltenham: Edward Elgar.

Winnicott, D. (1971). *Playing and Reality.* London: Tavistock.

10 Aquifer Analysis
Told and Untold Stories in Warwick Churches[1]

Vaughan S. Roberts

INTRODUCTION

In his novel *The Prague Cemetery* (Eco, 2011), Umberto Eco employs the device of using three narrators—the Narrator (capital N) who is relaying the diary of the central character Captain Simonini, which itself has interjections by Abbé Dalla Piccola. It is unclear throughout whether the Abbé is the alter-ego of Simonini or a separate person. Both the Narrator and Abbé Dalla Piccola offer their glosses on the main story. This mischievous narrative wash raises questions about which storyteller the reader can trust. In effect *The Prague Cemetery* is a novel about the process of storytelling which teases its readers about who is telling the story and which sources are feeding into the main narrative so that we are never sure which account can be relied upon.

Every narrative involves a process of choice between possibilities, between those stories that are told and others that remain untold, and who makes those choices. This chapter is an account of how multiple stories were collected for an organizational review and provides an analysis of which were 'told', which remained 'untold' and how those choices came about. Eco's novel has a single author disguising himself in different voices for the purpose of story as entertainment, whereas this account is one author seeking to identify different voices for the purpose of story as organizational sensemaking (Weick, 1995).

The image of an aquifer is used to explore the process of filtering told and untold stories from the pool of narrative communities, applying it to a worked example of a storied review undertaken in 2010 by a group of Warwick churches, where I was Team Rector. This metaphorical approach is informed by Janet Martin Soskice's understanding of metaphor as: "speaking of one thing in terms which are seen to be suggestive of another" (Soskice, 1985: 49). Her definition shares a good deal of common ground with the approach outlined by George Lakoff and Mark Johnson who argue similarly that the "essence of metaphor is understanding and experiencing one kind of thing in terms of another" (Lakoff & Johnson, 1980: 5). Later they broaden this definition by talking about understanding "one domain of experience" in terms of another (Lakoff & Johnson, 1980: 117) and these domains of experience are conceptualised as "experiential gestalts" which are structured wholes recurrent within human experience. According to Lakoff and Johnson metaphors play a key role in the coherent organization of our experience, which extends into the world of organizations.

The use of analogy and metaphor is widely attested in organizational literature, for example in understanding the nature of organizations (Morgan, 1997), forms of strategy (Cummings & Wilson, 2003) and types of leadership (Alvesson & Spicer, 2011). An aquifer is a body of permeable rock which can contain or transmit water and in the process of the water flowing underground and rising to the surface it is filtered. Water is also a frequent image for many aspects of organizational life. Morgan uses it to describe organizational change (Morgan, 1988, 1997),[2] Cummings to portray the process of managing change (2002), and Weick uses the notion of filtering in describing the process of organizational sensemaking (1995).[3] Interestingly, he also uses an explicitly geological image when outlining his understanding of the overall process of sensemaking:

> Research and practice in sensemaking needs to begin with a mindset to look for sensemaking, a willingness to use one's own life as data, and a search for those *outcroppings* and ideas that fascinate.
>
> (Weick, 1995: 191—my emphasis)

In writing this chapter I needed to address the question of whether places and people described here should be done so anonymously. I thought about using the fictional name of 'Greyden' for Warwick and as a reference to the opening chapter of *The Prague Cemetery* ('A Passerby on that Grey Morning'). However to my mind it was important, in Weick's terms, to use outcroppings from one's own life so that others might be free to come to these stories and openly critique this narrative. Names of individuals have been omitted but this account is of real places located at real points in time.

Turning then to the guiding metaphor, Figure 10.1 describes one example of an aquifer which gives an idea of the ways in which water is stored in porous rock beneath the earth's surface and how it interacts with other geological features within which it is set. This chapter uses the natural feature as an analogy for the ways in which stories can be filtered in organizations so that some are 'told' whilst others remain 'untold'. We need to keep in mind that, like all forms of language, analogy and metaphor have their limitations. Morgan has described metaphor as a kind of 'constructive falsehood' which has "an inherently dialectical quality that binds truth and falsehood into the same process, creating powerful insights that, if taken too literally or too far, can become counter-productive" (Morgan, 1996: 232). In this chapter the aquifer's vertical dynamic of water passing through a process of filtration will remain the principle focus for this image as a means of understanding the filtration from untold to told stories. Of course, the image could be extended into exploring how stories might flow horizontally as underground streams or rivers across the surface, be held as standing water, or be sites of conflict as water itself can be fought over as a valuable resource. But that would take us well beyond a single chapter and the scope of the original paper.[4]

It is worth noting that although the chapter is about how a group of six churches was asked to review their work, it is not a theological reflection on that process. Rather it seeks to analyze how it came to be that some stories were told whereas others remained untold. It is in three parts: (1) Organizational Backstories—examines some of the narrative context for the review; (2) Aquifer Analysis of the *Review* (Roberts et al., 2010)— applying the aquifer analogy to the told and untold stories that were collected; (3) Aquifer Filters—identifying some of the filters of organizational storytelling that were in play during this process, in particular: (i) The Storyteller, (ii) Other Participants, (iii) Potential Audiences, and (iv) Wider Narrative Culture.

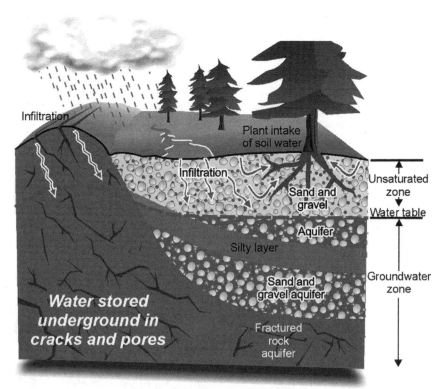

Figure 10.1   An Aquifer—Regional District of Nanaimo (British Columbia).

ORGANIZATIONAL 'BACKSTORIES'

The Church of England

For those not familiar with the structure of the Church of England, a brief outline might be helpful. Its website states:

> The Church of England is organised into two provinces; each led by an archbishop (Canterbury for the Southern Province and York for the Northern) . . . Each province is built from *dioceses*. There are 43 in England and . . . each diocese is divided into parishes. The parish is the heart of the Church of England. Each parish is overseen by a parish priest (usually called a vicar or rector). From ancient times through to today, they, and their bishop, are responsible for the 'cure of souls' in their parish. That includes everyone. And this explains why parish priests are so involved with the key issues and problems affecting the whole community.
>
> (Church of England, 2014)

One of the untold stories hidden in this official statement is that within those 43 dioceses there is an evolving organizational complexity that includes: elected bodies (one diocesan synod for each diocese plus several local or deanery synods), clergy with managerial roles (bishops, archdeacons, area deans), and executive officers (diocesan secretaries, directors of finance, legal and HR advisors). Each diocese configures these roles in slightly different ways but Figure 10.2 gives a general overview of this structure and how stories move within it:

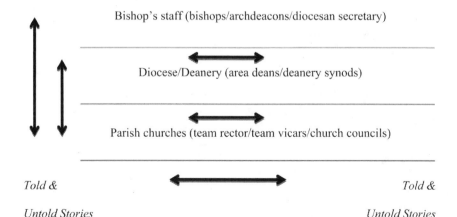

Figure 10.2   Church of England: Organizational Levels & Flow of Stories.

Some parishes are clustered together in teams or groups. This has been done in an ad hoc manner, so there is no nationally recognised system or structure for such clusters as each diocese has gone about this in its own way. There have been some official reports and guidelines but the fact that the most up-to-date report listed on the website at the time of writing is *Good Practice in Group and Team Ministry* published in 1991 highlights not only the lack of structure but that this area of collective church life seems to be noticeably under-researched[5] with this chapter being one of the very few pieces of detailed, published analysis of team ministry in the Church of England.

THE WARWICK TEAM

The new Warwick Team came into being in 2003 consisting of four Anglican parishes (All Saints, St Mary's, St Nicholas, and St Paul's) and a conventional district served by a Local Ecumenical Partnership (Christ Church). This succeeded the old Warwick Team of 1976, which had brought together Christ Church, St Mary's, and St Nicholas as a single parish. The new Team was established with five stipendiary (salaried) clergy, each responsible for one place of worship, plus a designated Team-wide role. At the time of the review in 2010, one of these posts was vacant (St Nicholas) following the early retirement of the Team Vicar based there, which was the stimulus for an appraisal of how the Team was working. A review of the new Warwick Team and Budbrooke Parish was a diocesan requirement for a new appointment.

In 2003 Budbrooke was in a different administrative unit (Deanery and Archdeaconry) and, although the then Team Rector met with certain parish representatives to explore joining the new team, there appeared to be a mutual agreement that the institutional complexities were too great at that time for the parish to join. Since that meeting Budbrooke has become part of the Warwick and Leamington Deanery and a new stipendiary appointment was made in 2005 with a view to the parish exploring the possibility of becoming part of the Warwick Team. Some of the institutional complexities remain but the relationship between Team and Parish has grown over time and the *Review* has played a significant role in that development. We turn to examine that review in more detail.

AQUIFER ANALYSIS OF THE REVIEW

This section is my account of key aspects of the review process, which led to the finished document. In addition, it includes my analysis of some of the untold stories that did not rise to the surface through the narrative aquifer.

The review document is clear about the ambiguity which greeted the original request for such a review:

> The proposal for a review was met with a degree of concern within the Warwick Team given that there had already been a number of recent opportunities for self-examination and appraisal—including the setting up of the Team itself, the mapping of the Team's ministry onto the Deanery values in 2006 and individual reviews (e.g., the creation of a parish profile for Budbrooke in 2005 and the review of Christ Church for its Revised Declaration of Intent and Constitution in 2006). This unease was expressed in the observation that we were frequently being asked to 'dig up the plant and examine the roots in order to see how it was growing'.
>
> (Roberts et al., 2010)

However, two of my clergy colleagues were more enthusiastic about such a project providing we could bring a narrative approach to the undertaking, so they were asked to prepare a brief for such a storied review. Their position paper stated:

> All communities hold their share of foundational stories and myths, and many of these stories are held in common. However, individual takes on these stories can be quite different. This can become problematic when a community considers its identity and its mission. If key members of the community are working from different foundational stories (a different sense of how they began, where they are, and where they're going) then looking at who we are and what we are doing can be fraught with unforeseen anxiety and tension. Unless handled sensitively, tension between individuals and groups as they strive to promote their story as the 'correct one' can lead to quieter voices being marginalised, and others being entirely alienated by the process.
>
> (Roberts et al., 2010: 4)[6]

The document went on to set out four questions they felt the review should address:

- *Where we've been.*
- *Where we are.*
- *What makes us 'tick' (personal skills, knowledge and experience)*
- *Where we're going and how the team can best be configured to serve God and all of God's children in this place.*

> (Roberts et al., 2010: 4–5)

The Warwick Team and Budbrooke Parish would then create an exhibition and account of our stories which would weave "personal narratives with [church] community narratives and wider community narratives" and would "encourage people to bring something of their own story and faith journey, passions and interests in prose or picture form" (Roberts et al., 2010: 5).

A formal proposal was taken to the Bishop and after some discussion it was agreed to proceed with this narrative approach provided we could find an external consultant to moderate the project. We found a consultant from the Cass Business School who agreed to fulfill this role and who had a professional interest in narrative approaches to organizations and leadership. In the event the Bishop made a further response to our proposal, asking us to address four additional questions:

- *What does the ministry and mission of the Church in the town of Warwick as a whole require at this point in time?*
- *What makes for the flourishing of the Church and what is the shape of ministry to best serve this?*
- *How can we help to ensure that the best use is being made of the resources available to the Team?*
- *In what ways may the Team serve the Diocese beyond Warwick?*

These were noticeably different to the four questions that we had identified. and in addition, he provided a diagram for how he saw the review progressing, see Figure 10.3.

These questions changed the framework for the review because in addition to facilitating a process of listening to each other's stories, we also had to provide responses to these more specific queries. The self-description and evaluation, together with the external audit effectively

Self-description and evaluation

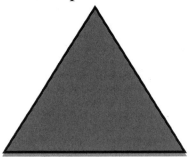

External audit   **Diocesan response**

Figure 10.3 The Bishop's Process of Review.

became the review document which sought to bring told stories within the Warwick Team and Budbrooke Parish into conversation[7] with the Bishop's questions. In the course of encouraging certain stories to surface through a process of listening, recording and discussion, other stories remained untold. There were three levels of told and untold stories: (A) Individual communities' own narratives; (B) Organizational meta-narrative; and (C) The review document's final narrative. The image of the aquifer can help in configuring the different narrative strata, see Figure 10.4.

This analogy will now be used to explore told and untold stories within the context of the review, before going on to examine how stories from the narrative pools were filtered into the final review document. In my capacity as Team Rector, I met with each of the church councils to listen to their accounts of how the expanded Warwick Team came into being; how they came to join it, or not (as in the case of Budbrooke Parish), and what their experience was of being/not being part of the Team. With the permission of each council the conversations were recorded and I also had a long telephone conversation with my predecessor who had brought the new Team into being, during which I made notes. In addition to the process of listening to the communal stories, I also sought each council's responses to the Bishop's four questions.

I wrote up those meetings in a draft report that wove together congregational stories and their responses to those questions, which I took to a meeting of clergy colleagues for their comments and critique. It was also sent to our external moderator at this stage for his observations. Afterwards, I re-worked aspects of the review before taking that to an open meeting of the six church councils to which all interested parties were invited for

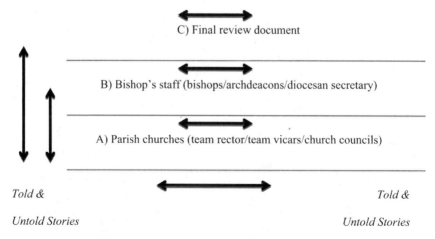

Figure 10.4 Aquifer Analysis: Flow of Told and Untold Stories.

their reflections and appraisal. The document was re-worked once more as a final draft, which was presented again to colleagues before being sent to the Bishop, with the caveat that: "this document is intended to stand alongside the exhibition of the churches' ministry" which was being prepared for the Bishop's visit later that month.

The final version of the review is a public document for the Bishop and those churches involved in the process itself. In terms of the aquifer analogy it is the 'surface' or that place where a number of the organizational stories emerged into the open. The review itself is stratified, containing six sections: (i) Introduction, (ii) Our Stories & the Bishop's Questions, (iii) Future Options, (iv) Summary & Conclusion to the Questions, (v) Questions & Responses from the Congregational Meeting, (vi) Conclusion. Each response under section (ii) included three parts: a background statement, an account of the discussion at the church councils, and a summary response to the specific question. Using the aquifer analogy this chapter will explore three levels of told and untold storytelling in the *Review* (Roberts et al., 2010)—communal narrative (A), organizational metanarrative (B), and the *Review*'s own narrative (C). In particular, we will examine the relationship between the told story (the *Review* itself) and some of the untold stories which remained in the aquifer and did not make it to the surface.

INDIVIDUAL COMMUNITIES' OWN NARRATIVES

One of the parts of the final review document where its narrative nature is richest can be found in the conversations relating to Question 2: *What makes for the flourishing of the Church and what is the shape of ministry to best serve this?*

Discussion of this issue was framed by the independently developed, theological writings of Irish Anglican David F. Ford and American feminist Grace Jantzen on the nature of 'flourishing'. We shall examine below the implications of this upon the process of organizational storytelling within the context of the review but, in different ways, both Ford (1999) and Jantzen's work (Graham, 2009) introduced themes of birth and death, which informed the *Review*'s overall narrative arc.

Thus, in the account of the discussion regarding Question 2, the *Review* states:

> The death of the first Warwick Team (Christ Church, St Mary's and St Nicholas) and the birth of the new Warwick Team (All Saints, Christ Church, St Mary's, St Nicholas and St Paul's) are remembered as protracted and painful. There are a small number of people on the present Team Council who recall the setting up of the first Warwick Team in 1976 and how All Saints and St Paul's opted to remain as individual parishes but many more can remember the labour pains of the new

Warwick Team and some of the words used about that period of transition from death to birth give a sense of how people felt at the time. For instance, one member of the Team Council describes the process as 'fraught' and another spoke about the 'animosity' of those discussions. A member of Christ Church depicted it as a 'battle' and the final Team Rector of the first Warwick Team says that the clergy team he inherited at the start of the process of exploring a new team was 'horrendously dysfunctional'.

(Roberts et al., 2010: 13)

The *Review* continues:

Whatever the rights and wrongs of these perceptions, such recollections paint a consistent picture of a team facing conflict amongst laity and clergy. At this distance little is gained by reliving those events but it is agreed this was not a time when either the Team or individual churches were particularly 'flourishing'. However it was a time which had a significant impact on the type of team which came to birth.

(Roberts et al., 2010: 13)

In this section of the *Review* we can see a great deal of bitter water bubbling up from the narrative aquifer. The animosity referred to in the *Review* is indicative of the lingering sense of mistrust, which was part of the untold story about the birth of the Warwick Team. A good example can be found in the early part of the meeting with the church council at Christ Church, which is a local ecumenical partnership on a 1970s housing estate built on the edge of Warwick between the town and the by-pass. Many of their early questions at that meeting reflected concerns about being on the geographical and ecclesiological margins. In particular, the council wanted to know: what organizational definitions were in play ("what is 'the Church' that's in mind with the first question—the Anglican Church or the wider Church"[9]). Some warned about too much emphasis being given to the churches at the centre of Warwick ("danger of focusing on the Church as located in the centre—it should be broader than this"), whilst others asked if there were hidden agendas ("we are on a journey towards a destination we don't know yet—does someone else have a destination in mind?"). The council was clearly concerned about Christ Church's relative smallness ("worry about sense of competition") and the implications any review might have for Christ Church's future. Similar and additional anxieties were expressed in the other meetings but none were recorded in detail within the final review document. They are part of the pool of untold stories, the narrative aquifer, lying beneath the report yet with the potential to still irrigate the organizational landscape. At this point the process of filtration comes into sharp focus—who filters these stories so that some become told whilst others remain untold? Why and by what criteria are such decisions made? To what purpose are these choices between told and untold stories being put? We shall identify some of the key elements of how stories are filtered through this narrative aquifer in the final part of this chapter.

However, it is worth noting here that in this account of the discussion surrounding the Bishop's Question 2 (*What makes for the flourishing of the Church and what is the shape of ministry to best serve this?*) we can detect a mixture of what Emery Roe calls 'story' and 'counterstory' (Roe, 1994). Significantly Roe describes his approach to the analysis of narrative as 'hydraulic' and it begins with detailed analysis of the story or stories being presented in a certain situation before proceeding to identify and examine those narratives which run counter to the prevailing story (counterstories) or those that are not included within the dominant narrative (nonstories).

A good example of this dynamic lies on the surface narrative of the review in the statement that:

> the final Team Rector of the first Warwick Team says that the clergy team he inherited at the start of the process of exploring a new team was 'horrendously dysfunctional'. Whatever the rights and wrongs of these perceptions, such recollections paint a consistent picture of a team facing conflict amongst laity and clergy.
>
> (Roberts et al., 2010: 13)

There were some from that period who disputed the previous Team Rector's account. Once again, there is a large pool of untold stories here. On coming into the role of Team Rector, I was struck by the fact that numerous stories were told by clergy and lay people alike testifying to the dysfunctionality of the Team that my predecessor inherited. Other clergy who have been Team Rectors or had experience of teams frequently attested to the severe friction which can exist in Anglican teams. Yet there were numerous other stories told about this time some of which painted diametrically opposite pictures of events.

Not only was it impossible at that distance to do due justice to these competing narratives and counter-narratives, I felt that in my role as 'storyteller' I had to provide a coherent narrative for all the different constituencies 'above ground' and therefore filter the told and untold stories for those different audiences. It is clear, therefore, that a key filter in the aquifer model of organizational storytelling will be the judgments of the storyteller, which must themselves be open to scrutiny.

ORGANIZATIONAL META-NARRATIVE

In addition to the pools of local stories, we can extend this model of aquifer narrative analysis to an organization's meta-narratives, in the sense that there will be a well of 'grand' stories which individuals and groups draw upon to make sense of their circumstances. This may include: documents of past times, organizational folklore, academic analysis, leadership myths, and more. In the Church these will include scripture, magisterial teaching,[10] theology, stories of the saints, and teachers of the faith. Once again the filtered water, the choices made in this respect will determine what grows on the organizational surface and what plants reach up through the institutional layers. In other words, there are told and untold stories at the level of meta-narrative where different filters could have been applied and alternative stories told.

As already noted, this review employed the convergent yet contrasting work of theologians David F. Ford and Grace Jantzen on the theme of flourishing to address one of the Bishop's questions. The interaction of their thinking and the stories collected for the *Review* had a major impact on the final document. Jantzen was Professor of Religion, Culture and Gender at the University of Manchester until her death from cancer at the age of 57 in 2006. Ford has been Regius Professor of Divinity at Cambridge since 1991 and, amongst other things, is a significant theological voice in global Anglicanism.

The *Review* notes two key elements to Ford's theological description of flourishing. First, the sacraments of baptism and eucharist are signs of birth and death—for example: (a) the birth and death of Christ; (b) the birth and death of the Church; (c) the dying and living of individual members of Christ's body; (d) birth and death in congregational life. Second, from Ford's perspective, the abundance of the eucharist and flourishing of human life means (in the words of the *Review*) "we have to take seriously the diversity of the Church and all its wider relationships" (*Review*, 2010: 12) This is what Ford calls living in a "multi-dimensional habitus" which is "formed through repeated celebration of the eucharist and interweaving that with the rest of life" (Ford, 1999: 4). The *Review* drew a link in this affirmation of diversity between notions of 'flourishing' and the model of a 'mixed economy' Church which had emerged from discussion of the Bishop's first question: *What does the ministry and mission of the Church in the town of Warwick as a whole require at this point in time?*

A similar dynamic is at work in Grace Jantzen's elaboration of 'flourishing' where she also identifies the importance of birth and death, and notes how to enter into the life of God involves a similar engagement with the web of our relationships. For Jantzen birth is more powerful than death and therefore: "Birth is the basis of every person's existence, which by that very fact is always material, embodied, gendered, and connected with other human beings and with human history" (Jantzen in Graham, 2009: 6). So once again the importance of human diversity is being underlined. According to Elaine Graham 'flourishing' is revealed in Jantzen's writing as a "life well-lived" and by cultivating those virtues which promote "the values of life, creativity, diversity and justice" (Graham, 2009: 9).

In the *Review* Ford and Jantzen's ideas drawn from the pool of theological metanarrative were brought together with Charles Hampden-Turner's work on corporate culture—in particular, his ideas about socially destructive and creative circles—and defined in this way: "Vicious and virtuous circles can be distinguished by whether the dilemmas or tensions within the circle are unreconciled and fiercely adversarial, or reconciled and synergized" (Hampden-Turner, 1994: 30). The Team Review established the virtuous circle in Figure 10.5 for a flourishing team.

The three parts of the circle were summarised as follows:

(a) **birth and death—sacramental lives:** Sacramental lives treat the embodied beginnings and endings (births and deaths) of individuals and groups with proper care and attention, recalling that all we are and all we have is through the grace of God.

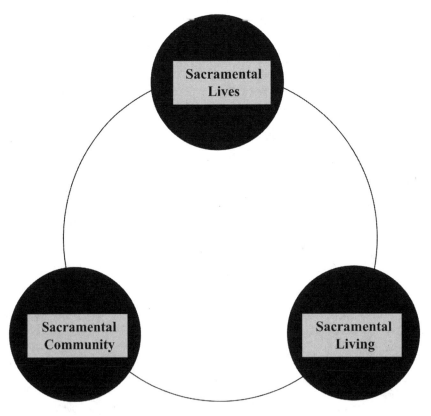

Figure 10.5   A Virtuous Circle for a Flourishing Team (*Review*, 2010: 18).

(b) **lives well-lived—sacramental living:** Sacramental living recognises the place of God in the life and worship of others within the Body of Christ and in all Creation, which has its embodied beginning in God.

(c) **diversity and individuality—sacramental community:** Sacramental community is the Body of Christ in action seeking healthy relationships within the body and with the wider social body which we seek to serve.

(Roberts et al., 2010: 18)

This summary represents part of the theological narrative about flourishing that was told in the *Review* and was referred to directly by the Bishop when he came to preach at the exhibition on 22nd July.[11] Other stories could have been told. For instance, it could have begun by examining historical research into the life and work of Jesus and its implications for the contemporary Church (Wright, 1996); or by recent understandings of the Church's mission and their implications for notions of flourishing (Bosch, 1992) or through influential writing on ideas about church leadership and analysis of its embedded principles of success (Hybels, 2002). These possibilities and many others remain in that part of the aquifer of untold stories for the review document as they were not part of localised storytelling (A) which was the main narrative source of the review.

THE REVIEW'S FINAL 'NARRATIVE'

Part of the untold story of the *Review* includes two significant comments from our external auditor about the first draft which were not included in the final version. In his annotated copy of the original edition, against the *Review* statement that reads: "One of the aims of this review is to provide a rich, narrative account of how the Warwick Team and Budbrooke see their individual and collective ministries at this point in time", the auditor has written: "But there has hardly been any narrative" (Statement and external auditor's comments from page 21 of the first draft of the review document).

Then further on, when the first draft considers "Future Options" it states on page 26:

if we continue this journey and our story together along such lines there are various issues which could usefully be addressed and examples include:

i. Does the Warwick Team wish to continue as a team?

ii. If the response is 'yes' does this review provide a helpful foundation on which to build?

iii. How can we develop the Team?

    iv. How to strengthen the Team—Possibilities might include existing ideas (*Take 5*, Lent groups) and new suggestions (taking a theme each year to explore individually and collectively—*Finding God* has been suggested for 2011)

    v. What should we do about the clergy Team-wide roles?

    vi. How should the relationship between the Team and Budbrooke be nurtured?

Once again the auditor observes: "A good set of conclusions, though the narrative idea has disappeared." (External auditor's comment on page 26 of the first draft of the review document).

The auditor is right at one level—the review became less concerned with collecting, collating, and analysing stories within the Team as it progressed. I would contend that the *process* of review became an important part of the story in itself and the final review document was a means of recording some of that narrative and telling a version of its story. An important comment at this stage of *Review* was the auditor's observation that: discovering that some people were expecting to find a single coherent story for the Team is a "big diagnostic finding". The reason for this is that within organizations (including the Church) "single purposes are always mistaken" (Roberts et al., first draft: 9). In other words, we *became* aware that we were a diverse group seeking to tell various stories from different perspectives some of which overlapped. A key aspect in the *Review*'s narrative approach was to allow as many voices as possible a say in the telling of the story.

The model of team working that the review then identified was that of a 'mixed economy' approach. The term was being used at the time by the Archbishop of Canterbury to encompass traditional organizational forms and "fresh expressions" (Williams, 2010—quoted in the Roberts et al., 2010: 11, 19, 29) but it seemed to many of those involved in the ministry of the Warwick Team and Budbrooke Parish that the mixed economy analogy also encapsulated our organizational relationships. It was in itself, a metaphor that would work with the diverse stories and counter stories (Roe, 1994) which had been filtered through the narrative aquifer of the review. The congregational meeting on 10th June 2010 explored the collective answers that we had provided to the Bishop's questions in the context of a mixed economy team.

We submitted the final *Review* document to the Bishop who came to the exhibition of their ministry mounted by the six churches but there was never any further or formal response to the *Review* as originally envisaged (Figure 10.3, above). One can speculate on the reasons why there was never any official reaction. One possibility is that the Bishop and his senior staff were entirely content with the outcome and saw no need to proceed further. Another is that they were happy enough and saw no need for further action. Alternatively, it may have lodged in the middle of a busy in-tray and never rose far enough up the ever-lengthening list of jobs that any bishop needs to address. Or it may be that the approach taken by the *Review* was very different to the Diocesan approach of identifying and encouraging the eight essential qualities for growing healthy churches.[12]

So in the absence of a response from diocesan senior staff and a conclusion as envisaged by the original process, the intriguing question presents itself: was the *Review* a told or untold story? In one sense it was clearly told as many voices spoke and were recorded sharing their perspectives. Yet in another sense, it is a story that seems to have no clear audience and no conclusion. In terms of the analogy of the aquifer (Figure 9.4) the water has emerged from below ground but has not risen through the organization to become part of the organizational culture.

AQUIFER FILTERS FOR TOLD AND UNTOLD STORIES

This chapter has examined three pools of told and untold stories in the process of reviewing the Warwick Team and Budbrooke Parish: (A) Narratives from within the communities; (B) The organizational metanarrative; and (C) The *Review*'s own narrative. The final part of this chapter will develop the aquifer analogy further and explore what kind of filters are at work, sifting those told and untold stories as they rise to the surface. We can identify four such filters: (i) the storyteller; (ii) other participants; (iii) The potential audience; (iv) wider narrative culture.

THE STORYTELLER

At one level, the main narrative voice in the review process was mine, in my capacity as Team Rector and principle author of the story. My research experience of organizational storytelling and sensemaking for my PhD meant that this was a process I was comfortable with (Roberts, 1999). If my background had been electrical engineering or international development it is likely that the *Review* would have taken a very different course. However, throughout the process of review there were also other significant contributors, e.g., papers prepared by Team clergy, the Bishop's four questions, the experiences garnered from the various church councils, and the input from the open congregational meeting.

Nevertheless, choices were made and some stories were included whilst others were omitted. A good example is provided by the meeting with St Paul's Church Council. A preparatory paper for the review described five models of the Church drawn from the work of Avery Dulles—institution, herald, servant, sacrament, and mystical communion (Dulles, 1974/1987). The image of the Church as a servant, attending to and serving its local community was a significant part of the emerging narrative stream. At the St Paul's meeting members of the council spoke about how that church began life as the place of worship for the servants of those who attended the large civic church of St Mary's but in the process of reclaiming this aspect of their story they speak of how the 'servants' church' now sees itself as the 'servant church' serving their local community.[13] Speaking personally, this vignette appeals to me at many levels—not least with its sharp word play and clever juxtaposition of organizational imagery. Yet as the narrative arc of the *Review* progressed this significant story for the community at St Paul's remained untold within the much broader narrative of the story I was seeking to tell about the Team.

OTHER PARTICIPANTS

The filter of other participants can work in different ways, so it is perfectly possible for various storytelling contributors to hold stories back because they either do not want to be known or feel awkward about putting them into the public arena. In the memorable words of the then Secretary State for Defense, Donald Rumsfeld: they are the "unknown unknowns—the ones we don't know we don't know" (Rumsfeld, 2002).[14] Of course, in the process of analyzing organizational storytelling, it may be possible to pick up hints about these hidden narrative streams and with careful searching discover their courses together with the springs and tributaries which feed them. In the course of such exploration untold stories are told. They are revealed and opened to scrutiny.

However, the withholding of untold stories may not be such a conscious or deliberate act. In the meeting with the Budbrooke Church Council I raised the matter of the meeting that St Michael's had with the previous Team Rector at the turn of the millennium over the creation of the new Team. All those around the table who had been involved with the church at that time were adamant that no such discussions had taken place.[15] This was in direct contradiction to the account given to me by my predecessor and the story which had been in widespread circulation within the Warwick Team. Since there seemed to be no obvious reason for either church council members or the Team Rector to be dissembling about this matter, what did this told/untold story mean? It could be that PCC members had forgotten the meeting or that both sides had misremembered. Perhaps the Team Rector had had a meeting with the previous Vicar of Budbrooke, who had now moved on. As the facilitator of the *Review*, the significance of this story was that in my mind, during the process of reviewing the Warwick Team and Budbrooke Parish, we would be returning to a prior conversation and picking up earlier threads of a discussion. In the event there was no shared story here and what I had thought might be significant common ground was filtered out of the *Review*'s narrative and became a "nonstory" (Roe, 1994).

POTENTIAL AUDIENCES

There would appear to be a number of potential audiences for this review. Most immediately the six churches, their church councils, and their congregations. Another key audience was the Bishop and his senior staff. Other potential onlookers would be more distant and might include posterity—would the Team churches return to this document a decade hence to consider these discussions and what had changed in the meantime? And what about other teams in the Church of England—could this review contribute to the debates about team-working elsewhere?

As 'lead' writer of the *Review*, I was conscious of all four potential audiences acting as filters on the narrative. So for instance in terms of the six churches, a principle narrative aim was to encourage as many voices as possible to be represented in the final draft so that there was potential for many untold stories to percolate through aquifer's filters. The Bishop's questions were another important filter because they focused the *Review* and storytelling in a certain direction. There was potentially less opportunity to range over the full terrain of the narrative aquifer and as the storyteller I faced a choice—should I extend the project to include the fullest collation of organizational narrative and then subsequently engage with the Bishop's questions or should I try and run both tasks together?

My judgment in this matter was that over time these two filters might end up in conflict, i.e., if we extended the project the patience of the first audience might be exhausted (the churches) before achieving what was required by the second (the Bishop). Therefore, it would be prudent to run the two together.

WIDER NARRATIVE CULTURE

The aquifer of what might be called a narrative ontology has many streams, which can be seen in a number of detailed analyses of Western culture and belief. For example, when Charles Taylor asks rhetorically: why was it virtually impossible not to believe in God in, say, 1500, while in 2000 many of us find this not only easy but inescapable? He responds: "One important part of the picture is that so many features of their world told in favour of belief, made the presence of God seemingly undeniable. I will mention three, which will play a part *in the story I want to tell*" (Taylor, 2007: 25—my emphasis). Similarly, Brad S. Gregory's sweeping account of the same period includes the statement:

> As we shall see in *filling out this story*, the secularization of knowledge in the West was not inevitable . . . it was a thoroughly contingent process derived from human interactions that involved assumptions, institutions, metaphysical beliefs, the exercise of power, and human desires

beyond the desire to discover and to learn. The *dominant narrative* of modern Western intellectual history, of course, suggests otherwise.

(Gregory, 2012: 307—my emphasis)

My aim is not engage directly with Taylor and Gregory's different retellings of the last 500 to 600 years of Western thought but to note their overt *narrative* framework.[16]

The metanarrative framing of communal storytelling is, as George Mead contends, biographical[17] but it is much more than that. It extends into the deepest wells of culture and identity. Therefore, although this review may be about six churches located in a specific place and time, its narrative context is extensive. In addition to streams of story identified in the work of Taylor and Gregory, there are a number of narrative flows operating here. These include: (i) *biblical narrative streams*—how do participants in the review understand Old Testament concepts (such as being the People of God, the Kingship of God, the role of the Prophets), (ii) *New Testament developments* (such as Jesus' ministry, the emergence of Paul and the early church); (iii) *theological narrative streams*—understanding of the Church (ecclesiology), ministry and priesthood; (iv) *management narrative streams*—how are local churches and church leadership understood in terms of contemporary organizational thinking?[18] All of these are being filtered here so that some accounts are told, whilst other stories remain untold.

CONCLUSION

This chapter has described how the Warwick Team and Budbrooke Parish set out to undertake a narrative review of their shared ministry in 2010. As the author of that review and one of the filters for the told and untold stories, I have sought to reflect critically on that process and bring to the surface some of those 'nonstories' (Roe, 1994) that were originally omitted. This has involved exploring how the Bishop's directive to identify: 'What makes for the flourishing of the Church and what is the shape of ministry to best serve this?' (*Review*, 2010: 5) was a significant narrative filter for (A) individual stories; (B) the organizational meta-narrative; and for (C) the narrative of the review itself. From this, I have identified four further filters which might shape any process of organizational storytelling: (i) The storyteller; (ii) Other participants; (iii) The potential audience; (iv) Wider narrative culture.

This is not merely an esoteric matter for churches or other religious bodies. As Keith Grint reminds us, imagination: is "crucial in the construction of what may be the most important element of leadership: the community narrative . . . the sense of narrative that roots a community in the past, explains its present, and conjures up a future" (Grint, 2000: 14). The process of filtering organizational stories is fundamental to understanding organizations and to leading them. I noted earlier that presently there is little quantitative or qualitative research into how teams function within the

Church of England. Such a deficit must be urgently remedied in order to better understand both how such organizational storytelling works and what implications this has for leadership. It is also important to bear in mind that narrative itself is socially constructed and that what counts as a story in one culture (or organizational culture) might not count as a story in another (Brown, Gabriel, & Gherardi, 2009: 329).

This chapter began with a reference to Umberto Eco's work of fiction *The Prague Cemetery*. At one point in the novel the central character is receiving reports from two colleagues about their battles whilst fighting with General Garibaldi. Captain Simonini asks himself:

> How can I rely on these two fanatics? They are young and this is their first experience of war. They had worshipped their General from the start and in their own way are storytellers like Dumas, embellishing their recollections so that all their geese are swans. (Eco, 2011: 123)

Through the device of getting Simonini to compare those reports of battle with the historical fictions of Alexandre Dumas, Eco is inviting us to reflect upon the whole process of reportage and storytelling, and to be aware of the filters that are at work as we read narratives of any kind. In this account my aim has been to give an open and critical account of some of the ways in which stories filter to the surface from one particular narrative aquifer, providing lakes and ponds where both (to use Eco's analogy) geese and swans will continue to swim.

NOTES

1. Thanks to my clergy colleagues in the Warwick Team and Budbrooke Parish, David Sims, and Claire Spivey for their comments on earlier drafts of this chapter.
2. See also Trompenaars and Hampden-Turner's *Riding the Waves of Culture* (Trompenaars & Hampden Turner, 1997)
3. I have variously considered water as a poetic metaphor for change (Roberts, 1997), a theoretical metaphor for change (Roberts, 2002), and a practical metaphor for change (Roberts, 2008).
4. Used with permission from the Regional District of Nanaimo (BC, Canada), artwork by Richard Franklin.
5. A research project into cathedrals, team ministries, and amalgamation of benefices has been established at the University of Durham but has yet to post results from its work, see Church Growth Research Programme at http://www.churchgrowthresearch.org.uk/cathedrals_amalgamations
6. For a theological discussion of a storied approach to church and embodied meaning see Smith (2013) which draws upon MacIntyre (1981) and bears comparison to Gabriel's description of stories as 'symbolically endowed material artefacts' and 'repositories of meaning, a meaning that both changes and is timeless' (Gabriel, 2000: 88).
7. On the place of conversation within church leaders narratives see Simpson (2012).

188   *Vaughan S. Roberts*

8. Correspondence to the Bishop dated July 5, 2010.
9. Quotations from my notes of that meeting.
10. Or in academic terms reviewing 'the literature'.
11. This is my personal recollection. As part of writing this chapter I approached the Bishop's office for the text of his sermon but no copy of his notes had been retained.
12. Empowering leadership, gift-orientated ministry, passionate spirituality, inspiring worship, holistic small groups, need-orientated outreach, loving relationships, and functional structures.
13. From the Team Rector's notes of the meeting at St Paul's Church.
14. US Department of Defense News Briefing (2002) available at http://www.defense.gov/transcripts/transcript.aspx?transcriptid=2636 (accessed 5th March 2013)
15. From the Team Rector's notes of the meeting at St Michael's Church.
16. For a critique of the 'narrative turn' particularly in North America (see, Salmon, 2010).
17. 'History is nothing but biography, a whole series of biographies' (Mead, 1962: 36) cf. Weick's comment about using 'one's own life as data' (Weick, 1995: 191 see above p 253).
18. On applying the biblical metaphor of a 'canon' to organizational narrative see Sims (1999: 41–57).

REFERENCES

Alvesson, M., & Spicer, A. (2011). *Metaphors We Lead By: Understanding Leadership in the Real World*. London: Routledge.
Bosch, D.J. (1992). *Transforming Mission: Paradigm Shifts in Theology of Mission*. Maryknoll, NY: Orbis Books.
Brown, A.D., Gabriel, Y., & Gherardi, S. (2009). Storytelling & change: An unfolding story. *Organization, 16*(3): 323–333.
Church of England, The. (2014) Structure. Retrieved from http://www.churchofengland.org/about-us/structure.aspx.
Cummings, S. (2002). *ReCreating Strategy*. London: Sage.
Cummings, S., & Wilson, D. C. (Eds.). (2003). *Images of Strategy*. Oxford: Blackwell Publishing.
Dulles, A. (1987). *Models of the Church* (Expanded ed.). New York: Doubleday. (Original work published in 1974)
Eco, U. (2011). *The Prague Cemetery*. London: Harvill Secker.
Ford, D.F. (1999). *Self & Salvation: Being Transformed*. Cambridge: Cambridge University Press.
Gabriel, Y. (2000). *Storytelling in Organizations: Facts, Fictions, & Fantasies*. Oxford: Oxford University Press.
Good Practice in Group and Team Ministry. ABM/ACCM Occasional Paper No. 39 (1991). London: Church House Publishing.
Graham, E.L. (Ed.). (2009). *Grace Jantzen: Redeeming the Present*. Farnham: Ashgate.
Gregory, B.S. (2012). *The Unintended Reformation: How a Religious Revolution Secularized Society*. London: Belknap Press.
Grint, K. (2000). *The Arts of Leadership*. Oxford: Oxford University Press.
Hampden-Turner, C. (1994). *Corporate Culture: From Vicious to Virtuous Circles* (2nd ed.). London: Piatkus.
Hybels, B. (2002). *Courageous Leadership*. Grand Rapids, MI: Zondervan.

Lakoff, G., & Johnson, M. (1980). *Metaphors We Live By*. London: University of Chicago Press.

MacIntyre, A. (1981). *After Virtue: A Study in Moral Theory*. London: Duckworth.

Mead, G. H. (1962). *Mind, Self & Society: From the Standpoint of a Social Behaviorist* (C. W. Morris, Ed.). Chicago: University of Chicago Press.

Morgan, G. (1988). *Riding the Waves of Change: Developing Managerial Competencies for a Turbulent World*. London: Jossey-Bass Publishers.

Morgan, G. (1996). An afterword: Is there anything more to be said about metaphor. In D. Grant & C. Oswick (Eds.), *Metaphor & Organizations* (pp. 227–240). London: Sage.

Morgan, G. (1997). *Images of Organization* (2nd ed.). London: Sage.

Roberts, V. S. (1997). The sea of faith: After Dover Beach. *Modern Believing*, *xxxviii*(3): 25–34.

Roberts, V. S. (1999). *Sensemaking, Metaphor & Mission in an Anglican Context* (Unpublished PhD thesis). University of Bath, Bath, UK.

Roberts, V. S. (2002). Water as an implicit metaphor for organizational change within the Church. *Implicit Religion*, 5(1): 29–40.

Roberts, V. S. (2008). Riding waves of liturgical change. In J. Nelson (ed.), *How to Become a Creative Church Leader* (pp. 53–67). Norwich: Canterbury Press.

Roberts, V. S. (2010). *A Review of the Warwick Team and Budbrooke Parish*. An organisational report commissioned by the Bishop of Coventry (unpublished).

Roe, E. (1994). *Narrative Policy Analysis: Theory & Practice*. London: Duke University Press.

Rumsfeld, D. (2002) Secretary of State Press Briefing US Department of Defense. Retrieved from http://www.defense.gov/transcripts/transcript.aspx?transcriptid=2636.

Salmon, C. (2010). *Storytelling: Bewitching the Modern Mind*. London: Verso.

Simpson, P. (2012). Complexity & change management: Analyzing church leaders narratives. *Journal of Organizational Change Management*, 25(2): 283–296.

Sims, D. (1999). Organizational learning as the development of stories. In M. Easterby-Smith, J. Burgoyne, & L. Araujo, (Eds.), *Organizational Learning & the Learning Organization* (pp. 44–58). London: Sage.

Smith, J. K. A. (2013). *Imagining the Kingdom: How Worship Works*. Grand Rapids, MI: Baker Academic Press.

Soskice, J. M. (1985). *Metaphor & Religious Language*. Oxford: Clarendon Press.

Taylor, C. (2007). *A Secular Age*. London: Belknap Press.

Trompenaars, F., & Hampden-Turner, C. (1997). *Riding the Waves of Culture: Understanding Cultural Diversity in Business* (2nd ed.). London: Nicholas Brealey.

Weick, K. (1995). *Sensemaking in Organizations*. London: Sage.

Williams, R. (2010). *The Archbishop of Canterbury's General Synod response to Mission-shaped Church: Report from the Mission & Public Affairs Council*. Retrieved from http://rowanwilliams.archbishopofcanterbury.org/articles.php/1955/mission-shaped-church-report-from-the-mission-and-public-affairs-council.

Wright, N. T. (1996). *Jesus and the Victory of God*. London: SPCK.

11 How Stories Make It
Antenarrative, Graffiti, and Dead Calves

Gillian Hopkinson

INTRODUCTION

There is substantial support across the social sciences for a view of homo narrans (Fisher, 1985) in which story is at the centre of society. Broadly, this view asserts that we make sense of the world in our stories, communicate that sense through story, and learn of the world as others make sense of it when we listen to story. Consequence and credibility are important ingredients in this 'narrative turn'. Stories are consequential because we live in the world according to its shape and logic as produced and re-produced in our stories (Sarbin, 1986). To be credible a story must possess narrative logic (Polkinghorne, 1988) and by establishing such logic must be seen by its audiences as credible (Bruner, 1986).

Without denying the importance of a story seen by others as credible, some authors have pointed to the difficulty of establishing such a story. Amongst organizational scholars, David Boje in particular has expanded upon the fragility of story. He offers the concept of the antenarrative (Boje, 2001) which both precedes the settled narrative and is a speculative bet upon how we might make sense of the world. The idea that alternative stories exist which have the potential to disrupt a settled narrative is well evoked in seeing the antenarrative as a rhizome that throws down roots and is able to erupt in unpredictable ways. According to this metaphor, antenarratives have their own life and lurk around, with an ability to change more dominant storylines where and when they come into contact. In order to understand narrative processes, then, we should look at the interaction between multiple stories, those widely told and those with more restricted credibility, untold in a wider arena. This chapter is concerned with this interaction between told and untold and with how public understanding is shaped through these narrative and antenarrative interactions. The chapter looks at how an antenarrative might 'make it' to become a narrative, by which I mean to establish coherence and become the basis of action for multiple actors. The chapter looks also at the contest among and between narratives and antenarratives since, where contact is made, multiple stories support, undermine, or divert one another. One crucial element of this contest lies in the successful assertion of a distinction between what can be told here and now and what is untellable. The chapter aims to demonstrate the precarious nature of narrative given its continuous vulnerability to the emergence of the untold. The chapter develops these themes.

The chapter is organized as follows. Firstly, I develop the concepts that inform my approach by expanding upon the concept of antenarrative and then offering graffiti (or more accurately 'graffing') as a metaphor that depicts the process of story interaction. I argue that this captures aspects of the intentional insertion and deletion of elements in the narrative, that is, graffiti helps us conceptualize storytelling contest. Then, I turn to look at how one object (the male calf in the UK dairy system) has been storied since around 1990. Here I consider the relationships between two antenarratives that account for the object in different ways. My focus is upon identifying the included (told) and excluded (untold) elements in each and, drawing on the metaphor of graffiti, I demonstrate the lurking presence of the untold by tracing the relationship between the stories. The discussion returns more explicitly to the theme of graffiti and draws out the ways in which this allows us to relate the told and the untold. In conclusion I summarise my arguments and point to the potential and pitfalls of the approach that I have advocated.

ANTENARRATIVE

The more prevalent approach to story, within organizational studies as elsewhere, focuses upon narrative. Definitions of narrative highlight the role of sequence and emplotment (Czarniawska, 1997; Watson, 2009) so that a narrative offers an ordered account of a flow of events. Narratives also provide explanation in establishing the links between events and characters. Within a narrative we are told, albeit often implicitly, how something was caused, who is responsible and who is able to, or should, act upon a situation (Gabriel, 2000). Additionally, narratives portray characters and 'types', inviting or compelling the audience to place themselves within this or similar situations (Gabriel, 2000). These are the features that enable 'narrative logic' (Polkinghorne, 1988) so that narratives are credible and powerful devices through which we understand the world.

The power of narrative to construct and communicate meaning is well recognised in the study of organizations. Early contributions emphasised the role of the narrative in providing a unitary meaning (e.g., Clark, 1972). Subsequently researchers have highlighted difference across the narratives told by different organizational groups about one topic (e.g., Brown, 1998). The latter approach depicts narrative as sufficiently persistent and shared to provide a common understanding within a group that legitimises a certain course of action and furthers the group's interests. Such narratives accord with the idea of a 'petrified' narrative (Czarniawska, 2004) that seeks to control and convey a singular meaning.

Derrida (e.g., 1979) and Bakhtin (e.g., 1973) criticise the view of a monolithic narrative and provide the basis to see meaning as fragile and multiple. Accordingly, storytelling may be seen as more active, since meaning is always contestable. Also it is more difficult to establish credibility and have that accepted by others in the face of alternative accounts, with alternative emplotments, characterization, and so on. Boje (1995) therefore depicts the organization as a storytelling system in which stories emerge from collective contributions and are differentially understood by diverse audiences according to their own individual engagements with the events. In place of the stabilised and shared meaning of the narrative, Boje (2001) proposes the antenarrative. Drawing on the dual meaning of ante, the antenarrative is both a tentative attempt to give meaning to a situation and a bet upon the ability to provide a credible account. The intervention of antenarrative in storytelling systems is evident in the following definition that also richly portrays the dynamic and agentive qualities of story-telling attempts. Antenarrative is "a gambler's bet that a before-story (pre-story) can take flight and disrupt and transform narrative practice" (Boje, Rosile, & Gardner, 2004: 1).

Boje emphasises insecurity and speculation in our attempts to create meaning in the storytelling system. This arises because no story is isolated but must be reconciled in some way with other stories with which it shares some terrain. The multiple stories that confront each attempt to tell a singular story are those told both by others (Izak, 2014), and by the storyteller (at other times or about related topics) that interact with the current telling. The fragmented audience, wherein each person's engagement relates to their diverse involvements with stories told elsewhere, both complicates the possibility of communicating a solid and singular meaning and also provides the possibility for the antenarrative to "take flight" (Boje et al., 2004: 1) in multiple directions. This is illustrated by Sims, Huxham, and Beech (2009) who write of "snippets" de-contextualised by the audience of one telling and re-contextualised for their audiences in other arenas. In effect this means that stories (within and across tellers) are networked within a system. There are innumerable connections to other stories (Hitchin, 2014) and the boundaries between stories are porous.

Contrast and contest both feature in the relationships between antenarrative and narrative. Antenarratives are improper, fragmented, polyvocal, and lack the clear linear structure of narrative. The two are opposed "in 'story space' that is contested collective memory" (Boje et al., 2004: 6). Struggle to align the fragmented elements in order to create a clear structure that can be accepted in a collective space underpins the contest between narrative and antenarrative. "Antenarratives are bundles, weakly linked assemblages, not yet petrified into a tight narrative frame" (Boje, 2011: 9). The tighter bonding of elements into a coherent explanation casts those elements in a new light or modifies them, calling into question the way they are constructed and accounted for in other stories. Antenarratives thus interact with narrative and either has the potential to undermine the other in what might be seen as a contest for broader acceptance, that is, a contest for narrative status. This contest is a political site in which meanings are made, rather than seeing the more petrified narrative as the vehicle to further interests formed outside narration (Brown, 1998).

Antenarratives are often contrasted to narrative through characteristics such as being improper, fragmented, and polyvocal. The active depiction of antenarratives is more relevant to consideration of the told and untold. Narratives provide a coherent and linear account and that which lies outside the line "gets erased out of awareness" (Boje, 2011: 13). Yet, descriptions of the antenarrative suggest that what has been erased from current telling both remains and is active. We have already seen that antenarratives "take flight and disrupt and transform" (Boje et al., 2004: 1). Antenarratives also "morph and coalesce" (Boje, 2011: 1) and "cling to other fragments" (Boje, 2011: 3). "Antenarratives involve a form of re-packaging—where new characteristics are recognized and old characteristics are minimized" (Boje, 2011: 1). In this way, the untold remains a threat to the coherence of the narratives from which it was excluded precisely because it was necessarily excluded to permit coherence. The ever present untold is particularly well evoked through Boje's metaphor of the rhizome. Boje (2011) describes how underground tubers send out runners and appear above ground in unpredictable ways to form new plants. Many are pervasive 'weeds' that wrap their roots around those of other plants making it near impossible to remove in its entirety.

Despite the richness of metaphor in the extant literature, I shall now introduce graffiti as a metaphor that foregrounds the political and ideological workings within narrative processes. Antenarratives are agential, as Boje argues and the rhizome enables us to see, but their use, appearance and disappearance involves social negotiation to an extent that is more clearly visible in the metaphor of graffiti.

GRAFFITI

The metaphor of graffiti is inspired, in part, by Colville and Pye (2010) who respond to the idea that sense is made in picture form. To emphasise process and the continuously tentative character of understanding, they argue that we should instead consider pictur*ing*. Here I explore graffiti as a form of picturing. Graffiti offers conceptual insight into narrative processes and in particular emphasises fragility and continuous struggle in the movements of antenarrative and the making of narrative. More accurately, and to draw on terms used within graffiti communities, the processes are demonstrated in the graffing activity of graffers in the production of graffiti. Graffiti is thus faithful to the idea of picturing and antenarrative and avoids the 'petrified' meaning of the linear narrative which is evoked in the picture metaphor.

Several features of graffiti are pertinent to its application. Firstly, the practice of graffing, as well as the specific content of particular graffiti, is ideological in that it expresses and communicates an interconnected and deeper set of beliefs and values about the nature of shared space and of society. Secondly, the nature of its location in public space means that graffiti is ephemeral. Thirdly, graffiti is relational, by which I mean that it establishes meaning through its relationship to other or previous works. Finally, graffiti is read differently by diverse audiences. Graffiti therefore allows us to locate meaning making within the social world and to see meaning built and read through a cumulative inter-play of complementary or competing contributions that themselves derive their meaning making potential from their usage elsewhere. The metaphor enables a view of antenarrative processes and the possibility of disruption of a narrative through the introduction of the untold or the reintroduction of the no-longer-told-here. I shall expand upon these points in this section.

Firstly, an introduction to the terms I shall be using. *Graffiti* (from *graffio*, a scratch) is applied to several 'art' forms that vary in sophistication and include *tags* (signature markings, or iconographic logos), *pieces* (masterpieces that are more elaborate and multi-coloured), *murals* (that cover an entire wall), and *aphorisms* or sayings as found in restroom graffiti. The various forms are typically located in public space. The 'artist' is often referred to as a *graffer* and their activity as *graffing*.

The contested nature of terms, including those used in the previous paragraph such as *art* and *public*, is a key theme in literature that addresses graffiti. Many writers (see especially Halsey & Young, 2000; McAuliffe & Iveson, 2011; Schacter, 2008) depict a struggle over how commerce, ownership, authority, aesthetics, and vandalism are defined in the activities of graffers and counter activities of commerce (through advertising) or authorities (through graffiti removal). To graff at all is therefore a public expression of particular meanings and ideas that are grounded in a broader understanding of society, or ideology, and it asserts a right to speak on a topic in a certain place and time and in a certain way. The ideological content of graffiti is particularly explicit in the graffiti of the conflict zone (such as Northern Ireland or Palestine) that re-produces the beliefs appropriate to a specific zone. Symbolic elements, with a particular local resonance and meaning, instantiate and authorise the versions of identity, history, and beliefs appropriate to the locale (McCormick & Jarman, 2005). The use of graffiti to claim rights to speak in a locale and to define what may be said is also found in the practice of tagging where a crew (or gang) marks its territory by repetition of its logos and in order to exclude others (Lachmann, 1988). Graffing highlights, therefore, an assertion of the right to contribute to a story and alerts us to negotiated conventions concerning who may speak, what may be said and where it may be said.

Despite the conventions that operate at one time and in one place, the literature also highlights the ephemeral character of graffiti arising from its public setting. McCormick and Jarman (2005: 64) elaborate the various ways in which graffiti 'is disappeared' which may relate to the decay or destruction of its physical environment, weathering or its removal by authorities, as well as partial or complete overwriting by graffers. Overwriting may subvert or re-enforce a message and the message itself may become inappropriate either because a community has moved or because circumstances have changed or the space may be sufficiently desirable for others to want to occupy it. The term 'being disappeared' is used to "connote the lack of public discourse over the removal" (McCormick & Jarman, 2005: 64). Use of the passive transitive verb emphasises the hidden agency as well as the unknown outcome of removal or overwriting. The apparent destruction of previous work may, however, be taken as proof of its efficacy. Weathering makes a work look more 'at home' and removal or overwriting of graffiti evidences the success of the provocation or the desirability of location (Schacter, 2008). Even where graffiti is disappeared it leaves "aftershocks and tremors . . . disappearance from actual sight but perhaps not from active memory" (Schacter, 2008: 46). Therefore, previous use of a site intrudes upon future attempts to create meaning.

The movement of meaning within graffing is evident in practices which include the insertion of additions, the use of aphorisms or familiar images, the copying and mimicking of styles and topics between pieces, and the incorporation of local features. What is particularly pronounced in these borrowings are the subversion and diversion of meaning where, for example, Banksy incorporates street furniture in his work (Dickens, 2008) or in the multiple contributions to restroom 'conversations'. In these practices, pre-existing elements are rearranged and the construction and communication of meaning draws upon the audience's prior familiarity with those elements. These ideas are in keeping with Boje's (2011) description of the reassemblage of elements and the creeping and unpredictable recurrence of the rhizome. The graffing metaphor encourages us, however, to explore the process as one in which intentional agents work to reassemble elements in antenarrative.

Finally, the ambiguity of meaning for multiple audiences is highlighted by the idea that graffiti draws meaning from a pre-existing familiarity with its images and styles amongst audiences. Established understandings amongst some groups may render the piece unintelligible or give the piece an alternative meaning to others. This same ambiguity makes the graffiti versatile in its use. That is, just as Sims, Huxham, and Beech (2009) describe how an audience extract snippets which they may endow with new meaning in other contexts, the ambiguity of graffiti encourages such re-contextualisation of elements according to the viewer's engagement within conversations elsewhere.

For the reasons outlined here, graffiti provides a metaphor that invites us to consider how meaning is made through the assemblage of elements in a story network. Specifically, it focuses attention upon who is allowed, or makes a claim, to say what, where, and when. The metaphor also high-lights the de-contextualisation and re-contextualisation of story elements in alternative antenarratives. The ideological power of narrative is recognised along with the often obscured agency through which antenarratives are cre-ated, developed, or removed as they fight for narrative status. Accordingly, I illustrate these elements through the antenarratives pertaining to male calves in the UK dairy sector.

AN ILLUSTRATIVE CASE—DAIRY BULLOCKS

Background and Methods

I shall apply the metaphor of graffiti to an illustrative case regarding the treatment of dairy bullocks in the UK. The topic is apposite since there is a tension between the need for continuous calf production in the dairy industry and the absence of veal (calf meat) in the contemporary British diet. Accordingly the problem arises: what is to be done with dairy bullocks? Mixed and publicly available sources including TV, print media, and orga-nizational websites document different ways of understanding and solving the problem. Using these sources it is possible to identify several distinct but linked storylines or antenarratives that address the situation. In this analysis I shall focus upon only two antenarratives concerning dairy bullocks and my aim is to show the interaction of the two and the vulnerability of each to the other.

I developed my database by following the traces between texts across times and arenas. An initial text search for 'veal' in UK print media data-base (Nexis) rapidly became more confused since texts reference others. For example, a newspaper report may use quotes from other organizations and establish relevance by commenting on recent TV coverage and evidence a stance by profiling a particular farmer and their practices. True to the notion that interaction, de-contextualisation, and re-contextualisation are central to the construction of meaning in graffiti, I followed these traces to the websites or other press comment upon cited organizations (a similar method and intent is used by Izak, 2014). Clearly such a snowballing technique has no natural boundary and rapidly leads through to antenarratives about, for example, other aspects of food production. Therefore, I have selected mate-rial and traced contributions through to the extent where I felt able to pres-ent the antenarratives and draw out aspects of interaction without claiming to exhaust the field of interacting antenarratives.

In my analysis I pay attention to contributions from diverse organiza-tions within the storylines and report documented events that indicate the pervasiveness or otherwise of the antenarratives on a broader social stage. I also pay attention to 'disappearance' and to what is excluded that enables coherence. My approach is structured around the idea of problem and solution because, as Grint (2005: 1470) explains, "the environment is not some objective variable . . . but rather an 'issue' to be constituted into a whole variety of 'problems' or 'irrelevances'". The antenarratives constitute different issues of the dairy bullocks and the antenarratives account for the problem and solution.

I shall be looking at narrative processes focusing on two antenarratives. These are not neatly bounded to sequenced periods, but overlap and interact over an extended time frame. Nevertheless, it is possible to see a period when each gained more widespread credibility and at least reached towards narrative status. The first antenarrative, in which the issue is live transport, was dominant between 1990 and 1996—a period marked by relevant legislation as I shall show. However, the antenarrative had circulated since the 1960s and continues to do so to this day, albeit garnering less attention. The second antenarrative, in which the issue is the lack of a market for veal within the UK, can be traced at least to 1994 when the term 'rose veal' was applied to denote a high welfare, British product. This antenarrative has gained some prominence and credibility since about 2006 through media exposure. My analysis explores in more detail the narrative processes through which these antenarratives became settled and gained wider circulation with a focus also upon the interaction between the two.

ANTENARRATIVE ONE: AN ISSUE OF ANIMAL WELFARE

The first antenarrative constitutes the issue as one of animal welfare and focuses upon systems of veal production (in dark, single animal crates) and live transportation. A key narrator is Compassion in World Farming (CIWF), a group founded in the UK in 1967 to address farm animal welfare. Although the group campaigned against crate rearing in the 1970s and 80s the issue received scant attention in the national press. During this period veal featured occasionally in cookery columns and rather more in restaurant reviews and travel features. This changed in 1990 when legislation banned the crate rearing of calves, ahead of similar European legislation in 2007.

Ironically, the ban on crate rearing, an aspiration of the CIWF, greatly increased the live export trade creating conditions for the emergence of the CIWF antenarrative into a broader arena. Continued comment from the CIWF now met with the visible transportation of nearly half a million calves a year on the roads and through the ferry ports of the UK. This led to a 'virtuous spiral' through which the antenarrative reached greater prominence and gained support. Newsworthy port protests increased reportage of the CIWF story which swelled protestor numbers making the protests all the more newsworthy. The spiral intensified when, in 1992, continental concerns about BSE (mad cow disease) in Britain led to the relaxation of elements of the law that had been intended to protect animal welfare during transport. With a public alerted to the transport, calves now had to be transported in sealed trucks and without any periods of break to prevent contamination of continental stock. "This should be the final nail in the coffin for this horrendous and evil trade", said CIWF (*The Guardian*, 1992, November 16). However, as the trade continued the protests increased in size and, accordingly, so too did press coverage. At its height, a port picket had drawn approximately 2,500 protestors per night (*The Independent*, 2006, March 6).

Through the early 1990s, the antenarrative that constituted animal welfare as the issue and focused in particular upon the poor welfare standards of live transport gained sufficiently widespread credibility to effect material change amongst a variety of market actors. In July and August 1994, P&O, Brittany Ferries and Stena Sealink announced that they would not transport live animals. New companies (e.g., Ferrylink) were established solely for animal transport, and these operated out of lower profile ports. Freight airlines (e.g., Pheonix) also entered the market. In 1994, a flight carrying calves crashed. In the next year a protestor against air haulage of live animals was killed by a cattle truck at Coventry Airport. Both incidents generating additional media coverage. Various regional airports agreed and then pulled out of cattle freight contracts. Calves were shipped to Ireland, from where they were then flown to Europe.

There was some response also from the retailers, although this was less widely reported. On 10 January 1995, *The Times* reported that veal sold at Waitrose was sourced from British farms, naming Tesco as one store that stocked continental veal. *The Daily Mail* on 12 January 1995 reported that Tesco would discontinue imported veal and stock only British veal within one month. In these ways the retailers signalled some intention to enable a UK market that might reduce calf transport, although, as previously noted, UK sales of veal were minimal.

In presenting my narrative account, I hope to have demonstrated that a narrative developed and grew in credibility through the interaction of antenarratives told in different arenas. Such arenas include policy conversations within the CIWF, conversations amongst the protestors at the ferry ports, the media coverage, and discussions within the board rooms of commercial organizations. The key point, for me, is that whilst elements were undoubtedly somewhat differently understood and expressed within such contexts, each conversation was shaped by conversations taking place elsewhere. Just as graffiti can be used to instantiate a particular belief to a locale and may also draw on and adapt or subvert recognised slogans and images to current purposes, so each antenarrative is suited to context but takes shape from the way it draws off a broader storytelling space.

Through the 1990s, growing coalescence around at least sufficient ground for a widely tellable narrative to form was established such that it became a basis for actions across multiple types of organizations. We may see the retailers' and ferry operators' actions as commercial responses to public concern. The actions are also indicative of the narrative status of this particular rendition of the calf problem which was repeatedly graffed in the national media through coverage of port protests. At the same time, as corporate actions were reported, they too became part of the assemblage, giving further credibility to the narrative. We can only speculate upon how elements of the narrative were re-contextualised in the antenarratives of the board rooms of ferry companies and retailers. It is clear, however, that board room talk was networked to the public narrative.

The antenarrative gained strength to take on narrative status in public arenas, but it did so through what was excluded from the assemblage of elements. The processes of exclusion are similar to the conventions surrounding which graffers, styles, and images are acceptable to a locale and to the overwriting, white washing or graffiti removal through which such conventions operate. Exclusion of the untold had two effects. Firstly, it allowed the production of a relatively settled narrative that could circulate and gain a wider community of narrators. Secondly, that which would have unsettled the coherence of the explanation was excluded. The untold elements lurked in antenarratives told elsewhere.

There is evidence of elements from antenarratives told elsewhere that intruded upon the narrative but failed to unsettle it. For example, elements that would construct the calf question as an issue of consumption were excluded from a narrative about animal welfare. Discussion about the moral rights and wrongs of meat consumption, vegan and vegetarian antenarratives were suspended or set aside from the dominant narrative of calf export (*The Independent*, 1995, January 6). In the same way, differences between a moderate mainstream (with which the CIWF was identified) and more violent protestors were noted (*The Independent*, 1995, January 6). This article elaborated upon the similarity between the more militant wing and those attacking medical research facilities using animals and even to "American pro-life activists who have taken to killing the staff at abortion clinics". Such differences amongst protestors were nevertheless excluded from much of the reportage in which the protestors were referred to collectively, implying shared understandings and objectives and coalescence around one narrative. In a similar vein, the dairy industry was largely excluded from the narrative and it was only some time after the commencement of protests that an attack upon milk tankers was reported (*The Observer*, 1995, June 4). What was revealed, as the protests intensified and more violent methods were deployed by some, was the permeability of the narrative. Antenarratives surrounding 'animal rights' with respect to, for example, vivisection and medical research, the ethics of consumption, the rights and wrongs of the food production system all could be linked to the narrative. Audiences had diverse pre-existing understandings of these antenarratives that would be carried through were they to be inserted in the narrative. Not only would their inclusion unsettle the narrative but it would fragment those able to narrate it. Through 1994 and 1995 this narrative began to look increasingly unstable and vulnerable to those elements that had to remain untold in order for the narrative to be coherent and widely tellable. Yet the exclusion of such elements in many renditions allowed the narrative to persist until legislation in 1996 made this construction of the issue problematic.

In 1996, calf export was banned by the European Union due to the increased incidence of BSE in the UK and growing concerns about its effect upon human health. Since the narrative that treated calf transport as the issue became irrelevant this opened the way for greater contest between alternative antenarratives. The legislated ban exposed the problem brought about by realization of the former narrative; no adequate and accepted element explained what should be done with dairy bullocks if they are not to be exported. This issue had never been satisfactorily addressed in the former narrative and to have done so would have necessitated engagement with contested antenarratives which gave greater prominence to, for example, the ethics of meat consumption and the role of the dairy industry.

The public media turned to coverage of political debate surrounding levels of compensation paid to the farmers now they had no market for the calves and to the abattoirs in which the now worthless calves were slaughtered. "This is the slaughter of the innocent. The government is treating these tiny animals like trash instead of respecting them as sentient creatures capable of feeling pain and fear," said CIWF (*The Times*, 1996, April 24). As we have seen, multiple antenarratives that circulating around but were largely excluded from the narrative might see the correct treatment of animals in different ways.

On the resumption of live calf transport in June 2006, the CIWF relaunched a campaign against the trade, broadening this to a more general attack upon global animal transport (*The Independent*, 2006, May 1). However, in the interim period the acceptance of the narrative had subsided and its influence is notably lower. Whilst there have been some port protests, these have not reached previous levels. The incoherence of such a narrative and the exposure of the absence of an alternative treatment of dairy bullocks through reportage of slaughter and incineration opened a space for alternative antenarratives to gain greater traction. Of the alternative antenarratives about male dairy calves, I shall examine one in order to draw out the narrative processes running between the two accounts.

ANTENARRATIVE TWO: AN ISSUE OF THE MARKET

The second antenarrative centres upon 'rose veal', which, according to the Nexis database is first used in UK print media in 1994 in an article that locates its origins in relationship to the first antenarrative. *The Glasgow Herald* (1994, December 2) reported protests at Prestwich airport near Glasgow and presented two alternatives to live transport, namely slaughter or the development of a market for 'rose veal'. Rose veal calves are not reared in crates and are fed a mixed diet instead of a milk based diet. The development of a market for this 'high welfare' meat is central to the second antenarrative in which the issue is the lack of a viable UK market for veal. Thus the second antenarrative began to form whilst the first antenarrative was dominant and has, throughout, been shaped by its relationship to the first.

Within the early period of development of this second antenarrative, like graffers partially overwriting a piece, some narrators sought to insert alternative narrative elements to the assemblage of the, then rising, first antenarrative. For example, The Times (1995, February 8) quoted a rose veal farmer, Mr O'Connell, who feared for his safety in the light of a possible ban on live export: "I think that what we are doing here is what the concerned middle-class protestor would accept was the real way out of the problem". Here, Mr O'Connell implies a distinction between the concerned moderate and the violent militant of whom he is scared. For Mr O'Connell it is possible to subvert elements and thus re-shape the story whilst still appealing to (many of) its followers. Other farmers, however, sought to remove the first antenarrative without replacement. The National Farmers' Union (NFU) focused its comments upon the practical difficulties and physical dangers farmers faced because of the protest activity. The NFU 'poured scorn' on the idea of a UK market for higher welfare veal for which the British consumers had no taste (*The Independent*, 1995, January 10).

The antenarrative gained greater attention from around 2006 when it was taken up by celebrities able to bring it to television and other media. TV programmes included Gordon Ramsey's *The F Word* in August 2006 featuring also Janet Street Porter, well known journalist (*The Grocer*, 2007, November 26). Long standing radio soap opera *The Archers* featured a storyline in summer 2010 in which Vicky, unused to country life, attempted to 'save' her new husband's dairy calves from slaughter at birth to rear them instead for rose veal (*The Daily Telegraph*, 2010, July 24). Chef Hugh Fearnley-Whittingstall's Good Veal Campaign launched in 2006 was widely reported in the press (see The Independent, 2006, articles). High profile TV or radio coverage was amplified by reports of such programmes in other arenas such as the print media. Increased use of rose veal within the food and cookery sections of the newspapers was evident in the period.

Through the growing circulation of the second antenarrative, the inevitability of a relationship to the first antenarrative becomes apparent. The second antenarrative is informed by traces from the first. Specifically, veal is seen as unethical and carries meanings arising from the stress placed upon unethical treatment of calves in the first antenarrative. That the ethical discussion hinged around features of transport and rearing that are eliminated in the higher welfare product may well not be recognised. The Grocer (2008, August 23) aptly summarises: "public opinion . . . generally regards veal as ethically somewhere between dodo omelettes and panda fritters". That is, a meaning has been instantiated that is difficult to dislodge regardless of 'the facts'. This provides the context with which any narrative promoting veal consumption must engage.

The difficulty of constructing a viable narrative for a high welfare market in the face of the aftershocks from the first antenarrative is recognised by the celebrities and other narrators in the general media. Predominant features of TV and print media coverage in all these arenas included the recognition of the significant UK consumer barriers to rose veal due to ethical sensitivities and lack of product familiarity. Rose veal is storied as an ethical alternative to the destruction of calves within their first 24 hours of life. In this way, attempts to construct meaning recognise the ethical barriers to consumption, but seek to detach these ethical concerns from live transport and attach them to slaughter at home. We have already seen that, in introducing rose veal, farmer O'Connell drew upon instabilities in the first antenarrative by presenting a solution acceptable to 'the concerned middle class protestor'. I have discussed how the first antenarrative accommodated differences between 'concerned moderates' and 'extreme activists' and between vegetarians, vegans, and meat eaters through exclusion of elements in the narrative. The second antenarrative stories the issue as lack of a market and in so doing seeks to re-contextualise and re-assemble the ethical sensitivities of a more moderate, meat eating mainstream. The intended audience that might propel the growth of the antenarrative includes many of those who engaged with the former narrative.

However, the second antenarrative also struggled with questions of fissure amongst the potential audience. In many ways this story told by celebrity chefs was about the alternative: the lone farmer, the farmers' markets, the 'foodie'. In summer 2012, *Jimmy and the Giant Supermarket* (JGS) was broadcast on Channel 4 in an appeal to the mainstream (Sheahan, 2012). Jimmy Doherty (well known TV food and farm campaigner) documented his attempt to introduce veal meatballs to Tesco's own label range. The programme sought to address both consumer acceptance and mainstream retail availability by developing an affordable rose veal product.

JGS presented footage of three one-day old calves being shot, juxtaposed at other times of the programme with 'happy' calves in large barns or on pasture. Rose veal, we are told, will prevent the calves being shot, rendered down, and shipped to Holland for use in energy production. The programme gained print coverage, focusing especially upon the suitability of the slaughter scene, but in this way the story gained wider telling. Internet searches on 'rose veal' peaked over the period of broadcast (http://www.google.co.uk/trends/) to decline shortly afterwards.

The inclusion of the mainstream remained, however, difficult. We see the enthusiastic consumer response to the veal meatballs in film shots where Jimmy vividly recounts the antenarrative in public arenas. The relevance of the antenarrative to the world of the mainstream consumer is implicitly critiqued by Tesco. Jimmy can produce an economically viable meat ball through the addition of herbs and stuffing. Tesco abruptly counter that these inclusions will 'turn kids off in their thousands' and limit the versatility that is the key selling point of meatballs. With more limited market potential, Jimmy nevertheless succeeds in gaining a listing for rose veal fillets under the Tesco brand. Thus, tension remains surrounding the possibility of incorporating the mainstream to the antenarrative and detaching this from a story that should exist only in the more foodie contexts and the, for many, fantasy contexts of celebrity cooking.

The broader currency of the antenarrative may also be considered through the actions of diverse organizations. An article in *The Observer* (2008, January 20) focused upon celebrity telling of the antenarrative, citing Hugh Fernley-Whittingstall, Rick Stein, Gordon Ramsey, and John Torode. The article also shows how the antenarrative is being used in other spheres and enabling some alignment amongst previous adversaries as is seen in the selection of quotes provided in the article. According to the NFU "The more veal you eat in this country, the greater the incentive for farmers to rear veal calves here in Britain". CIWF qualified the statement that "there's nothing inherently cruel about veal" with a desire in the long term to see reform of the dairy sector. Tesco claimed "recent TV shows such as The F Word have done a lot to explain that it is OK to eat veal if its production meets strict welfare standards". Waitrose, who we are told have been selling British veal for 20 years, explained that the fast cooking time makes this appeal to "a new generation of foodies who are time poor" (all quotations from *The Observer*, 2008, January 20). What becomes apparent here is that, as one antenarrative emerges and gains wider telling it incorporates elements of other, previously existing antenarratives. For example, NFU's previous assertion about the lack of a UK market can be converted to suggest that farmers will follow if consumers lead the way. Similarly, Waitrose insert their target market of time poor foodies into the narrative and the CIWF qualify their acceptance of veal with a concern for dairy practices. Each can contribute to this antenarrative by inserting elements that maintain a level of coherence. However, elements that would break down coherence of narrative amongst this disparate and temporary coalition of narrators are, at least for the moment, excluded. Whether there is sufficient agreement upon an assemblage of shared tellable elements to form a narrative that excludes those elements on which there is not agreement remains in question.

Retailer actions provide an indication of the growing strength of the antenarrative. Waitrose initially sold 'British veal' or 'English farmhouse veal', according to *The Times* (1995, February 8). The Grocer documents other introductions—of rose veal by Marks and Spencer's (*The Grocer*, 2003, July 5), by Tesco (*The Grocer*, 2007, November 26), Sainsbury's use of veal in processed beef products (*The Grocer*, 2009, August 15), and Asda's sale of 'young beef' (The Grocer, 2008, November 29). Such actions intensified following JGS. Fillet rose veal was introduced under the Tesco label and later Tesco stocked a branded veal meatball from Brookfield Farm (*The Grocer*, 2012, November 10). Sainsbury's extended rose veal to their Taste the Difference label and then expanded the range (*The Grocer*, 2012, December 4).

The extent to which an assemblage of elements has emerged and gained acceptance across various audiences is, however, questionable. Tensions remain within the antenarrative. These relate both to the ethicality of eating veal, arising either from the longstanding view of veal as unethical or from a more thoroughly developed critique of the treatment of animals as sentient beings. Amongst farmers, tensions are also evident between seeing the raising of veal calves as merely a hobbyist activity or one for the mainstream. This mirrors the tension between 'foodies' and mainstream consumers. Farmers' blogs demonstrate the distance emerging between farmers (often depicted as hobbyists) wanting to rear a few bull calves, and others who reiterate the poor economics. For example, someone posts a question on Farmers' Weekly interactive (Veal!!, 2012) about raising bull calves. Three months after the broadcasting of JGS, 'Bovril' (2012) replies (emphasis added).

> Before you get too excited, have a look at the price of cattle food . . . the amount of feed . . . the cost of the calf, *the shooting of bull calves is an out of date story now* . . . I've reared . . . bull calves over the years . . . an expensive way to keep busy in the winter!

DISCUSSION: GRAFFITI AND NARRATIVE PROCESS.

I shall now look at some of the key features of graffiti that I previously argued make this a useful metaphor to understand narrative process. I shall relate these explicitly to the case material before relating these also to my engagement as both audience and narrator of antenarratives.

Initially I highlighted the ideological character of graffiti. Making a mark at all asserts a right to 'speak' and graffiti establishes conventions about what may be said, where and by whom. This is illustrated in various ways. The analysis has focused upon certain narrators or graffers who have been able to tell the story in highly visible arenas, including the CIWF as a spokesperson to the media and, latterly, celebrity chefs. These have been particularly powerful actors in defining what may and may not be told here and now and what is not tellable. In so doing a certain ideological stance is forwarded at the expense of another. I have shown how the struggle to create and maintain a coherent story involves inclusion and exclusion of elements within antenarratives. What gets included and accommodated within an antenarrative as well as what remains largely untold has effects in terms of whether the story can be more broadly told and speak to and for a broader constituency. Recently, celebrity chefs have assumed the right and been able to obtain a high profile space to tell the second antenarrative. To relate to graffiti, these celebrity chefs have, in effect, 'tagged', at least temporarily, this topic as their area to speak publicly on. In this space they portray a certain form of production as high welfare and a certain form of consumption as ethical. Additionally, they have determined the assemblage of elements suggesting what can and can't be told by, for example, screening killings of day old calves and excluding screening of nine month old calves. Here other ideologies informing other critiques of, for example, the contemporary food and dairy system form are untold. As with graffiti, were elements introduced from alternative ways of storying the situation, and such alternative stories exist, or were the extant elements subverted by, for example, juxtaposing images of calves at different ages, this would destabilise the second antenarrative. What this analysis has also revealed is the material consequences attaching to the different antenarratives as these gain strength: a claim to speak, an ability to gain and audience and successful inclusion and exclusion has, in this case, shaped supply chains, influenced the activity of farmers as well as ferry companies, amongst others.

The right to speak and instantiate a reality is also evident in the interactions between Jimmy and Tesco and this documentary film allows us to see graffing within a specific interaction. Both claim the authority to know and say what it is that consumers want. Jimmy sees this as underpinned by ethical concerns, Tesco's by family lifestyles. The fly on the wall film shows each developing their account of consumer motivation and shows Jimmy's vision being overwritten by Tesco through whom Jimmy had hoped to reach a mass market. This occurs whilst the film itself contributes to antenarrative and causes us to question what guides our own consumption. Therefore, I propose that graffiti allows us to move analytically between the multiple levels at which a graffiti-like process is constructing the world.

The ephemerality of graffiti enables a conceptualisation of narrative process. Graffiti de-contextualises and re-contextualises elements with pre-existing meanings. In so doing it reinforces, diverts, or subverts meaning. Graffiti is disappeared in several different ways yet it leaves aftershocks and tremors—the way meaning is made of something draws upon previous usage of the space. The potentially de-stabilising effects of insertions have been highlighted already. What graffiti highlights, in particular, is that such insertions carry with them pre-existing meanings that can, in theory, be re-contextualised in the calf story. For example, a vocabulary of 'animal rights' developed largely in the 1990s when calf transport was problematised. Moving to this vocabulary within the anti-transport movement brings into the graffiti the various meanings that different audiences would have about a host of other 'animal right' issues. More recently there are antenarratives about food authenticity, traceability, and the connection between farm and fork. These are available insertions to the second antenarrative but the manner of their incorporation has consequences upon the antenarrative, moving it perhaps towards a more foodie or a more mainstream narrative. The case also illustrates the obscurity surrounding being disappeared or, indeed, being appeared. Without denying the importance of some narrators or graffers, tracing the origin of an idea is impossible. Conceived of through graffiti we may see narrative emergence and disappearance is of uncertain origin because it is always built through the bringing together of and re-assemblage of previous meanings.

The case analysis also illustrates well the tremors and aftershocks left by disappeared graffiti. The first antenarrative that did become so powerful was disappeared by unanticipated government actions. The destruction of the environment in which this narrative was credible exposed the untold, but always relevant 'ending' to the story and presented a problem of valueless calves. In effect this dissolved a community of storytellers who needed to re-configure meaning. The second antenarrative lives in the wake of the first. That is, the strong belief in the unethical nature of veal has become detached from questions of transport—but remains a strong belief with which the second antenarrative interacts. This is so even if many consumers have forgotten or never knew the first narrative. Noticeably, the former narrative is minimised in many tellings of the second antenarrative with an attempt to establish a distance between the two. Within this the displaced community built through the first narrative arguably has fractured with the possibility that the second antenarrative may be credible for some, but not for others.

Finally, I argued that graffiti is ambiguous, in part because of the re-contextualisation of meaning. Here I have presented a case and sought to build credibility into my antenarratives in my re-contextualisation of others' words. I have turned to graffiti as a metaphor because of the dominance of the more static picture metaphor in my own field of research—interorgani zational networks. I became interested in the case through watching Jimmy and the Giant Supermarket and because of my own teaching activity in retail supply chains. As I traced out from that story through databases and websites, I remembered things I had forgotten such as the port protests. I learned things I had never known, for example, about dairy production. I reflected on the beliefs and understandings that led me first to being a veg-etarian and, 25 years later, to resume meat consumption. As my understand-ings developed they were certainly coloured by the widespread questioning of meat production systems occasioned by the then recent horse meat scan-dal. My point here is that we researchers are graffers too. In this we are no different to anyone else. Our understandings develop though what is very likely a unique route of memories, snatches of information, juxtaposi-tion of engagements in multiple arenas—and we re-contextualise elements in an assemblage in order to communicate to others. Through all this we are part of multiple conversations defining the tellable and the untellable. As researchers we can, however, pay more explicit attention to the processes whereby understandings are created and communicated and how these inform organizational actions and shape the world. I hope, in this chapter to have stimulated greater interest in this endeavour.

CONCLUSIONS

The aim of this chapter was to develop a deeper understanding of narrative processes through a focus on the interactions between antenarratives. I have argued that antenarratives may gain strength and coherence only through the definition of what may be told here and now and what shall be untold. The inclusions and exclusions are a point of precariousness so that narrative coherence can be unsettled when antenarratives come into contact with each other. In introducing the graffing metaphor I have sought to conceptualise these as social and political processes and recognise not only the agential character of narrative but the intentional actions and ideological commitments of narrators as narratives develop.

The chapter has looked only at two antenarratives that account for one object. This could be usefully extended, since these antenarratives interacted with others that have only been briefly mentioned in this chapter. Certainly I have simplified much complexity. Nevertheless, the chapter has conceptualised and illustrated methods of reading between multiple data sources to search for complexity and interactions of difference, rather than to converge and triangulate in the pursuit of one narrative. Herein there is a tension since any attempt to account for complexity tends towards reification of certain narrative lines. The production of a coherent account is central to research, whether or not it accords with the researcher's view of the world. I have shown that the graffing metaphor can, nevertheless, be reflexively applied and I have argued that researchers can recognise that their engagement across academic arenas and more broadly shapes the particular narrative they tell.

The concepts developed in this chapter might form the basis for further research that admits greater complexity and traces the negotiation of meaning in narrative processes. Such an endeavour will help researchers to study organizations as participants in sensemaking in broader society and overcome a tendency to see, or at least treat, the organization in isolation. An extension of this work to consider other narratives of food seems especially pertinent in this regard. This is because of the cacophony of voices from government and celebrity, as well as both commercial and more informal organizations that tell us stories of food—and this study has considered only a very restricted area. Where coherence is created and broader arenas of telling are claimed within the competition between antenarratives of food this has important consequences, not least for food security and health.

REFERENCES

Bakhtin, M. (1973). *Problems of Dostoevsky's Poetics* (R. W. Rotsel, Trans.). Ann Arbor, MI: Ardis.

Boje, D. M. (1995). Stories of the storytelling organization: A post-modern analysis of Disney as Tamaraland. *Academy of Management Journal, 38*(4): 997–1035.

Boje, D. M. (2001). *Narrative Methods for Organization and Communication Research*. London: Sage.

Boje, D. M. (2011). Introduction to agential antenarratives that shape the future of organizations. In D. Boje (Ed.), *Storytelling and the Future of Organizations: An Antenarrative Handbook*. London: Routledge.

Boje, D.M., Rosile, G.A., & Gardner, G.L. (2004, August 9). *Antenarratives, Narrative and Anaemic Stories.* Paper presented at the All Academy Symposium, Academy of Management. Retrieved from http://peaceaware.com/McD/papers/2004%20boje%20rosile%20Gardner%20Academy%20presentation%20Antenarratives%20Narratives%20and%20Anaemic%20ones.pdf.

Bovril (2012, September 3) RE: Farming Veal [Online forum comment]. Message posted to http://www.fwi.co.uk/community/forums/farming-veal-73446.aspx.

Brown, A.D. (1998). Narrative, politics and legitimacy in an IT implementation. *Journal of Management Studies*, 35(1): 35–59.

Bruner, J.S. (1986). *Actual Minds: Possible Worlds.* Cambridge, MA: Harvard University Press.

Clark, B.R. (1972). The organizational saga in higher-education. *Administrative Science Quarterly*, 17(2): 178–184.

Colville, I. & Pye, A. (2010). A sensemaking perspective on network pictures. *Industrial Marketing Management*, 39(3): 372–380.

Czarniawska, B. (1997). *Narrating the Organisation: Dramas of Institutional Identity.* Chicago: University of Chicago Press.

Czarniawska, B. (2004). *Narratives in Social Science Research.* London: Sage.

Daily Mail, The. (1995, 12 January). Tesco 'kind veal' pledge.

Daily Telegraph, The. (2010, 24 July). Veal back on the menu, minus the guilt; It's long been associated with animal cruelty, but the British version of this delicious meat is in fact a more ethical choice Recipes for the weekend.

Derrida, J. (1979). Living on: Borderlines. In H. Bloom, P.D. Man, J. Derrida, G. Hartman, & J.H. Miller (Eds.), *Deconstruction and Criticism* (pp. 75–176). London: Continuum.

Dickens, L. (2008). Placing post-graffiti: The journey of the Peckham rock. *Cultural Geographies*, 15(4): 471–496.

Fisher, W.R. (1985). The narrative paradigm: In the beginning. *Journal of Communication*, 35(4): 74–89.

Gabriel, Y. (2000). *Storytelling in Organizations: Facts, Fictions and Fantasies.* Oxford: Oxford University Press.

Glasgow Herald, The. (1994, 2 December). Despite the protests of animal welfare groups, Prestwick Airport has decided to continue with the export of live calves.

Grint, K. (2005). Problems, problems, problems: The social construction of 'leadership'. *Human Relations*, 58(11): 1467–1494.

Grocer, The. (2003, 5 July). Back in the pink.

Grocer, The. (2007, 26 November). Tesco trialling organic rose veal in 10 stores.

Grocer, The. (2008, 23 August). RSPCA gives its veal of approval.

Grocer, The. (2008, 29 November). Dairy calves reared for Asda's beef range.

Grocer, The. (2009, 15 August). Sainsbury's puts calves' meat to use.

Grocer, The. (2012, 10 November). Jimmy's veal meatball buzz leads to new line in Tesco.

Grocer, The. (2012, 4 December) Sainsbury's to launch new veal range.

Guardian, The. (1992, 16 Nov). Mad cow fear leads to stock rule breach; Calves suffer as ministry 'covers up' BSE spread.

Halsey, M. & Young, A. (2000). The meanings of graffiti and municipal administration. *The Australia and New Zealand Journal of Criminology*, 35(2): 165–186.

Hitchin, L. (2014). Fabricating methods: Untold connection is story net work. *Tamara—Journal for Critical Organizational Inquiry*, 12(1): 59–73.

Independent, The. (1995, 10 January). Pressure builds on Waldegrave over calves; Sir Richard calls for a British veal market, but the NUF and the Meat and Livestock Commission say consumers don't like the taste.

Independent, The. (1995, 6 January). How scarves and woollies slaughtered a trade; Animal libbers, radical vegetarians, soppy pet-lovers and RSPCA die-hards have joined forces to cripple Britain's pounds 200m livestock export business.

Independent, The. (2006, 1 May). Joanna Lumley to lead protest against export of veal calves.

Independent, The. (2006, 2 Sept). The appeal of veal. It's been banished from British menus for nearly 20 years. But now Janet Street-Porter has spoken out to change our minds about this most succulent of meats. And celebrity chefs are queing up to join the campaign.

Independent, The. (2006, 6 March). Export of live veal calves to resume despite protests.

Izak, M. (2014). A story-in-the-making: An intertextual exploration of a multivoiced narrative. *Tamara—Journal for Critical Organizational Inquiry, 12*(1): 41–57.

Lachmann, R. (1988). Graffiti as career and ideology. *American Journal of Sociology, 94*(2): 229–250.

McAuliffe, C., & Iveson, K. (2011). Art and crime (and other things besides . . .): Conceptualising graffiti in the city. *Geography Compass, 5*(3): 128–143.

McCormick, J., & Jarman, N. (2005). Death of a mural. *Journal of Material Culture, 10*(1): 49–71.

Observer, The. (1995, 4 June) Militant animal rights activist celebrates milk tanker attack.

Observer, The. (2008, 20 January). Veal back on a guilt-free British menu: After farming reforms, animal welfare lobbyists and top chefs are endorsing a once shunned dish.

Polkinghorne, D. (1988). *Narrative Knowing and the Human Sciences.* New York: State University of New York Press.

Sarbin, T. (1986). *Narrative Psychology: The Storied Nature of Human Conduct.* Greenwood Press.

Schacter, R. (2008). An ethnography of iconoclash. *Journal of Material Culture, 13*(1): 35–61.

Sheahan, T. (Series Director). (2012). *Jimmy and the Giant Supermarket* [Television series]. London: Channel 4.

Sims, D., Huxham, C., & Beech, N. (2009). On telling stories but hearing snippets: Sense-taking from presentations of practice. *Organization, 16*(3): 371–388.

Times, The. (1995, 10 January) Production of veal in Britain a 'vast improvement' on continental system.

Times, The. (1995, 8 February) Veal farmer on hit list turns home into fortress.

Times, The. (1996, 24 April) Protesters to picket abattoirs in calf cull.

Veal!! (2012, September 3) Farming Veal [Online forum comment]. Message posted to http://www.fwi.co.uk/community/forums/farming-veal-73446.aspx.

Watson, T. J. (2009). Narrative, life story and manager identity: A case study in autobiographical identity work. *Human Relations, 62*(3): 425–452.

Part III
Untold Story and Methodology

12 Method and Story Fragments
Working through Untold Method

Linda Hitchin

Suppose you are contemplating an island. It is not an island known to you. You are looking at it from a great height. . . . At this height your viewpoint is more like that of an angel than any islander . . . the position of a reader in a book is very like that occupied by angels in the world. . . . Yours is, like theirs, a hovering gravely attentive presence observing everything . . . nothing is concealed, for angels are very bright mirrors.

(Paton-Walsh, 1994: 9–10)

. . . all eyes, including our own organic ones, are active perceptual systems, building on translations and specific ways of seeing, that is, ways of life. There is no unmediated photograph or passive camera obscura in scientific accounts . . . there are only highly specific visual possibilities, each with a wonderfully detailed, active, partial way of organizing worlds.

(Haraway, 1988: 583)

INTRODUCTION

This chapter attends to untold story and specific research methods. There is no intention to review methodological choices or problems across the whole domain of organizational storytelling research; rather this chapter demonstrates challenges raised by a specific approach to story and research methods in practice. In line with the theoretical approach adopted here I use first person as a reminder that all stories are complicit and composed.

In terms of methods for researching **untold** stories, I am interested in methods that address the 'untold' in terms of boundless magnitude and scale. The sense of story adopted here has much in common with the storytelling interests of David Boje and draws on Boje's contribution to untold story research in some detail. In this context I pay specific attention to two motifs that Boje has developed: storytelling in Tamara-Land (1995) and story as quantum fragments (see Boje, 2011, 2012). The chapter considers the valuable theoretical imagery in these terms and the implication of such imagery for untold story research methods and practice. Whilst Boje is a central and seminal thinker informing this study, my approach to untold story is also heavily influenced by science technology studies (STS) and this warrants a little discussion.

It is never easy to adequately capture an entire field of study, especially one, such as STS, that has been a lively empirical and theoretically productive field for over four decades. Any attempt to capture such a field is inevitably selective and limited. Nonetheless, I will simply note that STS encompasses diverse interests from across the social sciences in techno-scientific knowledge production processes, techno-scientific practices, and techno-scientific applications (see for example Hackett, Amsterdamska, Lynch, & Wajcman, 2008). Over time influential contributions have emerged from empirical works in sociology (see for example Latour, 1987; Latour & Woolgar, 1986; Lynch, 1985; Haraway, 1989), anthropology (such as Rabinow, 1996) and history (illustrated well by Shapin & Schaffer, 1989). Notwithstanding differences over theory, method, and practice each discipline has contributed to a now tacit recognition of science as organized, cultural and situated practice (see Knorr-Cetina, 1999; Hackett et al., 2008). Hence it is hardly surprising that STS shares many matters of concern with organization studies.

There are various sociological approaches adopted in STS and my interest here is a particular collection of studies within or following an approach typically referred to as actor network theory or ANT (see Hassard & Law 1999). Theoretically, ANT shares some common interests with Boje's developing approach to organizational storytelling where he is paying increasing attention to story in terms of multiplicity, materials, socio-material relationships, energy, action, and situation (Boje, 2012). Our common interests in matters of sociomateriality, multiplicity, and relational situated action offer many opportunities for productive cross over and exchange, particularly in terms of how, historically, materiality and politics have been addressed in ANT. In this context, within STS, story has become a useful device for thinking, surfacing, and representing the flux of interacting, complex and unfinished organizing projects (see Latour, 1996a; Law, 2002 by way of illustration). My interest here is in how such work may inform untold story research.

There are three key reasons why I have opted to focus on method and links between Boje's matters of concern and ANT rather than over a methodological review.

My first reason relates to the liberal and diverse character of organizational storytelling research (see for example Brown, Gabriel, & Gherardi,

2009). There is no unified approach to either organizational storytelling or the untold. In terms of storytelling, one can find significant contrast across theorists such as Gabriel (1991a, 1991b, 1993, 1995, 2000), Mishler (1999), De Cock and Volkmann (2002), Brown (2004), and Boje (2011). Closer to home, this volume itself reveals quite specific and yet different notions of the untold. In place of unity, organizational storytelling research is an interesting and vibrant multidisciplinary field of study. A field represented by a variety of different traditions and approaches each with their own cherished foci. It is through attention to contrasting approaches that, as researchers, we find a home to work from and write into. Comfortingly, a theoretical home provides both the conceptual devices that we use to form our research objects along with particular technical imagery that colours how these conceptual forms may be operationalised in practice. It is in such contexts that method is shaped in practice by bodies that are working with and through particular ways of knowing whilst attending to particular matters of concern.

Whilst localness matters, it is under theorized in the literature. It is easy to find wide-ranging literature that plays out theoretical debates and so distinguishes one approach from another. There are also highly accessible methodological debates ranging across qualitative research methods. However, far less is written from within storytelling research on the choices and consequences of method once a position may have been taken on knowledge and knowledge production and the thinking body is out there working with 'the field' (see Donnelly, Gabriel, & Özkazanç-Pan, 2013). In this context, there is explicit attention to Haraway's 'partial way of organizing the world' and method is a matter of praxis. Even if we put aside any reservations we may hold in regard to positioning (Haraway, 1988; Woolgar, 1992), this lack of specificity and localness in method dialogue is disturbing as any empirical *finding* inevitably reflects those local and cherished professional assumptions used to conceptualise a research object/problem and the tools used to cut into, decompose, model, or forensically dissect the objects or phenomena under study (see Bloor, 1991; Cornelissen, Oswick, Christensen & Phillips, 2008; Haraway, 1988, 1994; Knorr-Cetina, 1999; Latour, 1986; Lynch, 1985; Shapin & Schaffer, 1989). These tools are situated in practice and any seemingly local specificity of method warrants attention.

A second reason for a focus on situated method over methodology is in response to increasing concern over the limited range of methods deployed in storytelling research. Protagonists in these discussions have observed an over-reliance on post-hoc interview techniques as a typical source of qualitative story data. Typically, this observation is a prelude to a call to conceptualise story as situated performance and practices (Gherardi & Nicolini, 2002; Mano & Gabriel, 2006). The desire for a practice turn in storytelling research has also led to calls for attention to both materiality (see for instance Boje, 2012) and deep field ethnographic study (see Hitchin & Maksymiw,

2012). The focus adopted here responds to such general interest in action and materiality and offers insights into specificity of such field practice.

The third reason for theory/method particularity is in response to a general concern over method in qualitative organization studies (Cornelissen et al., 2008; Rhodes, 2009) and accompanying interest in reflexivity and the politics of academic explanation. Where reflexivity and politics of explanation are concerned specificity matters: a lot. In reflexivity we fold-back onto our own practice the very theoretical and analytic tools that we deem valuable in examining the organizing of others. Hence, the shape, form, and behaviour of those tools in use influence our options for reflexive work. Concerns over politics of method and explanation have a relatively recent history in social science research, something a little over three decades. However, in that time, there have been particularly strong contributions. For example, anthropology responded to a crisis that occurred within the discipline when various 'fields' politicised, protested, and wrote back (Asfcroft, Griffiths & Tiffin, 2002; Biolsi and Zimmerman, 1997). One response to this crisis was increased attention on the textualization of the others and otherness (see Clifford, 1997; Clifford & Marcus, 1986; Marcus & Cushman, 1982; Geertz, 1988; Tyler, 1986; Wolf, 1992). Social studies of science also made early and valuable contributions which, given that this field is an extension of the sociology of knowledge and favours ethnographic practices informed by anthropology, is probably not surprising (see Haraway, 1988; Latour 1988, 1996b; Law, 2004; Woolgar, 1988).

Storytelling research is taking much the same route as STS in confronting politics of explanation. There is clearly an increasing interest in apparently multi-voiced representational forms, denaturalising representational forms such as fiction (see Rhodes & Brown, 2005, for commentary and critique) and *reflexive* or 'confessional' methodological reflection (Donnelly et al., 2013). However, whilst STS has enjoyed some notable success with denaturalising forms (see for example Latour, 1996a; Mol, 2002), working in STS has also provided some useful lessons. Lesson one: multi-voiced approaches are subject to criticism of ventriloquism (Pinch & Pinch, 1988) or delusion. Lesson two: literary forms are risky. Denaturalising novel, fictional, or poetic forms demand specific skills in the author if they are to be empirically convincing. Yet, as with poets ". . . there are many wandbearers but few inspired" (Okri, 1997: 14). Good sociology turned into bad fiction is a problem. Lesson three: at its worst, a reflexive approach can tend toward epistemological hypochondria (Geertz, 1988: 71) leading to self-absorption. The danger here is that the researcher becomes the object of study and the field a site for self-analysis. There is space for a focused discussion of how story method in practice might attend to politics of explanation whilst keeping these three lessons in mind. This chapter responds to that need.

Finally, and quite simply, I have adopted a show and tell strategy reflecting one approach as I wish to hold conversations on intransigent problems in story research when storytelling is messy, multiple, boundless, and political fabrication work (Hitchin, 2014).

To begin I draw on David Boje's work on the hidden and untold stories of organizations. Boje has developed a particular sensibility and imagery that has local and specific consequences for method. In developing this discussion I pay attention to particular analytic imagery to be found in Tamara, antenarrative and quantum fragments. I then introduce four specific theory/method fragments of my own into the discussion. These interruptions are drawn from STS literature and develop the discussion of theory/method. To bring a degree of closure I use the final to illustration to reflect back over the discussion and consider the problem of telling authoritative and empirically sound untold sociological stories of power, politics, and the social life of others whilst avoiding the 'god trick' (Haraway, 1988: 578).

THEORY, IMAGERY, AND METHOD: TAMARA-LAND AND QUANTUM FRAGMENTS

For readers already involved in organizational storytelling research the name Tamara, or the idea of a Tamara-Land, will represent both a particular approach to organizational storytelling and a particular contributor: Tamara has become synonymous with the work of *David Boje*. It is difficult to turn anywhere in storytelling research without finding authors making reference to Boje for either support or debate. Whilst I do not intend to follow Boje as such, I am turning to him here as his work with both Tamara and quantum fragments, offer accessible and plausible imagery to inform anti-foundationalist methods in untold story research. In other words, within the storytelling community, Boje has offered vivid imagery to think-with and use in research encounters. As we shall also see, these images make certain demands on method.

In putting Boje to use here, let me begin with a retelling of the play Tamara (Krizanc, 1989), a play that Boje offered as metaphor for organization (Boje, 1995). Krizanc's Tamara will always be its own best representation. Any version of Tamara taken and used by an academic is reshaped in the retelling. The new teller edits the original and puts the play to specific use. I will make my own adaptations, raise certain tropes convenient to my own story and quieten others. Note that, here is an adaptation made for a purpose rather than a copy faithful to either Krizanc or Boje: a variation on their interlacing themes.

So, Tamara and Tamara-Land. Firstly, imagine a play that was never intended for a conventional theatre. It is a radical drama and the imagery it evokes offers a radical insight into both theatre and drama. The primary and potent radicalism comes with Tamara's relationship with staging theatre. Tamara is a play deliberately and artfully composed such that it cannot be performed among the usual theatrical trappings. Instead of a conventional theatre staging Tamara demands a building, ideally a hotel, comprising many levels, rooms, internal spaces, and an extensive landscaped area leading to outbuildings and life beyond the fence. The play embroils building and landscape in story work not as a powerless apolitical backdrop or set but as active enabler: liberating multiple storylines for enactment in shifting contexts.

The challenge to traditional theatre landscaping is one move in Krizanc's radical turn. A further move is made against normative staging of theatre by way of how Tamara attends to audience. Note that again, Tamara attends-toward audience rather than manages 'them'. The audience members can choose where and how to travel around the play. Given that the convention of stage has disappeared audiences are now something of an itinerant friendly mob. Each member of the audience decides where to be from the outset: whether to be inside or outside; by a door or deep in a room; in a corridor or at the dining table. There is little in the way of a clue to location or suggestion of where one might begin. There is something potentially risky and adventurous in such audience work as it raises the uncertainty and decision making for all concerned. With audience and players suitably dispersed the action begins. The players follow through their roles and move through the play in time and across locations. Neither characters nor audience are monochrome and they change and adapt depending on the places they move to and the others they meet. Friends talk as friends to friends but not in the same manner to strangers or acquaintances; plotters plot together in plotting rooms but never apart or in public.

The drama plays on. An audience in one room may see a minor character enter at 7.23: an amiable quiet chap with a minor role, such as serving drinks. If the audience chooses to follow the quiet man as he leaves and moves up the staircase by 7.33 he may be revealed as a still amiable but now more powerful player in the drama. If we stay with the character, two moves later, by 7.48, we might witness a less agreeable shift in his character when crossed. Choosing whether to follow or not follow the amiable chap alters the trajectory of the play. Those who did not follow remain ignorant of this characters potential and activities. He remains the quiet man and his storylines remain those of the amiable quiet guy—hardly worth noticing, noting or retelling.

When the action stops 3 hours later, for each member of the audience, their version of the story of Tamara may be coherent but it is clearly their story and contingent on choices made across performances of landscape, play-smiths, actors, and audience. Tamara-Land, that is the landscape, people, events, lives, and stories that were available never come neatly together in a nicely ordered form. Rather, the distributed composites of Tamara are glimpsed in snapshots as the audience make their choices: what to notice and follow and what to select out of the gaze and the story.

Let us now take a momentary step away from the hotel play and reconsider Tamara as political practice. In creating Tamara the playwright dramatist ensured that tradition was overturned. In this case, the traditional theatrical infrastructure of staging the play incorporating sets, props (properties), dressing rooms, stage positions, audience seating, a presidium arch, orchestra pit, and safety curtains were rendered redundant. This single move of breaking tradition revealed the work that this infrastructure blithely performed in controlling actions, meaning, potential, and experience of theatre. Infrastructure is embroiled in story and in this case infrastructure was revealed as both political and inadequate by the play itself.

Similarly, undoing the materials and tradition of audience performances reveals further politics of theatre. The radical turn liberates the audience to make choices around the hotel/theatre. The effect is to make the production team, actors and audience aware of their positionality. By this I mean that all involved recognise the fabrication work involved in this play and understand that they are always coproducing a partial glimpse into 'the story'. The dynamic and energetic drama implicates the audience in any reading of social interaction as they follow characters that inhabit different, simultaneous, interconnecting, and disconnecting storylines of others. Here is play full of uncertainty, potential, and diverse trajectories that form 'stories'. A play of quasi plots, characters, events, and consequences—and these quasis refuse to stay still.

In a remarkable move, in 1995, Boje took the political intent of this play and put it to work as a metaphor for both organizing and organizational research: organizations as Tamara-Land. The analytic imagery this metaphor offers up to story research was dramatic and remains radical: a metaphor to capture the sense of organizations as full of variety, action, movement, disruptions, uncertainty, and shifting arrangements of people, places, and things. In this context, storytelling can no longer focus on interviewing across different perspectives as perspectives are seen to shift and actors perform rich and multiple characterisations. Instead, the method challenges that are revealed for storytelling research by Tamara, and developed over almost two decades since this piece, are concerned with movement, materiality, partiality, performance, and situation.

TAMARA'S MISSING POLITIC

However, and here is the crunch, there are some missing methods that require attention if we are to get the most from Tamara. I am thinking of methods that are surfaced if we return to Krizanc's intent: denaturalising politics of theatre. In practice Krizanc had to attend to infrastructure. Infrastructure mattered, it was an untold storyteller tucked away quietly doing its political work and for Krizanc the infrastructure had to be broken for its politics to be revealed. How to study infrastructure is a significant challenge, Krizanc knew what was controlling his storytelling and holding back stories. However, for untold story research, we need a better clue to infrastructure;

where it is, what it looks like, and how it behaves. The emerging interest in materiality is one way to address infrastructure (see Star, 1999).

Let me take a slight detour from Tamara to explain. In a recent piece of fieldwork I have worked with the Human Resource team in a large retail cooperative. The organization is a large employer and provides a range of services across an English county. These services range from supermarkets, department stores, post-offices, and pharmacies through to funeral services and include all the typical back-stage work of retail such as warehousing, distribution, marketing, and strategy. The HR Director wanted to develop their organizational wellbeing programme: it had been well valued on staff surveys and lauded across the sector. However, the Director also wanted to develop activities in a way that would not only work for the organization but attend to the organization's commitment to public health and wellbeing and I was invited to undertake this exercise as research.

Inevitably, there was some moving to and fro as we settled on the research aims and the rules of engagement. Typically, organizations are interested in timescales and interruptions to workflow. There is also an interest in research designs and methods: a design was required. The design I offered indicated that we would conduct qualitative interviews across the wellbeing provision, examine uptake and current evaluation data, and we would also map the organizational wellbeing infrastructure. The interviews and existing data sets were always going to happen but by putting infrastructure on the 'table' I had opened up the expectation that I would travel around the organization on a mapping exercise: a neat device to open up places and things at work. In terms of places, wellbeing was geographically distributed around the county. It required special rooms for meeting, consultation, health checks, and management. It required an owner: Human Resources. It required a space for experts to work: pharmacy, nutrition, and HR. It required the equivalent of a box office booking system. It required access to marketing. As with the theatre, it also required classifications and separations: in this case, experts, HR, divisions, coordinators, colleagues, and members. It required a budget. Once the spatial and classificatory requirements were met all manner of necessary materials were put to work. Just as conventional theatre arrangement created audience that led to rows of seats, tiers, circles, stall and boxes, seating plans, and so forth, the infrastructure of wellbeing demanded situated paraphernalia. The paraphernalia just kept on coming: policy documents, flu vaccines, vitamins, corporate newsletter production, utilisation spreadsheets, health check records, management structures, body-mass calipers, job descriptions, timesheets, rotas, blood-glucose meters, desks, shops, telephones, pharmacies, sphygmomanometers, scales, warehouses, rooms. . . . Here were untold numbers of materials holding wellbeing infrastructure stable and making its particularity. I put infrastructure on the method map as I wanted to examine its agential presence in wellbeing stories and to do that, I needed to get close to the sites where wellbeing was taking material form be that as a job description, a set of scales or a sphygmomanometer.

However, putting that infrastructure interlude to one side for now, let us return to the life of Boje's metaphor. As a metaphor Tamara continues to evoke organizations as messy and uncertain sites. The researcher (audience) of organizational Tamara is not reading organizational stories from the 'position of angels' summoned by Jill Patton-Walsh: hovering over the world able to see everything in a coherent and organized landscape (1994). For a researcher sensing organization as a Tamara-Land their story always depends on positionality and movement: who to travel with, what friends to bring, where to move to, when to move, and how to move. Whilst such conceptualisation of the field of research may be intellectually appealing and coherent, research practice is a different issue.

As it stands Boje's Tamara metaphor reveals organizations as complex en-scripted social constructs generated from particular positions and in particular locations. Notwithstanding certain long running scripts and performances, any improvisation or interruption on behalf of players, the set, or audience renders it unknowable. There are always different positions at work, different interpretations and multiple stories emerging at work. Answering questions such as 'what is going on here' or 'what is this organizational play about' becomes a significant problem. However, it is at this point that the Tamara-Land metaphor seems to reach its limits and lose power as it although complex for a play it is running to script with no improvisations or interruptions to distract. A scripted play, even a play like Tamara, demands containment: whilst the theatre is no longer containing in a particular way the playwright has maintained limits and boundaries that cannot be crossed. In terms of a metaphor for organizational studies, such containment is a problem and organizational limits are inevitably porous. Once these aspects of organizing are revealed Tamara fails to be an adequate metaphor for organizations. A further metaphor is required that can attend to porous boundaries, materiality, flux, and fragility of organization.

FROM TAMARA-LAND TO QUANTUM PHYSICS

As Boje develops his sense of contingency and storytelling his research imagination turns away from drama towards complexity theory, string theory and a multi-world view of quantum theory mechanics (Boje 2001, 2007, 2011, 2012). A turn to complexity and quantum physics offers up new imagery and opportunities to think about some sociological problems in new ways. Both complexity and quantum physics are concerned with uncertainty, relationships, forces, and movement. By appropriating elements from physics and mathematics in his analogical reasoning, Boje introduces a new conceptual vocabulary and imagery to examine organized uncertainties. A thinking world of attractors, entanglements, forces, fractals, virtual fragments, strings, and flux. In the emerging 'quantum' analogy, organizational stories were turned into living moving fragmented phenomena embroiled in messy dynamic social relationships (Boje, 2012). Now the Tamara metaphor has been subverted. Tamara, the servant of position, perspective, plays, and coproduction gives way to a new research imaginary, antenarrative, and fragments. This shift of imagery pulls away from Tamara-Land questions of epistemology and moves toward questions of multiple worlds: ontologies. The move made by virtue of imagined and untold hidden quantum fragments at work creating multiple uncertain organizational realities (Boje, 2012).

Whilst I may not fully buy into the selective use of physics, I would not seek to subvert the effort and it certainly offers space for thinking. Removing the sense of orchestrated drama (even a radical one) and focusing instead on complexities of fragmentary organizational stories has value. Storytelling method now might appear to be an itinerant collection of bits or snapshots (fragments) of storylines and stories' lives. The assumption guiding method now is that fragments are coherent only in limited times and spaces, organizational stories refuse to hold together, keep still, or have eternal stability. Indeed, rather than organizational common logic holding stories in place and fixing a unified meaning, Boje's work on story and ante narrative suggested that we should focus on multiple story fragments as they are made, circulate, cross spaces, and are put to diverse use: half told stories interfering with each other in a variety of ways (Boje, 2012; Rosalie, Boje, Carlon, Downs, & Saylors, 2013). The analytic imagery has developed from a radical dramatic metaphor for organizations into a relational metaphor for organizing realities, Boje's work looks at the political unfinished fragmented nature of organizational storytelling and the generative relationships that emerge between stories—where one fragment circulating among many actors and situations has agential potential to set multiple new story lines spilling out from its own trajectory (Boje, 2012).

I find the imagery of story fragments both intellectually compelling but also slightly worrisome. My concern is that the imagery suggests a particular type of attention to fragmented individualism that I would resist. I can remember a public lecture by Bruno Latour some years ago at Brunel University (UK) when he challenged any sociological satisfaction in the notion of fragmented culture or individualism. Typically, he was funny, forceful and convincing. He asked the audience to think of pottery fragments, a cracked vase, or potshards, and I think he had an image to show to help us imagine. Clearly, here were fragments and a broken thing. Then he simply posed a question—do we feel cracked or broken? Paraphrasing scandalously, I would say that he went on to wonder why social science would focus on fragments when a better question is what hidden (untold) practices and processes are reassembling the pot?

Notwithstanding my idiosyncratic reservations over physics and fragments, Boje is clearly pursuing an interesting and productive path and we share many concerns. His imagery of fragments and my STS informed concern for fabrication both assume that social reality is constructed through multiple, mobile, messy relationships. These assumptions have inevitable consequences for storytelling method. If story is generative and mobile then to understand organizational realities the research method must attempt to pursue multiplicity and attend to flux, interference and mobile situations.

FRAGMENTS AND NOTICING AS METHOD

In developing his concern for method Boje has indicated that research must attend to both materials (2012) and noticing (Boje & Tyler, 2009). To aid in developing this interest it is worth connecting Boje's interest in sociomateriality, uncertainty, and messy complexity to counterparts elsewhere in the social sciences. Inevitably, for me, that means STS, indeed, specific science studies, particularly those undertaken in and around scientists at work can offer some valuable insights into noticing—not least the empirical base to argue that attentiveness and noticing depend on specific sense, imagination and embodied sensibilities (Haraway, 1988; Latour, 1986, 1992). Boje's illustration of 'noticing' as method is a continuation of the dominant imagery of gaze, perspective, and lens that is used in social and natural sciences. It probably is hardly surprising that science study became interested in vision when they were spending so much time in laboratories or hospitals watching as knowledge was crafted and used through the assisted gaze of microscopes, imaging technologies, and other real/virtual lenses. Unlike the natural sciences, the social sciences do not tend toward prosthetic lenses to aid vision. Nonetheless, vision is a powerful imagery for thinking about the construction of research data and their methods: the methodological imperative is to improve the gaze and see better or through any obscuring or distorting interferences with lucid and informed thinking. This is not straightforward, as Haraway suggests "Vision is *always* a question of the power to see—and perhaps the violence implicit in our visualising practices. . . . Self-identity is a bad visual system" (1988: 585). Working with visual imagery demands attention to position and the relationship between cognition, body, and knowledge production is ever present (Latour, 1986). Whilst Haraway asked social science to move against visual imagery and turn our research centre toward situated objectivity (1988), there is a danger here. Storytelling research needs to increase its powers to see. Better research vision and skilled noticing offer a disruptive research method in an otherwise phonocentric domain. So, whilst we can only notice what we can notice, any suggestion that stories involve action, things, and worlds beyond speech is valuable.

Let me take you back to the wellbeing study for a moment. We are now some way into the research and I am meeting again with a young woman, let us call her Faith, an early career HR officer. Faith has been given coordination of organizational wellbeing as her special project and, whilst she continues with her routine work of providing HR support to retail stores and pharmacy, wellbeing is Faith's *baby*. In doing her wellbeing work, Faith bypasses the HR structure and works directly with the HR Director: wellbeing is a special relationship.

Today, Faith and I meet in a meeting room with a large boardroom table. Faith's own desk is in an open plan office. The office limits us, it feels public, we could annoy co-workers, and there is no room to lay things out on Faith's desk. So, today we move to the booked meeting room to look over and work with some wellbeing material. Today we are handling 'stuff' that came from a particular noticing.

To explain, in an early interview, just as I was finding my way with Faith, I asked about how she builds the annual programme of wellbeing events. As she started to talk me through I asked if we could take a look at schedules. She popped out of the small meeting room we had booked and returned with a folder. This was her file of events. It was originally the hand-over file she had received from the HR Officer who had held her post previously. Faith had updated regularly and it was a nice resource. As we looked over the material together we looked at previous schedules of events and Faith talked me through the inclusions, deletions, and modifications made in the new plans. I was grateful to this file, we had moved beyond settling in talk.

Over the next 10 minutes or so we looked at how Faith's calendar reflected another unseen calendar of events. We did not know where the unseen calendar was made but speculated on its existence. Indeed, we knew it existed somewhere in some other organization and someone managed it. The unseen calendar had a big impact on Faith's organizational wellbeing programme of events. This unseen calendar arose as Faith walked me through how she puts her programme together and who else is involved—this was helpful as it gave clues as to places to go and people to visit. However, I noticed how some scheduling work involved the climate—that is the seasons—but how even more scheduling work involved health charities and Public Health. At this point we were standing looking down on the schedules as I asked about how the seasons impacted on her schedule and why the names of charities appeared in slots. With her hands traversing the schedule, pointing here and there, Faith answered with a flow:

> . . . after Christmas we run the weight-loss challenge its really popular. . . . this is when the British Heart Foundation are having a national fun run so we are doing that. . . . Hay fever season so we will run a campaign and have discount in the pharmacies; oh yes and a big skin cancer campaign with check-ups follow that . . . this is national no-smoking day so we will . . . here, oh its migraine awareness week . . . and this isn't marked up yet but I know it is when the National Health

Service (NHS) do chlamydia' and here . . . this is when we'll do the flu jabs again—mixed views on that.

(taken from field notes, February, 2012)

There were other local activities on the calendar too, including recurring opportunity for health checks and nutritional advice, and it was my intent to trace them all. But, in this meeting and at this point, I was noticing how porous the space was around wellbeing and getting a sense that these wellbeing stories were spinning off and away and I needed to follow in various ways.

So, when Faith and I were meeting again to look at stuff, the particular stuff in question was a resource bank that Faith composed and maintained of wellbeing matter from the NHS, health charities, and NGOs. There was a lot of material of all shapes and forms: pamphlets, advice booklets, lifestyle guidance, website links, cartoons, confidential telephone help-lines, posters, samples, invitation to screening, desk paraphernalia such as pencils, memo blocks and sticker, and on it went. What a lot of stuff. Faith and I went through the material and she selected material for forthcoming events. All the time I was intrigued: why this material, why these sources, and why here?

For Faith, this was material that helped her do a 'good job'. The mini-marathons run for cancer charity; the walk challenge with free pedometers supplied by public health were enrolled in Faith's organizational wellbeing work. As we talked and looked over 'stuff' Faith ran over the value of this material. Here were resources that were free other than the time taken to set up the contact and keep the flow running: Faith thought with budget logic at times. The resources were pre-screened for advice accuracy and they were part of a much larger 'campaign' for wellbeing: Faith also thought with responsible but non-specialist logic at times. The resources all targeted diseases with a demonstrable impact on organizational performance: Faith thought with an absence monitoring management logic at times. Indeed, it seemed that Faith thought with lots of logics lots of the time. Faith does not have one perspective on organizational wellbeing. No, tucked away in her sociomaterial coordination work, she has many.

Given what we have just seen in a compressed snapshot of work it is hardly surprising that materiality is becoming a hot topic across organization studies (Carlile, Nicolini, & Langley, 2013) and within organizational storytelling research methods (Boje, 2011; Boje & Saylors, 2013; Donnelly et al., 2013). STS has a long tradition of interest in theorising and examining relationships between the social and material that produce composite agency (see for instance Barad, 1998). Whilst many empirical monographs develop STS, ANT studies have been particularly potent in raising the material trope in social science. If you have an interest in materiality and STS is new to you then there is value to be found in monograph ethnographies that have adequate space to develop theory/method discussions (such as Latour, 1987, 1999, 2010a; Latour & Woolgar, 1986; Law, 2002; Mol,

2002). Alternatively if time is limited there is value in looking at short papers by Latour (1992), Callon (1986a, 1986b), and Callon and Law (1992) for thorough but short illustrations used to develop the arguments for sociomaterial agency.

In terms of sociomateriality and untold stories, STS studies use the notion of story to underline the **fabricated** (Hitchin, 2014) or compositional (Latour, 2010b) nature of both the field and the findings. Indeed story often appears in book titles and abstracts (see Lampland & Star, 2009; Rabinow, 1996). However, notwithstanding specific usage of terms and imagery there are useful ANT theory/method fragments that I wish to bring to the table, in a practical and applied way. I am using the notion of fragments here with a purpose. Firstly, Boje has spiked an interest in fragments: the circulating partial bits of things that collide, impact, and change story trajectories and I wish to keep faith with that line of thinking—using fragments to tell of fragments. Secondly, fragments carry a neat sense of incompleteness that I wish to hold to in general—rather than reflect on confessionally. Thirdly, I am keeping faith ANT by insisting that these highly selective 'snatches' of a significant collection of diverse work undertaken across three or more decades are indeed fragments—bits of the discussion circulating around. There are four fragments of STS work and ultimately they are here to extend our discussion of method for stories conceived as boundless untold or unfinished projects. Each fragment has been chosen to unsettle a little and to pose further questions in practice. Firstly, a fragment of John Law's discussion of what might come *after* method for those researchers drawn to work with uncertainty and flux. Law has an impressive history of empirical fieldwork in this tradition and his challenge to the politics and untold stories of conventional conceptualisations of method warrant attention. Secondly, a fragment of Anne Marie Mol's work to summon interest in interference and multiplicity. Mol has richly illustrated and theorised action in terms of the network of multiple relating realities. If, as Boje argues, stories are indeed networks of multiple and relating fragments, then Mol has illustrated method in action. The third fragment is from anthropology and this discussion knocks against Marilyn Strathern's concern over untold limits and analysis. Strathern poses a crucial challenge for anyone hoping to work with sociomaterial story fragments. If story is limitless network of relationships then Strathern is concerned over how we can cut the network in order to analyse it. Finally, a fragment of a fragment by summoning Donna Haraway and the imperative to avoid the god-trick.

FRAGMENT 1 AFTER METHOD

From an STS point of view Law has made exemplary contributions to social science. In pursuing questions raised by practising ethnography from an 'actor network and after' position (Hassard & Law, 1999), Law has developed particular sensibilities and raised awareness of the politics of method

(Callon & Law, 2005; Law, 2008; Law & Urry, 2004). In framing a research method project to support researchers attending to multiplicity and uncertainty, Law (2004) demonstrated a move beyond 'method' toward a situated practice appropriate to researching mess and messiness. Law points to the difficulties of researching phenomenon or research 'objects' that are conceived as multiple, heterogeneous entanglements possessing multiple threads and possibilities. In sharing his experience of practice, Law offers the researcher the opportunity to move away from the destructive safety nets of clearly articulated and mapped methods, imagining instead researchers sharing a sense of groping or feeling a way through the tangles and mangles of practice.

Now, Law is not alone in his concern over method. Anthropologist Paul Rabinow has also examined the illusion and appeal of virtuoso method in ethnographic practice (1997). In contrast to Law's stumbling imagery, Rabinow develops in his account a strong sense for *philia* (friendship), arguing that by forming relationships and being *interested* in the field we not only become complicit with the field, we are involved in ethical and epistemological practice. Arguing the legitimacy of politically interested fieldwork, Rabinow develops the case for the researcher as a cosmopolitan amateur "Although amateur is a somewhat clumsy term, it points to a practice that does not take mastery as its goal. . . . A cosmopolitan ethos entails a perspective on knowledge, ethics and politics that is simultaneously local and global, native and foreign" (Rabinow, 1997: 207).

In practice, I find myself agreeing with both Law and Rabinow. Given quantum stories or multiple fabrications story webs, a stumbling approach to method assemblages in practice is a more satisfactory and valuable image for method than the imagery of an engineer's toolkit. In tracing people and things on the move one is inevitably following certain traces whilst missing or ignoring other fragments. The terrain we are mapping appears alien, multi-dimensional, volatile, and fragile. Clifford Geertz used the image of a pilgrim cartographer and it is in an image I still cherish (Geertz, 1988: 10). The itinerant pilgrim and the cosmopolitan amateur both groping about in tangles of practice are not bad images for those researching boundless and innumerable untold stories. Researching untold stories is in these terms a case of feeling ones' way through a difficult terrain. Inevitably, this can produce disquiet when one first adopts the approach—as there are few if any benchmarks.

FRAGMENT 2 INTERFERENCES AND ONTOLOGICAL POLITICS

I have already suggested that we should notice action and relationships, which is a roundabout way of suggesting we notice inter-acting. Thus far, the social and theoretical imagery for researching interaction has come from Boje: that is story fragments that are on the move and energetic (the quantum imagery). These are stories that do not reside like labelled bottles secured in orderly wine racks—they bump about and interact with each other. The quantum suggestion is that the bumping about alters the fragments energy level, trajectory, possibilities and connections (Boje, 2011). So, story fragments have a powerful impact on each other. A strong and robust story has strong connections and coherence such that its interactions build resilience. Any connections, knocks, or prangs with less coherent stories or fragments have little impact. On the other hand some stories may have limited life as their composition is vulnerable. Knocks, prangs, and interferences from other fragments can destabilize the worlds of such stories: interaction has a disruptive effect.

Working in STS, Mol also adopts a focus on multiple ontologies interaction and develops her theorising through rich description in two separate monograph empirical health studies: one revealing multiple realities and logics of care (2008) and the other multiple medical realities and logics of the disease arteriosclerosis (2002). Both studies reflect and enrich earlier study of networks, fluids, and topographies (Mol, 1999; Mol & Law, 1994). Of particular use here is the way Mol notices different realities of a phenomena, in this case arteriosclerosis, interact:

> In their outpatient clinic vascular surgeons interact with patents. Here's what the doctors do: they ask questions . . . they look at the colour and texture of the skin of legs that hurt. They put hands on places where the patients' leg arteries should be palpable and attempt to feel whether or not the arteries pulsate with each heartbeat. They scribble down notes in their files while patients clumsily put on their clothes again and then they propose the next step in the patients' itinerary. . . . Then I wanted to know about pathology . . . the pathology resident had installed a double microscope . . . we sat down with the microscope on the table between us. Each looked into one of the eyepieces . . . 'there's a vessel, this here. And the purple, here, that's calcification, in the media. It's broken. They have done a bad job with decalcification. Not done it long enough, so the knife had a problem cutting . . . that's the lumen . . . that's the itima. Oh, wow, isn't it thick . . . look. Now there's your artherosclerosis. That's it. A thickening of the itma. That's what it really is . . . under a microscope'.
> (Mol, 2002: 29–31)

The deep fieldwork provided space for Mol to pursue the disease into the many places in which disease reality was performed and storied: sites such as laboratories, conferences, imaging technologies, surgery, pharmacy, homes, and walking. The 196 page monograph provided space to do justice to her academic intent and ethos. It can take a lot of words to capture how each location and reality of this disease offers different enactments: different work, materials, practice, and logic. Three pages of thick description on and away from the vascular surgeons outpatient clinic Mol observes

". . . pathologists do not make the thick . . . vessel walls they look at, not do they construct them. Those are clumsy words. . . . So I need a word that doesn't suggest too much . . . the English language has a nice one in store: enact" (Mol, 2002: 32).

Seeing, watching, being close to, and stepping back from these situated enactments become a means to examine multiplicity: a means that demands method responsiveness to changes in enactments, location, and scale. At times a shift of context or scale shows how realities connect in such a way that the network of the connections stabilises and secures certain realities and strengthens connections. In other cases a change of scale or location can show work being done to destabilise to one degree or another such that the some new work is required to offer additional shoring up of the internal logics if stability is to be maintained. Indeed, in numerous locations Mol has examined situations when one reality is subject to interference from another and difference is managed within both worlds such that a settlement is possible or one logic holds the interaction in place: these are political interferences across interacting realities.

I want to return now to my fieldwork for a moment and move around a few more locations and situation. As you know, I have the situated practice of my HR Director and HR Officer (Faith) close at hand. I have also indicated that I had to wander away from the location and get close to health education, health promotion, NGOs, and the NHS and look at their work and stories entangled in organizational wellbeing. One thing became evident in these travels: HR, organizational wellbeing, health education, health promotion, and public health are intimately related. They are not the same situations and when they interact different logics are enacted and decision making can turn on a coin. These interferences became apparent in around pharmacy wellbeing work.

If Faith is performing non-specialist custodian of wellbeing, pharmacists are experts. The time with pharmacy was fascinating. I spent time travelling to pharmacies, talking and watching pharmacists, and poring over plans for reconfigured pharmacy shops. In terms of the wellbeing programme the pharmacists were science in action. They managed the health check sessions: involving activities such as diabetes screening, weight check, BMI, blood pressure checks, health consultation, and medication review/guidance. In some instances staff were referred onward to consult their General Practitioner (MD). As you would imagine Faith and pharmacy were duly proud of the screening 'finds' and referrals.

In spending time around health checks one notices the materials used, the classifications at work and the analysis done on patient data across the programme. However, there are intervening and interfering logics, events, and peculiarities at work in pharmacy. These peculiarities repeated 'crop up' as special instances that demand that pharmacy reorder their pharmacy enactments of pharmacy. In this context organizational wellbeing was a powerful story of change. In following wellbeing to the pharmacy we found that it (wellbeing) had become a major storyteller in the reconfiguration of UK health services and pharmacy a central character in that story. Gathering wellbeing stories in action and within the retail pharmacy it became apparent that community pharmacy in the UK had become a liminal space in which situated professional work was being redesigned (H. M. Government UK, 2008a).

Pharmacists as a professional body operate under the auspices of the Minister of Health and have direct relationships with the National Health Service. Every prescription handled, exchanged across the counter, and dispensed is both income and relationship with the NHS. Until recently the work of the community pharmacy we worked with was deeply involved with pharmacology and the mixing, making, dispensing, and management of regulated prescription drugs. The debates from the 18th and 19th centuries around the role of pharmacists had been settled and the job role had closed down around pharmacology. Traditionally, and for many of the pharmacists we met, patient interaction was minimal and the role was not clinical—professional work required special paraphernalia and secure spaces but it did not require a clinic. Hence, pharmacy was nicely fixed in space. More recently, drugs companies have taken on traditional roles. The medicines came pre-packed and counted and much of the work of traditional role pharmacists has been deskilled or taken from the pharmacy and undertaken elsewhere and by others. The highly skilled and potentially under-utilised resource could however take on new forms of work. Hence, in the UK, community pharmacy as a 'profession' has been re-opened and subject to national consultation processes (H. M. Government UK, 2008b). These processes are part of a wider opening up of the UK notion of healthcare. It is in this context that organizational wellbeing stories connect outward.

Currently, for the retail pharmacist, health checks are both very new and not income. Health checks are changing the buildings that they work in and requiring that pharmacists meet 'patients' and consult and interact with them using a variety of clinical diagnostic devices. As the UK reconfigures national healthcare services, pharmacy will become one of a number of front line providers of healthcare (H. M. Government UK, 2008a). At the moment pharmacy work focus remains on pharmacology whether in terms of modelling and responding to public health, dispensing, ensuring safe practice, or reviewing prescribing patterns. However, increasing requirement to undertake wellbeing health checks falls outside such realities.

As my pharmacists had strong professional affiliations as healthcare providers, their robust and secure network connections were across the porous limit of organization. By this I mean that pharmacists were in strong, shifting and yet particular professional healthcare networks involving the UK government, UK health-workers, and drugs companies: their wellbeing stories are lengthy tales involving changing contracts and reconstituted profession.

FRAGMENT 3 CUTTING THE NETWORK

In tracing the strands of different stories and realties across locations Mol revealed untold stories of a disease (2002). The disease took her to conflicting behaviours where vascular specialists enact the disease in different ways. Take for example the debate over surgical intervention or a non-invasive response to the disease, such as requiring the patient to increase walking and follow dietary regimes. Possible strands of disease zoom out to owning a dog and suddenly veterinarians, dog breeders, and pet food manufacturers are now implicated in the story of the disease. The tangles of circulating worlds and highly situated but connected work seems to explode from agonised patient to hospitals, clinics, companion animals, and their limitless networks of care and value. Alternatively, if a surgical intervention is on the cards the network zooms out in other directions toward the trappings of theatres, anaesthesia, shunts, balloons, fluoroscopy, sepsis, and their attendant entanglements. So, here then is a new problem: if we are pursuing (boundless) untold stories how do we decide where to stop and how to stop? In chasing multiple realities stopping is a practical challenge as ". . . theoretically they are without limit. . . . Yet, analysis, like interpretation, must have a point; it must be enacted as a stopping place. . . . In coming to rest a network must be 'cut' at a point 'stopped' from further extension" (Strathern, 1996: 523).

Inevitably, taking an analytic cut changes the story. We may see a rich, material, multiple flow of people and things but the cut, even a textured thickly descriptive cut, uses cutting tools to shape and mould a story. We decide where and how to cut in practice, it is situated and subject to interference as much as any other practice. Ultimately, the research story is ours. If our commitment is to analysis (Strathern, 2004: 25–40) then surely that suggests an untold commitment in our own storying, a belief that 'One story is not as good as another' (Haraway, 1989: 331).

So, organizational wellbeing, where to cut the network? I have not written this chapter as a 'findings about wellbeing chapter', but with method as my key concern. I feel there is inadequate evidence here for demonstrating my cut as it demands thick description and a longer study but I will take the risk that you understand this and give you a glimpse (fragment!) of bits of the cut already hinted at here.

Working with organizational wellbeing was fascinating and the people I met a delight. Genuine and professional souls at work. However, my cutting hand was guided and my research noticing was situated. The sociologist in me wanted to understand what organizational wellbeing was doing. The cut is inevitably sociological. In surfacing untold stories and storytellers of organizational wellbeing I mapped out a particular terrain. If I had stayed close to Faith and invested all the research energy in HR worlds I would have a different tale to tell. But, I opted to be itinerant and follow some quasi stories. It is my relational, itinerant, and sociomaterial sensibilities that traced wellbeing from Faith to flu jabs and pedometers then through charities, organized healthcare, to the Office of National Statistics and classifications of wellbeing. Thence the network moves to the OECD Istanbul Declaration, and back down to UK Government, white papers, and to Ministerial consultations on the changing role of UK health services (see Figure 12.1). Always, but always wellbeing could scale back down to Faith and cut through untold story networks of organizational wellbeing:

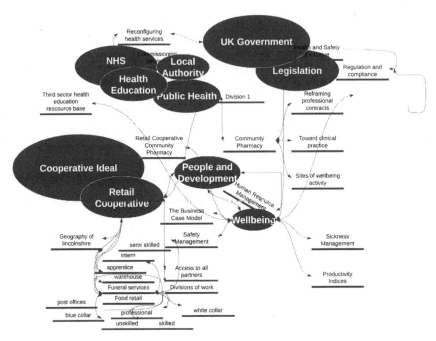

Figure 12.1   Story Interactions in Wellbeing: Messy Spheres of Healthcare, UK.

There is a coherence and resilience in these networks that is stabilising change and an individualisation of responsibility for health and wellbeing in the UK; a reconfiguration of practice and responsibilities from a National Health Service to a disaggregated fragile network of situated enactments where work is one active site:

> Employers are in a unique position of being able to educate, motivate and support their employees in understanding and actively maintaining their fitness and well-being. (Commercial Occupational Health Providers Association, cited in Black, 2008: Chapter 3)
> Government should work with employers and representative bodies to develop a robust model for measuring and reporting the benefits of employer investment in health and well-being. Employers should use

this to report on health and well-being in the board room and company accounts.

(Black, 2008: Recommendation 1 Chapter 3)

Here Black seems to be handing wellbeing over to employers in quite a formal manner. If this story fragment is connected with fragments from pharmacy and Faith's work with charities there seems to be an emerging shift from a coherent service model of healthcare to an incoherent cacophony of wellbeing.

FRAGMENT 4 AVOIDING THE GOD-TRICK

As Sir Walter Scott definitely did not say 'oh what tangle webs we weave . . . when we try to untangle the webs of messy worlds'. However, whilst there is far more to be refound, retold, and reframed about method and mess the final fragment that I offer here involves the god-trick. Throughout the 1980s and 1990s Haraway and others sought to develop alternatives to tradition research images, imagery and practice (Haraway, 1994; Strathern, 1995). The initial impetus came from feminist research into the political character of scientific knowledge production and particular research tools. This research surfaced an untold story of the particular potency of masculine, Anglo-Saxon, Judeo-Christian imagery and enactments in both the natural and social science research. Historically, this seems simply worth noting, a moment to pass through and into relative studies. However, whilst a radical constructivism of a postmodern persuasion might have offered up opportunities to feminists for an anything goes turn in social science, such an iconoclastic move is difficult (impossible) for social scientists who seek to attend to inequality and domination. We somehow want our analysis to have agency. Indeed, what feminist studies surfaced and confronted three decades ago remains a challenge for any anti-foundationalist research: namely where is our confidence located in claiming our analytic stories are valuable/legitimate. Returning now to those debates may be valuable, debates where Haraway using resources in science studies and Strathern using anthropological resources, applied considerable will to conceiving of alternatives to practice that did not fall into a relative regress yet did not assume supremacy: a god-like position over the world, hearts, and minds of (hu)man. Difficult!

For Haraway and Strathern the response to the god-trick is research conceived as situated objectivity. Knowledge production becomes a matter of shifting contexts and specificity. Over the last three decades confident empirical studies of Mol, Latour, and Law have steadily chipped away at method and demonstrated that confidence, knowing the story is a sociologically good one, resides in research praxis enacted in-situ.

LET THIS BE AN END TO IT: ON FRAGMENTS, POTSHARD, AND COPING WITH ONTOLOGIES

I began this chapter by focusing on the relationship between what we know, the imagery we have to work with, and methods that we deploy as researchers attempting to understand the social. The social is a difficult and debated term but even once we have fixed on our 'position' or approach there are hazards. In this context, the chapter stayed close to one approach to firstly examine the social imagery and theoretical assumptions that the approach contained before moving on to consider method in action.

In terms of approaching or imagining the social, the discussion followed the work of David Boje in organizational storytelling. Boje offered a valuable and safe anchor point from which to raise connections between untold storytelling research and untold stories found by actor network theorists (ANT) and their close companions working in science and technology studies. Here the social was extended and materials were rendered political: concerns for the social shifts toward concerns for the sociomaterial. At the same time, social/story heterogeneity shifts toward sociomaterial heterogeneity. In this context the sense of multiple stories as multiple social worlds that are themselves sites of interpretation and imagination alters. Multiple stories are now situated enactments in multiple realities.

The challenges that are raised in this chapter are shared by those who wish to study untold stories as sociomaterial, heterogeneous, and relational performances. In particular, this chapter on untold method has demonstrated the challenges of noticing mobile, situated performance whilst avoiding the god-trick.

Challenge 1: Noticing and untold story method. There is clear value in responding positively to the increasing encouragement to undertake observation studies in storytelling research. In this context, this chapter has demonstrated the value of ethnographic fieldwork as opposed to interview in surfacing boundless (untold) stories. Observation studies depend on visual capability that is intimately connected to our particular ways of knowing about the world. In this chapter I have used examples from deep-field ethnography to illustrate how the field might be constructed by sustaining an itinerant approach and following stories on the move. I have also illustrated that *seeing* stories in sociomaterial terms requires that materials are given a status over and beyond context or set dressing.

Challenge 2: Mobile, situated performances and untold story. Using the work of Mol, and snapshots from my own fieldwork, I illustrated that stories are lived out in situations. The chapter illustrates that situations are neither trivial nor value free. Physical sites might contain situations where people and things interact in particular arrangements such as we saw in the vascular clinic. However, situations can be carried into other spaces and interfere or cross cut with physical location, as we found when the reconfiguration of UK healthcare undertaken by the UK government travelled into the organizational wellbeing work of an HR officer in a retail organization in the guise of health checks and charity literature. Maintaining a sense of location, a willingness to travel and openness to twisting plots and confusion is a necessary challenge for 'quantum' story method.

Challenge 3: Avoiding the god-trick and untold story research.

I am arguing for politics and epistemologies of location, positioning, and situating, where partiality and not universality is the condition of being heard to make rational knowledge claims. These are claims on people's lives. I am arguing for the view from a body that is always a complex, contradictory, structuring, and structured body, versus the view from above, from nowhere, from simplicity. Only the god trick is forbidden.

(Haraway, 1988: 589)

REFERENCES

Ashcroft, B., Griffiths, G., & Tiffin, H. (2002). *The Empire Writes Back: Theory and Practice in Post-colonial Literatures*. London: Routledge.

Barad, K. (1998). Getting real: Technoscientific practices and the materialization of reality. *Journal of Feminist Cultural Studies*, 10(2): 87–128.

Biolsi, T., & Zimmerman, L. J. (Eds.). (1997). *Indians and Anthropologists: Vine Deloria, Jr., and the Critique of Anthropology*. Tucson: University of Arizona Press.

Black, C. (2008). *Working for a Healthier Tomorrow: Dame Carol Black's Review of the Health of Britain's Working Age Population*. London: The Stationary Office.

Bloor, D. (1991). *Knowledge and Social Imagery* (2nd ed.). Chicago: University of Chicago Press.

Boje, D. M. (1995). Stories of the storytelling organization: A postmodern analysis of Disney as "TamaraLand". *Academy of Management Journal*, 38(4): 997–1035.

Boje, D. M. (2001). *Narrative Methods for Organizational and Communication Research*. London: Sage.

Boje, D. M. (2007). The antenarrative cultural turn in narrative studies. In M. Zachary, & C. Thralls (Eds.), *Communicative Practices in Workplaces and the Professions: Cultural Perspectives on the Regulation of Discourse and Organizations* (pp. 219–238). Amityville, NY: Baywood Publishing.

Boje, D. M. (2011). *Storytelling and the Future of Organizations: An Antenarrative Handbook*. London: Routledge.

Boje, D. M. (2012). Reflections: What does quantum physics of storytelling mean for change management? *Journal of Change Management*, 12(3): 253–271.

Boje, D. M., & Saylors, R. (2013). Virtuality and materiality in the ethics of storytelling. In R. Todnum, & B. Burns, (Eds.), *Organizational Change, Leadership and Ethics: Leading Organizations towards Sustainability* (pp. 75–96). Abingdon Oxon: Routledge.

Boje, D. M., & Tyler, J. A. (2009). Story and narrative noticing: Workaholism auto-ethnographies. *Journal of Business Ethics*, 84(2S): 173–194.

Brown, A. D. (2004). Authoritative sensemaking in a public inquiry report. *Organization Studies*, 25(1): 95–112.

Brown, A. D., Gabriel, Y., & Gherardi, S. (Eds.) (2009). Storytelling and change: An unfolding story [Special Issue]. *Organization, 16*(3).

Callon, M. (1986a). The sociology of an actor-network: The case of the electric vehicle. In M. Callon, J. Law, & A. Rip, (Eds.), *Mapping the Dynamics of Science and Technology: Sociology of Science in the Real World* (pp.19–34). London: Macmillan.

Callon, M. (1986b). Some elements of a sociology of translation: Domestication of the scallops and the fishermen of St. Brieuc bay. In J. Law (Ed.), *Power, Action and Belief: A New Sociology of Knowledge?* (Sociological Review Monograph, 32) (pp. 196–233). London: Routledge and Kegan Paul.

Callon, M., & Law, J. (1992). The life and death of an aircraft: A network analysis of technical change. In W. E. Bijker, & J. Law (Eds.), *Shaping Technology/Building Society* (pp. 21–52). Cambridge, MA: MIT Press.

Callon, M., & Law, J. (2005). On qualculation, agency, and otherness. *Environment and Planning D, 23*(5): 717–733.

Carlile, P. R., Nicolini, D., & Langley, A. (Eds.). (2013). *How Matter Matters: Objects, Artifacts, and Materiality in Organization Studies.* Oxford: Oxford University Press.

Clifford, J. (1997). *Routes: Travel and Translation in the Late Twentieth Century.* Cambridge, MA: Harvard University Press.

Clifford, J., & Marcus, G. E. (Eds.). (1986). *Writing Culture: The Poetics and Politics of Ethnography.* Berkley: University of California Press.

Cornelissen, J. P., Oswick, C., Christensen, L. T., & Phillips, N. (2008). Metaphor in organizational research: Context, modalities and implications for research. *Organization Studies, 29*(1): 7–22.

De Cock, C., & Volkmann, C. (2002). Of language, limits and secrets. *Ephemera, 2*(4): 357–71.

Donnelly, P. F., Gabriel, Y., & Özkazanç-Pan, B. (2013). Untold stories of the field and beyond: Narrating the chaos. *Qualitative Research in Organizations and Management: An International Journal, 8*(1): 4–15.

Gabriel, Y. (1991a). On organizational stories and myths: Why is it easier to slay a dragon than to kill a myth? *International Sociology, 6*(4): 427–442.

Gabriel, Y. (1991b). Turning facts into stories and stories into facts: A hermeneutic exploration of organizational folklore. *Human Relations, 44*(8): 857–875.

Gabriel, Y. (1993). Organizational nostalgia: Reflections on 'the golden age'. In S. Fineman (Ed.), *Emotion in Organization* (pp.118–141). London: Sage.

Gabriel, Y. (1995). The unmanaged organization: Stories, fantasies and subjectivity. *Organization, 16*(3): 477–501.

Gabriel, Y. (2000). *Storytelling in Organizations: Facts, Fictions, Fantasies.* Oxford: Oxford University Press.

Geertz, C. (1988). *Works and Lives: The Anthropologist as Author.* London: Stanford University Press.

Gherardi, S., & Nicolini, D. (2002). Learning in a constellation of interconnected practices: Canon or dissonance? *Journal of Management Studies, 39*(4): 419–436.

Hackett, E. J., Amsterdamska, O., Lynch, M., & Wajcman, J. (2008). *The Handbook of Science and Technology Studies.* Cambridge, MA: MIT Press.

Haraway, D. (1988). Situated knowledges: The science question in feminism and the privilege of partial perspective. *Feminist Studies, 14*(3): 575–599.

Haraway, D. (1989). *Primate Visions: Gender, Race, and Nature in the World of Modern Science.* London: Psychology Press.

Haraway, D. (1994). A game of cat's cradle: Science studies, feminist theory, cultural studies. *Configurations, 2*(1): 59–71.

Hassard, J., & Law, J. (1999). *Actor Network Theory and After.* Oxford: Blackwell.

Hitchin, L. (2014). Fabricating methods: Untold connections in story net work. *Tamara Journal for Critical Organization Inquiry, 12*(1): 59–73.

Hitchin, L., & Maksymiw, W. (2012). Story spaces: A methodological contribution. *New Technology, Work and Employment, 27*(1): 65–77.

H. M. Government UK (2008a). *Pharmacy in England: Building on Strengths—Delivering the Future* (A White Paper). London: Stationary Office.

H. M. Government UK (2008b). *Pharmacy in England: Building on Strengths—Delivering the Future—Proposals for Legislative Changes* (A consultation document). London: Stationary Office.

Knorr-Cetina, K. (1999). *Epistemic Cultures: How Scientists Make Knowledge.* Cambridge, MA: Harvard University Press.

Krizanc, J. (1989). *Tamara: A Play.* Toronto: Stoddart Publishing.

Lampland, M., & Star, S. L. (Eds.). (2009). *Standards and Their Stories: How Quantifying, Classifying and Formalizing Practices Shape Everyday Life.* London: Cornell University Press.

Latour, B. (1986). Visualization and cognition: Drawing things together. *Knowledge and Society, 6*: 1–40.

Latour, B. (1987). *Science in Action: How to Follow Scientists and Engineers through Society.* Cambridge, MA: Harvard University Press.

Latour, B. (1988). The politics of explanation: An alternative. In S. Woolgar (Ed.), *Knowledge and Reflexivity: New Frontiers in the Sociology of Knowledge* (pp. 155–176). London: Sage.

Latour, B. (1992). Where are the missing masses? The sociology of a few mundane artifacts. In W. E. Bijker & J. Law, (Eds.), *Shaping Technology/Building Society* (pp. 225–258). Cambridge, MA: MIT Press.

Latour, B. (1996a). *Aramis: Or the Love of Technology* (C. Porter, Trans.). Cambridge, MA: Harvard University Press.

Latour, B. (1996b). On interobjectivity. *Mind, Culture, and Activity, 3*(4): 228–245.

Latour, B. (1999). *Pandora's Hope: Essays on the Reality of Science Studies.* Cambridge, MA: Harvard University Press.

Latour, B. (2010a). *The Making of Law: An Ethnography of the Conseil d'état.* Cambridge: Polity.

Latour, B. (2010b). An attempt at a "Compositionist manifesto". *New Literary History, 41*(3): 471–490.

Latour, B., & Woolgar, S. (1986). *Laboratory Life: The Construction of Scientific Facts* (2nd ed.). Princeton, NJ: Princeton University Press.

Law, J. (2002). *Aircraft Stories.* London: Duke University Press.

Law, J. (2004). *After Method: Mess in Social Science Research.* Abingdon Oxon: Routledge.

Law, J. (2008). On sociology and STS. *Sociological Review, 56*(4): 623–649.

Law, J., & Urry, J. (2004). Enacting the social. *Economy and Society, 33*(3): 390–410.

Lynch, M. (1985). *Art and Artifact in Laboratory Science: A Study of Shop Work and Shop Talk in a Research Laboratory.* London: Routledge Keegan Paul.

Mano, R., & Gabriel, Y. (2006). Workplace romances in cold and hot organizational climates: The experience of Israel and Taiwan. *Human Relations, 59*(1): 7–35.

Marcus, G. E., & Cushman, D. (1982). Ethnographies as texts. *Annual Review of Anthropology, 11*: 25–69.

Mishler, E. (1999). *Storylines: Craftartists' Narratives of Identity.* Cambridge, MA: Harvard University Press.

Mol, A. (1999). Ontological politics: A word and some questions. In J. Hassard & J. Law, (Eds.), *Actor Network Theory and After* (pp. 74–89). Oxford: Blackwell.

Mol, A. (2002). *Body Multiple: Ontology in Medical Practice.* London: Duke University Press.

Mol, A. (2008). *The Logic of Care: Health and the Problem of Patient Choice.* Abingdon: Routledge.

Mol, A., & Law, J. (1994). Regions, networks and fluids: Anaemia and social topology. *Social Studies of Science*, 24(4): 641–671.

Okri, B. (1997). *A Way of Being Free*. London: Phoenix House.

Patton-Walsh, J. (1994). *Knowledge of Angels*. London: Black Swan Books.

Pinch, T., & Pinch, T. (1988) Reservations about reflexivity and new literary forms or Why let the Devil have all the good tunes. In S. Woolgar, (Ed.) *Knowledge and Reflexivity: New Frontiers in the Sociology of Knowledge* (pp. 178–197). London: Sage.

Rabinow, P. (1996). *Making PCR: A Story of Biotechnology*. Chicago: University of Chicago Press.

Rabinow, P. (1997). Science as a practice: The higher indifference and mediated curiosity. In G. L. Downey, & J. Dummit, (Eds.), *Cyborgs and Citadels: Anthropological Interventions in Emerging Sciences and Technologies* (pp. 193–208). Santa Fe: School of American Research Press.

Rhodes, C. (2009). After reflexivity: Ethics, freedom and the writing of organization studies. *Organization Studies*, 30(6): 653–672.

Rhodes, C., & Brown, A. D. (2005). Writing responsibly: Narrative fiction and organization studies. *Organization*, 12(4): 467–491.

Rosile, G. A., Boje, D. M., Carlon, D. M., Downs, A., & Saylors, R. (2013). Storytelling diamond an antenarrative integration of the six facets of storytelling in organization research design. *Organizational Research Methods*, 16(4): 557–580.

Shapin, S., & Schaffer, S. (1989). *Leviathan and the Air-Pump: Boyle, Hobbes and the Experimental Life*. Princeton, NJ: Princeton University Press.

Star, S. L. (1999). The ethnography of infrastructure. *The American Behavioral Scientists*, 43(3): 377–391.

Strathern, M. (Ed.). (1995). *Shifting Contexts: Transformations in Anthropological Knowledge*. London: Routledge.

Strathern, M. (1996). Cutting the network. *The Journal of the Royal Anthropological Institute: Incorporating Man*, 2(1): 517–536.

Strathern, M. (2004). *Partial Connections*. Oxford: Rowman and Lichfield.

Tyler, S. A. (1986). Post-modern ethnography: From document of the occult to occult document. In J. Clifford & G. E. Marcus (Eds.), *Writing Culture: The Poetics and Politics of Ethnography* (pp. 122–140). Berkley: University of California Press.

Wolf, M. (1992). *A Thrice Told Tale: Feminism, Postmodernism and Ethnographic Responsibility*. Stanford: Stanford University Press.

Woolgar, S. (1988). Reflexivity is the ethnographer of the text. In S. Woolgar (Ed.) *Knowledge and Reflexivity: New Frontiers in the Sociology of Knowledge* (pp. 14–34). London: Sage.

Woolgar, S. (1992). Some remarks about positionism: A reply to Collins and Yearly. In A. Pickering, (Ed.), *Science as Practice and Culture* (pp. 327–342). Chicago: University of Chicago Press.

13 Afterword
Untold Story Futures

*Linda Hitchin, Michal Izak,
and David Anderson*

We began this volume by noticing that whilst organizational storytelling research is mature, after almost three decades of empirical research, some blank spots are evident on the theoretical and practical mapping of story-telling organizations. We suggested that it was now timely to ponder over the problem of what might be currently missing, invisible, or unsaid. So, in focusing this volume on the notion of untold stories we sought to provide an opening that could celebrate seminal insights into this vibrant field of orga-nizational storytelling whilst, at the same time, offer a threshold to glimpse future research trajectories. It was always our intention to discover what might happen if we raised the trope of the untold and allowed it to percolate and simmer. This volume is one product of such seepage and simmering. As this volume ranges across matters of time, space, consciousness, imagery, editing, and active imagination—it would seem that the glimpsed future for untold story studies is an inter-disciplinary space, somewhat messy, seem-ingly open, and rather precarious.

Inter-disciplinary work is a sword that cuts both ways. A virtue of inter-disciplinary working is the productive work that emerges when different disciplines converse and interact on matters of shared concern; an oppor-tunity for synergy and blending ideas. However, there are risks and if we take a turn to a more risqué rendering of interaction the hazards are put in sharp relief. For example, inter-disciplinary interactions are opportuni-ties for promiscuous thinking; a means to liberate thought and un-restrict thinking, whilst disciplines limit thinking a call for increasingly promis-cuous thinking might present something of a puzzle. At the very least it should certainly raise an important question: namely, is such deregulation really such a good idea? As we suspect that some productive futures for story research involve thinking-around, we will work through this question a little and examine certain virtues and attendant risks in thinking-around untold stories.

In terms of considering thinking-around as a potential virtue let us con-sider the notion of the *polymath*. In academic contexts this term is used to describe those with wide ranging expert, knowledge, and skills. In popular imagery the polymath is un-phased by specialism and specialist knowledge: they soak up and acquire specialisms. Traditionally, the polymath label is merited by learned and careful thinkers who demonstrate both depth of knowledge and skilled practice across three of more disciplines. In this sense, a polymath demonstrates far more depth than that required for simply handling, getting-by, or roughly translating across disciplines. If thinking-around demands reclaiming a professional necessity to acquire multiple expert knowledge, skills, and competencies—then seemingly there is no harm done.

On the other hand there is the risk that in supporting thinking-around we promote and legitimise the work of a dilettante dabbler. Exposure to opportunities to develop multiple expertise does not necessarily bring forth a polymath: ability has a part to play here. Further to this, our professional academic climates and employment arrangements do not foster polymaths: time and money is against most of us here. At best thinking-around arrangements allow space for collaborations with other experts or garner depth in a limited sphere—adding one further string to our bows. At worse the thinking-around motif can promote false confidence in theory tourism: short visits to other disciplines in a misguided attempt to absorb a little local colour.

Across the three editors of this volume we have a philosopher, sociologist, and educationalist. And we also each have our particular anxieties over partial appropriation of cherished disciplinary precepts, theories, and heroes. There is a sense then that sometimes broad-vistas and over confident appropriation of knowledge is not entirely satisfactory:

> Of all the causes which conspire to blind,
> Man's erring judgment, and misguide the mind,
> What the weak head with strongest bias rules,
> Is Pride, the never failing vice of fools.
> . . .
> Pride, where Wit fails, steps in to our deference,
> And fills up all the mighty void of Sense:
> . . .
> A little learning is a dangerous thing;
> Drink deep, or taste not the Pierian spring:
> There shallow draughts intoxicate the brain,
> . . .
>
> An Essay on Criticism Alexander Pope
> (circa 1711) see Pope (2003)

However, we must be cautious now that we do inflate the risks of thinking-around to the point where any value of inter-disciplinarity is lost. If we consider thinking-around and creativity the futures of untold story research may take some interesting turns.

FUTURES IN FLUX: A CASE REQUIRING MORE FOR THINKING-AROUND?

Across this volume the authors have demonstrated that researching untold stories requires attention to story in terms of both situations and specificities (Hitchin, Chapter 12; Hopkinson, Chapter 11). In some instances situations of untold story have been held in focus and the flux and flows or situation revealed from a central spot (Colón-Aguirre, Chapter 7). In other instances stories have been followed as they travelled sometimes changing and sometimes remaining remarkably immutable to flux (Daskalaki, Saliba, Vogiatzis, & Malamou, Chapter 8). Irrespective of whether the untold story has been rendered as a psychoanalytic concern for stories (Gabriel, 1995) or a sociological interest in the itinerant politics of story (Boje, 1995), situation has been found to be at work. One potential next step for researchers of untold story may be a return to theoretical debates of the 'practice turn' (see Knorr-Cetina, Schatzki, & von Savigny, 2005; Chaiklin & Lave, 1996; Gherardi, 2001)

The untold stories in this volume demonstrate a need to both show and share situation. These studies require thicker descriptions of a situated character of the untold if they are to be plausible. There have been calls already for a turn to thick description in storytelling research (Boje, 2012) and most refer back to anthropological reflections of politics of description (typically Geertz, 1988). However, accepting a need for thickness in untold story descriptions we wish to make two observations. Firstly, bar exceptions, thick descriptive pieces are not suited to the professional regulatory practices of academic journals. Anthropological studies that involve thick descriptions of situations, practices, experiences, and knowledge tend to be monographs emerging from deep field ethnographic studies. Whilst academic journal forms may well change over time we believe there is a pressing need now for ethnographic monographs that attend to *untold stories* based in lengthy, immersive studies of organizing work.

Secondly, rich description is not atheoretical. Rich description is a representational device designed to bring authority to anthropological claims. Descriptions draw a reader in toward ethno situations and offer a means to help readers *imagine* an anthropologists field; to summon, represent, or share a sense of particular ethnos. However, both realists and antifoundationalist anthropological studies adopt thick description—and much spins on how they approach evocation. Evocation carries a sense of both recall and conjuring. Consequently, evocation holds to acts of representational imagination. In pursuing the untold, closer attention to the practice of evocation rather than thick description may have considerable value—not least as it problematises description. Indeed, for anti-foundational researchers with literary abilities evocation offers significant potential:

> Evocation is neither presentation nor representation. It presents no objects and represents none, yet is makes available through absence

what can be conceived but not present. It is thus beyond truth and immune to the judgment of performance. It overcomes the sensible and the conceivable of form and content, of self and other, of language and the world.

(Tyler, 1986: 123)

Thinking-around with reflexive anthropological ethnographies (see for example Tyler, 1986; Crapanzano, 1986) and method (Clifford & Marcus, 1986; Wolf, 1992; Van Maanen, 1988) may prove highly productive for untold story research.

FUTURES IN ACTION: THINKING-AROUND AND THINGS TO COME?

The interest in practice is an interest in action. Consequently, a practice turn in storytelling research demands a concern for the activities that work in the making and life work of stories. In one sense this might be adequately captured as an interest in story as cultural industry and in untold story as industrial exclusion. Studies in this volume have focused attention on politics of story and in the process highlighted certain practices involved in making or killing stories. Editing is one such practice.

Once again we know that storytelling research is calling for increasing interest in editing in terms of both individual, self-editing, and social, organizational-editing (see Boje, 2012; Donnelly, Gabriel, & Özkazanç-Pan, 2013). In terms of thinking-around, there may be value in looking toward cultural industries studies, a site that has focused on politics of story production, including editing, for well over three decades. In this context, there is a considerable history on theoretical debate and empirical studies on editing. In some instances editing is a complicated if willful politic of domination and exclusion (see for example Gitlin, 2000). In other studies editing is a complex, messy and historically situated labour where any story-making is influenced by the editing in story-work of others (see Caughie, 2000). Once found, editing needs considerable thinking-around.

If editing is one emerging focus from the untold story research represented in this volume, so too is the notion of audience (Hopkinson, Chapter 11). For some time organizational storytelling researchers such as Sims (2003) have pointed toward the agency of audiences. In a study of middle managers, it was the diverse audiences of stories that revealed middle management as a particularly vulnerable space to practice. In this volume, audience again has been raised as a powerful actor in untold stories. There are stories that simply never reach an audience (Roberts, Chapter 10), and stories that are not intended for audiences (Sims, Chapter 2). Audiences are clearly an issue.

Again, in terms of thinking-around, cultural criticism studies has already invested significantly in trying to understand this tangled term audience

(Abercrombie & Longhurst, 1998). In this context, a turn to media and cultural studies for some valuable insights may be helpful. Audiences have been a hot topic for some time and a sub-field of audience research has formed. The empirical work in this area is impressive whether the focus is on motivated audiences consuming stories for use value and gratification (Chen, 2011; Clavio & Kian 2010; Shao, 2009) or a messier picture of heterogeneous audiences co-producing stories (Ang 1991, 1996a, 1996b; Messanger Davies 1997, 2001; Livingstone, 1998, 2013).

Inevitably, when audiences become a focus of research the relationships between audience and story are highlighted. Take for example the idea that storytellers differentiate audiences as when media broadcasts differentiate child as a specific category of audience. Such categorization of audience is at work with Sims' middle manager differentiating those 'above' and 'below'. Once categories are at work in audiences they become sociologically relevant. Oswell (1995) drew attention to the ideological meaning of a particular programming strategy of the 1950s and 1960s in the UK. This strategy positioned children, childhood, and motherhood in particular relationships by devising a deliberate 'watch with mother' schedule. Oswell traces children's broadcasting over time and identifies a shift from watching 'with mother' to 'without mother'. In the process he connects these shifts to a modified notion of 'child audience' emerging and changing politics of childhood, family, and motherhood. In this context, children are increasingly re-categorised as active and critical consumers of stories. Consequently, storytellers are required to respond to the sophisticated audience.

The critical child audience has been subject to longditudinal qualitative studies and whilst there remains considerable concerns over the effects of media 'on' child audiences the empirical literature reveals child audiences active consumers working in dynamic situations (Messanger Davies, 2001). Studies of audiences has the potential to be a fascinating political space to pursue for organizational storytelling and audience research methods are a useful space for thinking-around.

FUTURE TIMES AND PLACES: THINKING-AROUND AND MESSING WITH TIME?

Undoubtedly, this volume focuses attention on untold stories as 'work'. There is clear energy and effort involved in both living an untold story and keeping a story below audible levels. However, the volume also illustrates how time is implicated in notions of the untold. Time has been considered from a number of blank spots and literary theory has already proved a valuable resource in thinking about time and story. In this volume memorable time (Rae, Chapter 3); ephemerality (Hopkinson, Chapter 11), and mindful present (Sims, Chapter 2) have been surfaced as valuable foci in telling, untelling, and untellable work. Playing with temporal notions offers a multitude of challenges. For example, what might it mean for our analytic confidence if we fail to consider organizational stories as potentially seasonal in character? Sims' focus on the mindful present cannot be ignored, not least as it emerges from time itself and reflections on a considerable body of work. One question here perhaps is can story continue as a valuable concept if the focus is in the present: what might be required for studies of organized presents? There again, if time is constituted of moments: how are moments measured?

In terms of transient stories or the story that seeks to be erased, there may be value in thinking-around with empirical studies of on-line social communities and fora. In part by virtue of the sociomaterial arrangements of such communities, this research typically addresses time, place, and temporal/places (archives). The research here is suggesting that online time is volatile and different and so storytelling is also volatile. Tellers are coming, going, and interacting in a landscape that cannot draw on the old and well-rehearsed containment that measured time provides. In such social communities it is often difficult for researchers to hold time steady, and there is a need to refer backwards to the time accessed in the knowledge that it is quite possible that, in the next archive accessed, all traces of the story and storyteller may have disappeared.

RETROSPECTIVE FUTURES: THINKING-AROUND LOST WORLDS (LOST LITERARY CONNECTIONS)

One valuable future may well be fictitious and certainly literary. Storytelling research already has a long and laudable association with literary theory. Indeed, this volume continues that tradition with all chapters drawing in one guise or another on poetics, literary criticism, and literary theory. However, there is also a suggestion within this volume that a turn to literary fictions (Lait, Chapter 4; Rae, Chapter 3) and drama (Boland & Griffin, Chapter 6) has value. Whilst literary fiction and drama are not subject to the same politics of authorship as academic works, both are subject to other politics of authorship. Both literary and academic works have boundaries; they are just different boundaries. However, and here is the possible untold story future, literary fictions and dramas can attend well to un-concepts. By its nature fiction distances itself from 'reality'; that is one of its discriminating behaviours ". . . distancing, the pulling back from reality in order to see it better . . ." (Le Guin, 1973, cited in Le Guin, 1989: 13). Once seen, the literary spaces of the arts can mess about with retelling and in the process evoke that which is otherwise present but unsaid, unsayable, and untellable. Good literary works reimagine reality and create both effective and affective.

In his study of organizational moments David Rae plays with time, form, and fiction in order to reveal catharsis affect in workplaces. It would be inappropriate to recast David's concern as a concern over emotional labour as that term draws affect away from emotion. David used fiction to deal with affect such as tears, loss, hurt, and emotional resignation at work. Recasting his setting, his players and his story and drawing inspiration from fictional studies of University work, David reveals a major challenge; how might academic studies do gritty stories?

In the introduction to this volume we referred readers to a Special Issue of a Journal where the editors had taken inspiration from a work of Russian purist art, a study of whiteness. We believe that thinking-around with and within *the arts* is one potential future for untold organizational storytelling research. The future will not be easily gained as the constraints of both may interfere. One chapter in this volume has illustrated that it is possible to offer an academic rendition of an 'arts, organization studies and untold story' project (Daskalaki, Chapter 8): a synthesis difficult to capture and disseminate but inspired nonetheless. If we aim to pursue such cross over study we may require new sites in which to share and disseminate *findings*.

OWNING THE UNTOLD OR 'WHOSE LINE IS IT ANYWAY?'

Finally, in playing with futures some researchers have tended to play a simple game of utopia or dystopia. We have not even ventured there . . . only to suggest some potential opportunities and some hazards and dragons that are lurking in the shadows.

We close with one significant untold dragon, the dragon-in-the-mirror, so to speak. Almost all histories of England suggest that mapping is an important prerequisite to colonization: the powerful imperialist English of olde certainly invested heavily in competitive map making (Schmidt, 1997). Thankfully, Gabriel and others have suggested there is a difficult to occupy unmanaged territory (1995). Even so, if mapping is not always a good idea we might reflect on our purpose in map making.

Indeed, is it really so necessary to map every inch and chase all untold across organizations? Surely, one might say, there is the inevitable right to privacy for those who wish to keep secrets untold. On the other hand, the plausible and well-rehearsed riposte to such objections will play out the tension between public interests and privacy.

So, a sensible strategy now might be to ask one question of the dragon-in-the-mirror: a question of intent. Why are we pursuing such stories so assiduously? One answer might be that they are out there waiting to be found: subject of and to story collectors seeking out stories and looking for the satisfaction of a full set. For us, this is not a satisfactory intent, a questionable practice in moral and academic terms.

If we are not specimen collectors then what is our intent? It is at this point that the question turns to who is authoring the untold stories we raise and, ultimately, who values from the telling.

246   *Linda Hitchin et al.*

REFERENCES

Abercrombie, N., & Longhurst, B. J. (1998). *Audiences: A Sociological Theory of Performance and Imagination*. London: Sage.

Ang, I. (1991). *Desperately Seeking the Audience*. London: Routledge.

Ang, I. (1996a). *Living Room Wars: Rethinking Media Audiences for Postmodern World*. London: Routledge.

Ang, I. (1996b). Ethnography and radical contextualism in audience studies. In J. Hay, L. Grossberg, & E. Wartella, (Eds.), *The Audience and its Landscape* (pp. 247–262). Boulder, CO: Westview Press.

Boje, D. M. (1995). Stories of the storytelling organization: A postmodern analysis of Disney as "Tamara-Land". *Academy of Management Journal*, 38(4): 997–1035.

Boje, D. M. (2012). Reflections: What does quantum physics of storytelling mean for change management? *Journal of Change Management*, 12(3): 253–271.

Caughie, J. (2000). *Television Drama: Realism. Modernism and British Culture*. Oxford: Oxford University Press.

Chaiklin, S., & Lave, J. (Eds.). (1996). *Understanding Practice: Perspectives on Activity and Context*. Cambridge: Cambridge University Press.

Chen, G. M. (2011). Tweet this: A uses and gratifications perspective on how active twitter use gratifies a need to connect with others. *Computers in Human Behavior*, 27(2): 755–762.

Clavio, G., & Kian, T. M. (2010). Uses and gratifications of a retired female athlete's Twitter followers. *International Journal of Sport Communication*, 3(4): 485–500.

Clifford, J., & Marcus, G. (1986). *Writing Culture: The Poetics and Politics of Ethnography*. Berkeley: University of California Press.

Crapanzano, V. (1986). Hermes dilemma: The masking of subversion in ethnographic description. In J. Clifford, & G. Marcus (Eds.), *Writing Culture: The Poetics and Politics of Ethnography* (pp. 51–76). Berkeley: University of California Press.

Donnelly, P. F., Gabriel, Y., & Özkazanç-Pan, B. (2013). Untold stories of the field and beyond: Narrating the chaos. *Qualitative Research in Organizations and Management: An International Journal*, 8(1): 4–15.

Gabriel, Y. (1995). The unmanaged organization: Stories, fantasies and subjectivity. *Organization*, 16(3): 477–501.

Geertz, C. (1988). *Works and Lives: The Anthropologist as Author*. Redwood City, CA: Stanford University Press.

Gherardi, S. (2001). From organizational learning to practice-based knowing. *Human Relations*, 54(1): 131–139.

Gitlin, T. (2000). *Prime Time*. Berkley: University of California Press.

Knorr-Cetina, K., Schatzki, T. R., & von Savigny, E. (Eds.). (2005). *The Practice Turn in Contemporary Theory*. London: Routledge.

Le Guin, U. (1989). *The Language of the Night: Essays on Fantasy and Science Fiction*. London: The Women's Press.

Livingstone, S. (1998). Audience research at the crossroads the 'implied audience' in media and cultural theory. *European Journal of Cultural Studies*, 1(2): 193–217.

Livingstone, S. (2013). The participation paradigm in audience research. *The Communication Review*, 16(1–2): 21–30.

Messanger Davies, M. (1997) *Fake, Fact and Fantasy: Children's Interpretations of Television Reality*. Mahwah, NJ: Lawrence Erlbaum.

Messanger Davies, M. (2001) '*Dear BBC': Children, Television, Storytelling and the Public Sphere*. Cambridge: Cambridge University Press.

Oswell, D. (1995). Watching with mother in the early 1950's. In C. Bazalgette & D. Buckingham (Eds.). *In Front of the Children: Screen Entertainment and Young Audiences* (pp. 34–46). London: British Film Institute.

Pope, A. (2003). *An Essay on Criticism*. London: Dodo Press.

Schmidt, B. (1997). Mapping an empire: Cartographic and colonial rivalry in seventeenth-century Dutch and English North America. *The William and Mary Quarterly*, 54(3): 549–578.

Shao, G. (2009). Understanding the appeal of user-generated media: a uses and gratification perspective. *Internet Research*, 19(1): 7–25.

Sims, D. (2003). Between the millstones: A narrative account of the vulnerabilty of middle managers' storying. *Human Relations*, 56(10): 1195–1211.

Tyler, S. A. (1986). Post-modern ethnography: From document of the occult to occult document. In J. Clifford & G. Marcus (Eds.), *Writing Culture: The Poetics and Politics of Ethnography* (pp. 122–140). Berkeley: University of California Press.

Van Maanen, J. (1988). *Tales of the Field: On Writing Ethnography*. Chicago: University of Chicago Press.

Wolf, M. (1992). *A Thrice Told Tale: Feminism, Postmodernism and Ethnographic responsibility*. Stanford: Stanford University Press.

Contributor Biographies

David Anderson is a lecturer in Management at Lincoln Business School. He has edited a special issue of *Tamara Journal* and is a reviewer for *Journal of Management Education*. His research interests include methodological anarchism, network studies, sociomateriality, and relationality.

Tom Boland lectures in sociology at Waterford Institute of Technology. His interests include social theory, historical sociology, the sociology of critique, and unemployment. Recent articles appear in *Irish Political Studies*, *Anthropological Theory*, and *History of the Human Sciences*. His monograph *Critique as a Modern Social Phenomenon* was published in 2013.

Mónica Colón-Aguirre assistant professor at Simmons College and a native of Puerto Rico has a doctorate from the School of Information Science at the University of Tennessee. Her research interests include: organizational narratives in the academic library context, human resource management, information literacy, and professional development in information organizations.

Maria Daskalaki is an associate professor at Kingston Management School, Kingston University. Her research interests include urban social formations, identity work, social entrepreneurship, and alternative forms of organizing. She has published in several journals including *Organization Studies*, *Journal of Management Inquiry and Culture and Organisations*, and has contributed in edited books and conference proceedings.

Paul Donnelly (PhD, University of Massachusetts at Amherst) is a research fellow in Organization Studies at the College of Business, Dublin Institute of Technology, Ireland. His current research interests cover organizational forming, alternative ways of organizing, and the untold stories of those who inhabit the margins of organization studies.

Lucia Garcia-Lorenzo (PhD London School of Economics, UK) is an assistant professor in Organizational and Social Psychology at the Social Psychology Department, London School of Economics, UK. Her current research explores cultural changes and transitions in the world of work, with a particular focus on fragmented and liminal contexts.

Ray Griffin lectures in Management and Organization Studies at Waterford Institute of Technology School of Business. Ray researches in and around the sociology of organizing, with projects on multi-national corporations, fun workplaces, banks as hypermodern organizations, and unemployment as just another type of work, all underway.

Linda Hitchin is a sociologist of science and technology. She has a PhD from Brunel University and is currently interested in connecting Science and Technology Studies to organizational analyses of health and safety at work.

Gillian Hopkinson is a senior lecturer in the Marketing Department, Lancaster University. Her interests focus on narrative, discourse, and power, concepts that she applies particularly within retail channel contexts. Her work has appeared in journals including *The International Journal of Management Reviews*, *The Journal of Management Studies*, *Marketing and Psychology*, and *Industrial Marketing Management*.

Michał Izak, PhD, is a senior lecturer in Management at University of Lincoln. His research interests include emerging organizational discourses, Critical Management Studies, fiction as a reflection of organizational dynamics, and organizational storytelling. He publishes regularly in peer reviewed journals and is a member of the editorial board of *Organization Studies* as well as a guest editor of forthcoming issues of *Futures Journal* and *Tamara Journal for Critical Organization Inquiry*.

Jerzy Kociatkiewicz is Senior Lecturer in Management at The University of Sheffield. His current research interests focus on personal experience of organizational life and space, as well as on narrativity and fiction analysed as routes for understanding and explicating processes of organizing. His recent publications include articles in such journals as *Scandinavian Journal of Management*, *Organization*, and *British Journal of Management*.

Monika Kostera is Professor Ordinaria in Management in Poland, and Chair in Management at the University of Warsaw and Guest Professor at Leeds University. She has authored and edited 31 books in Polish and English and a number of articles published in such journals as *Organization Studies*, *Organization*, and *Management Learning*. Her current research interests include archetypes, narrative organization studies, ethnography, and the humanistic turn in management.

Angela Lait has completed a PhD at Manchester, alongside a career in journalism. The themes of class, identity, insecurity, and lack of voice have proved to be an enduring focus of her research. She currently works as a freelance author and researcher, most recently teaching at the Essex Business School at the University of Essex.

Thekla Malamou graduated from the Department of Photography and Audiovisual Arts in the Faculty of Fine Arts and Design of the Technological Educational Institute, Athens. She has been teaching photography in several colleges and foundations and works as a freelance photographer and director of photography in short films and documentaries. She has exhibited in countries such Israel, Morroco, Cape Verde, Thailand, and Sicily.

David Rae is Dean of Shannon School of Business, Cape Brenton University, Canada. He is a fellow of the Institute for Small Business & Entrepreneurship, having been a Board member and trustee from 2007–2013 and Vice-President for Education for 2008–2012. He was Editor-in-Chief of the *International Journal of Entrepreneurial Behaviour & Research* from 2012–2014.

Vaughan S. Roberts is Team Rector of Warwick. His PhD is in management from the University of Bath. He has contributed to *Managing the Church* (Sheffield Academic Press, 2000); *How to Become a Creative Church Leader* (Canterbury Press, 2008), and is co-author (with Clive Marsh) of *Personal Jesus* (Baker Academic Press, 2012).

Alexandra Saliba graduated from the Department of Cultural Technology and Communication where she studied Audiovisual Arts *(University of the Aegean)* and has an MA in Cultural Politics and Cultural Management *(Panteion University)*. She has worked as a documentary producer, researcher, and filmmaker for several projects as well as a freelance journalist for Greek and international media.

Lucia Sell-Trujilllo (PhD London School of Economics, UK) is a researcher and lecturer in social psychology at the University of Seville, Spain. Her current research interests are the social psychological aspects of long-term unemployment, the challenges and social construction of citizenship, and the social and relational aspects of gender.

David Sims is Emeritus Professor of Organizational Behaviour at Cass Business School, City University, London, and formerly Associate Dean and Head of the Faculty of Management there. His interests are in how people develop as leaders of change in different cultures and contexts; and in the relationship between leadership, identity, and the narrative processes of life.

Stratis Vogiatzis graduated in 2001 from the Department of Economic and Political Sciences in the Aristotle University of Thessaloniki and he received his master's degree in Social Sciences at the University of Amsterdam He has published *Chios* (2006), *From Athens to Beijing* (2008), *Inner World* (2009) and recently *People of the Sea*. He has taken part in various solo and group exhibitions and his work is included in various museum and private collections.

Index of Names

Index of Subjects